Welcome to Paris

1

Eiffel Tower
© Stéphane Lemaire/hemis.fr

Getting to Paris

BY TRAIN

Gare de Lyon (12th arrondissement), **Gare de Bercy** (12th arr.), **Gare d'Austerlitz** (13th arr.), **Gare Montparnasse** (15th arr.), **Gare du Nord** (10th arr.), **Gare de l'Est** (10th arr.) and **Gare St-Lazare** (9th arr.). *For access to stations by public transport,* 🤝 *p. 152, p. 160 and www.ratp.fr.*

BY PLANE

From Charles-de-Gaulle

Roissybus – every 15-20 min from 6am to 12.30am. Journey time: 60 min. €11.50; www.parisaeroport.fr. The Roissybus drops you at the Opéra Garnier (lines 3, 7, 8; RER A).

RER B – Direction St-Rémy-lès-Chevreuse - Massy, every 10-15 min on weekdays from 4.51am to 11.51pm (CGD2); 4.54am to 11.54pm (CDG1). Journey time: 30 min. €10. Stops at Gare-du-Nord, Châtelet-Les-Halles, St-Michel-Notre-Dame, Denfert-Rochereau, etc.

Le bus direct (shuttle bus) – Line 2 to Étoile - Porte Maillot, every 30 min from 5.50am to 11pm. Approximate journey time: 1h15m. €17 single; line 4 to Gare Montparnasse - Gare de Lyon, every 30 min from 6am to 10pm. Approximate journey time: 1h15. €17 single ; www.lebusdirect.com.

Noctilien (night bus) – see p. 158.

Taxis – €50 (fixed price) for Right Bank; €55 for Left Bank.

From Orly

Orlybus – From Orly Sud and Ouest terminals, direction Denfert-Rochereau (terminus), every 10-20 min from 6am to 12.30am. Journey time: 30 min. €7.50 single.

Orlyval and RER B – Automated train Orlyval to Antony (every 4-7 min from 6am to 11pm), then RER B to CDG2 - TGV or Mitry-Claye. Journey time: 35 min. €12.05 single (combined ticket). Stops at Denfert-Rochereau, St-Michel-Notre-Dame, Châtelet-Les-Halles, Gare-du-Nord, etc.

Le bus direct (shuttle bus) – To Gare Montparnasse - Invalides - Étoile, every 20 min from 6am to 11.40pm. Journey time: 45-60 min. €12; €20 return; www.lebusdirect.com.

Taxis – €35 (fixed price) for Right Bank; €30 for Left Bank.

Tram - Line T7 to Villejuif-Louis-Aragon (every 8-15 min from 5.30am to 12.30am; journey time: 45 min; €1.90 single), then metro (line 7).

From Beauvais

Shuttles between the airport and Paris - Porte Maillot, Times depend on flight timetable. Journey time: 1h15m. €17 single) - www.aeroportbeauvais.com.

3

Paris-Visite Pass
1, 2, 3 or 5 -day passes available; may save you money on transport 🤝 *p. 161.*

Gare du Nord
© Phil Robinson/age fotostock

Unmissable
Our picks for must-see sites:

Notre-Dame ★★★
Map F 6 - 🕯 p. 14

Eiffel Tower ★★★
Map AB 5 - 🕯 p. 63

4

Louvre ★★★
Map E 4-5 - 🕯 p. 22

Musée d'Orsay ★★★
Map D 5 - 🕯 p. 66

Champs-Élysées ★★★
Map BC 3 - 🕯 p. 74

The Seine, quais and bridges★★
👣 p. 14

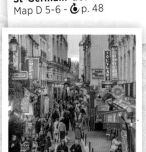

St-Germain-des-Prés ★★★
Map D 5-6 - 👣 p. 48

The Marais ★★★
Map FG 5 - 👣 p. 25

5

Latin Quarter ★★★
Map E 6-7 - 👣 p. 38

Montmartre ★★★
Off map E 1 - 👣 p. 85

Our top picks

♥ Stop in one of the many tucked-away little squares behind the façades of the Marais's historic hôtels particuliers (Soubise, Albret and Marle) and take a coffee break at the Centre Culturel Suédois. Steal into the courtyard of Hôtel de Sully: cross the gardens and emerge onto Place des Vosges. ☙*See p.26.*

♥ Contemplate the Seine from Pont Neuf, with the Institut de France and Monnaie de Paris on one side and the Louvre on the other — equally lovely in daylight or at night. ☙*See p. 20.*

♥ Pull up a chair opposite the Bassin Octagonal in the Tuileries and admire the Triumphal Way, a perspective taking in Concorde, the Champs-Élysées and La Défense to the west and the Tuileries Gardens and Louvre to the east. ☙*See p.74.*

♥ Make the most of car-free Sundays on Canal St-Martin and cycle its length from République to Parc de La Villette. Stop for a picnic at the park; on the way back, grab a drink at La Rotonde or play a canal-side round of pétanque.

♥ Visit the Louvre during Friday late opening, when the museum is less busy. When you leave, you'll have the magnificently floodlit Cour Carrée practically to yourself. Follow Rue de l'Amiral-de-Coligny, facing St-Germain-l'Auxerrois church; turn around and admire the colonnade. ☙*See p.22.*

♥ Climb the "butte" of Montmartre using the narrow staircases on its north side; wander the small, winding roads and make a stop on the tiny

Pont Neuf

© Brian Jannsen/age fotostock

♥ Head to **Musée Rodin** and take a break under the trees, surrounded by the sculptor's stunning masterpieces: *Le Penseur, Les Bourgeois de Calais, La Porte de l'Enfer.* ☙*See p. 62.*

Jardin du Luxembourg

Place du Calvaire overlooking the steps leading down to Paris. Take in the sweeping.

♥ Take a stroll in the gardens of the Palais Royal and wander the galleries. Head north to explore the charming Passages des Panoramas, taking in Passage Jouffroy, Passage Verdeau and Galerie Vivienne. See p. 81-82.

♥ At first light, head to Rue des Barres, one of the prettiest roads in Paris, for a coffee *en terrasse* at L'Ébouillanté. See p. 122.

♥ Explore the delights of the Jardin du Luxembourg in the heart of the Latin Quarter and take a seat in front of the Medici Fountain. See p.43.

♥ Stroll through the **park of the banks of the Seine** in front of the Louvre or in front of the Musée d'Orsay, or at the **quai St-Bernard** where locals dance outdoors on summer evenings.

♥ Ride the 75 bus to the end of the line. Hop on at Perrault's Colonnade at the Louvre, then pass through the Marais, along Canal St-Martin and across the Parc des Buttes-Chaumont, before stopping at the Philarmonie de Paris in La Vilette. See p.95.

Paris in 3 days

Paris is always packed with tourists and the queues to enter monuments can be very long indeed: bear this mind when arranging sight-seeing and consider booking timed skip-the-line tickets in advance.

DAY 1

▶ Morning
Start at the birthplace of Paris: Ile de la Cité★★★ (p. 14). Visit Gothic jewel Notre-Dame★★★; go at opening time to avoid crowds. Pass by Place Louis-Lépine, site of the charming flower market (and bird market on Sundays). Continue past Ste-Chapelle★★★ and La Conciergerie★★before crossing Pont-Neuf★. Wander St-Germain-des-Prés and stop for lunch (p. 48). ★★★.

▶ Afternoon
Discover the historic Quartier Latin ★★★ (p. 38) : Eglise St-Séverin★★, Musée du Moyen Âge, La Sorbonne★, Jardin du Luxembourg★★ (perfect for a little break), Panthéon★★, Eglise St-Étienne-du-Mont★★, Rue Mouffetard★.

▶ Evening
Walk the banks of the Rive Gauche and cross onto Ile St-Louis★★ (p. 20), admiring the superb 17th century architecture ; get dinner in Le Marais★★★, just across the water (p. 25)or head to the buzzy Montparnasse★ (p. 54), district, known for its cafés, cinemas and theatres.

DAY 2

▶ Morning
Depending on tastes, opt for a visit to the Musée d'Orsay★★★ (p. 66) or a section of the Louvre★★★ (the Passerelle Solférino links the two museums). If the weather is good, picnic in the tranquil Jardins du Palais-Royal★★ (p. 81) or the Tuileries★ (p. 74). Or try out a Japanese restaurant on Rue Ste-Anne, a ten-minute walk from the Louvre.

▶ Afternoon
Head on foot to L'Étoile : Tuileries★, Concorde★★★, Champs-Élysées★★★ (p. 75). At the top of the avenue, climb to the top of the Arc de Triomphe★★★ for a breathtaking view over the capital.

▶ Late afternoon and evening
From Charles-de-Gaulle-Étoile, hop on the metro to Pigalle (line 2). Climb the butte of Montmartre★★★

If you have an extra day

Opt for either the Centre Georges-Pompidou (p. 33) and the covered passageways (p. 82); or exploring eastern Paris and its buzzy neighbourhood haunts, popular with young Parisians : Canal St-Martin (p. 92), the villages of Belleville and Ménilmontant (p. 101), Parc des Buttes-Chaumont and La Villette (p. 94).

8

Musée d'Orsay

(p. 85). Wander the narrow winding roads, lined with little country-style houses, delight at the giant mosaic that decorates the Sacré-Cœur★★ and the panoramic view over Paris. Head back down via Abbesses, where you'll find an abundance of charming restaurants (R. des Abbesses, des Martyrs and des Trois-Frères).

DAY 3

▶ *Morning*

If it's a clear day, head for the Eiffel Tower★★★ (p. 63) and the neighbouring Musée du Quai-Branly★★ (p. 64). Preserve your energy (and enjoy a trip up the Seine) by taking the Batobus (hop on and off with a day pass) at the Tour-Eiffel stop. Look out over the riverbanks, the Grand★ and Petit Palais★★, Esplanade des Invalides★★★, Concorde★★★, Musée d'Orsay★★★, the Louvre★★★ and Ile de la Cité. Stop at Hôtel-de-Ville for lunch in the Beaubourg district or hit Le Marais★★★.

▶ *Afternoon and evening*

Take a stoll in Le Marais★★★ (p. 25) , with its exquisite architecture. Don't miss Place des Vosges★★★ and the sumptuous *hôtels particuliers*. Make time for at least one museum: Maison de Victor Hugo★, Picasso★★ or Art et Histoire du Judaïsme★★. There's ample opportunity for shopping, too, and a stop-off in one of the area's abundant bars and restaurants.

Discovering Paris

Paris viewed from Tour Saint-Jacques
© Pascal Ducept/hemis.fr

Paris today

There is no city quite like Paris, with its picture-perfect looks, but beyond its elegance and sophistication, Paris is a city of delicious contrasts: both bourgeois and gritty, intellectual and cosmopolitan – and with an ever-present streak of rebellion. The architectural and cultural riches of the "City of Light" are exceptional, while its social diversity can be seen in its many neighbourhoods, each with its own distinct identity.

The 'quartiers' of Paris

Paris is made up of twenty "arrondissements", each one with its own administration and its own distinct characteristics. Each arrondissement comprises four "quartiers" (neighbourhoods), whose boundaries have historically been set by inhabitants — so when you cross a road you may not necessarily be in the same quartier, or even the same "village".

Different trades

Historically, the Right and Left Bank have been associated with different spheres of activity, the former being dedicated to trade and business and the latter the seat of learning with its universities and publishing houses (though the difference is less marked today). Meanwhile, political power has spread out from its origins on île de la Cité. Today, political institutions can be found on both the Right Bank (the presidential residence, the Élysée Palace on Faubourg St-Honoré) and across the Left Bank (the government ministries, the Senate in Luxembourg and the National Assembly).

Following the example of the medieval guilds, the various crafts and trades were grouped together in different "quartiers" and the results of this differentiation can be seen to this day: haute couture on the Faubourg St Honoré, avenue Montaigne and rue Francois-Ier; luxury goods around Opéra; jewellers on rue de la Paix and place Vendôme; cabinetmakers at Faubourg Saint-Antoine (even if there are fewer today); clothing wholesalers in the Sentier and Temple; antique dealers in Rues Bonaparte and La Boétie; music sellers and makers of stringed instruments on rue de Rome and in Pigalle; purveyors of crystal glass on rue de Paradis and seed sellers on the quai de la Mégisserie. Finally, waves of immigration throughout the 20th century created new commercial districts specialising in goods from different parts of the world: Chinese in Arts-et-Métiers, Belleville and the Chinatown of the 13th arrondissement; African and Caribbean around Château-Rouge; North African in Barbès, la Goutte d'Or and Belleville; Jewish in the Marais and Sentier and Tamil (Sri Linkan, south Indian) at la Chapelle.

The character of each 'quartier'

Each of Paris's districts has its own unique character. You can wander the Latin Quarter, between Maubert and the Seine, weaving among the crooked houses, dinky squares and inviting café terraces before walking the narrow, winding alleys that lead to the riverside, revealing splendid vistas of the towers of Notre Dame above and the iconic green boxes of the bouquinistes that line the quais below. The traditionally minded should explore St-Germain-des-Prés and the maze of little streets between the Seine and St-Germain, taking in the market in the rue de Buci, Café Procope, the rue St-André-des-Arts, the Cour Saint Germain; or St-Sulpice with its fashion boutiques. Aesthetes will appreciate Île-St-Louis, with its enchanting 17th and 18th century architecture and tranquil atmosphere (except on weekends): stop to explore its small galleries and shops before taking a stroll along the Seine, surrounded by vestiges of the city's rich history. Around the Place des Vosges and rue des Francs-Bourgeois, in the Marais — Paris's centre of gay culture — majestic mansions have been repurposed in style, while ultra-hip fashion boutiques, bars and bookshops make the area thrum with life (especially on Sundays). In the north of the city, the staircases up to the "butte" of Montmartre lead to expansive views and charming country touches, hidden away behind touristy streets. In the east, the once working-class districts have transformed. Ménilmontant and Belleville are now filled with artists' studios, bars and restaurants; the area is less grand than some of the capital's more famous sights, but is nonetheless lively and full of charm. This is also the case of the Canal St-Martin and the Bassin de

© Bertrand Gardel/hemis.fr

Place de la République

13

La Villette – the area is still down-to-earth but also undeniably trendy and it's an excellent spot for a stroll on a sunny day.

The festivities surrounding the city's various annual events are another big draw. Summer highlights include Paris Plage ("Paris beach") and festivals including Paris Quartier d' Été, the open-air cinema at La Villette and the fun fair at the Tuileries; Nuit Blanche provides creative revelry in autumn and holiday illuminations and decoration delight visitors during the festive period.

Paris continues to evolve as times change, ensuring it retains its idiosyncratic charm and its status as the "most beautiful city in the world".

La Cité★★★
and Les Quais★★

The Île de la Cité is the birthplace of Paris and remains incontestably one the most beautiful spots in the city. It is very popular with sight-seers, drawn by two of Paris's most iconic monuments, Notre-Dame and the Sainte Chapelle. Be sure to explore neighbouring Île Saint-Louis with its tranquil atmosphere and sublime 17th-century mansions.

▶**Access:** M° Cité (line 4), Châtelet (lines 1, 4, 7, 11 and 14; lines A, B and D) – RER St-Michel-Notre-Dame (line C).
Area map *p. 16-17.* **Detachable map** *EF5-6.*
▶**Tips:** Start the day with a visit to Notre-Dame. See Ste-Chapelle on a sunny say to fully appreciate the magnificent stained glass. Consider booking a combined Ste-Chapelle/Conciergerie ticket.

14

NOTRE-DAME★★★

F6 Metro Cité or RER B St-Michel-Notre-Dame - 6 square Notre-Dame-pl. Jean-Paul-II- ℘014234 5610 - www.notredamedeparis.fr - 7:45 am - 6:45pm, Sat-Sun 7:30pm.The queue may be long to enter; come early and leave ample time.

Maurice de Sully began the construction of Notre-Dame around 1163 to give the capital a cathedral worthy of its standing. The work was completed around 1300. Notre-Dame was one of the first large churches with flying buttresses, extended by the famous gargoyles, designed to spout rainwater away from the church. The portals of the facade are extraordinary. To the left, the portal of the Virgin is adorned with a tender Dormition of the Virgin Mary and the Coronation of Mary in heaven.

The central portal is dedicated to the Last Judgment. The figures in the vaults represent the heavenly court, while down below, heaven is symbolised by Abraham receiving souls, hell by terrifying demons. The portal of Saint Anne is on the right, where the Virgin sits in majesty on her throne and presents the infant Jesus, in traditional Romanesque style. Above the portals is the Gallery of Kings, showing the kings of Judah and Israel, ancestors of Christ. With a diameter of almost 10m/32.8ft, the immense rose window forms a halo around the statue of the Virgin and Child.

On the interior, the scale and sheer elevation of the nave are testament to the talent and pre-eminence of the French school at the beginning of the 13C. In the 13 and 14C, to allow extra light into the chapels, the windows that covered the high tribunes were

Façade Cathédrale Notre-Dame

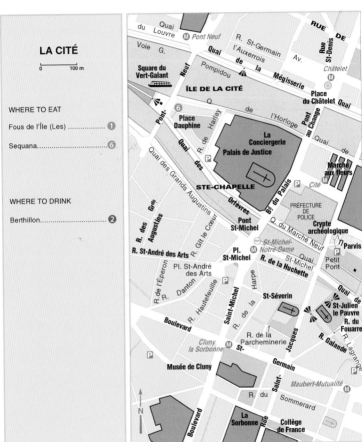

LA CITÉ

0 ——— 100 m

WHERE TO EAT

Fous de l'Île (Les) .... ❶

Sequana .... ❻

WHERE TO DRINK

Berthillon .... ❷

enlarged. To support the thrust of the nave and vaults, flying buttresses at a lower elevation were added, meaning all the weight of the construction rested on the outside of the church, allowing for a maximum of space and light on the inside.

Towers – *1 r. du Cloître-Notre-Dame - ℘ 01 53 40 60 80 - Jul-Aug: 10am-6.30pm, Fri-Sat 10am-11pm; Apr-Jun and Sep: 10am-6.30pm; rest of the year: 10am-5.30pm; closed 1 Jan, 1 May,*

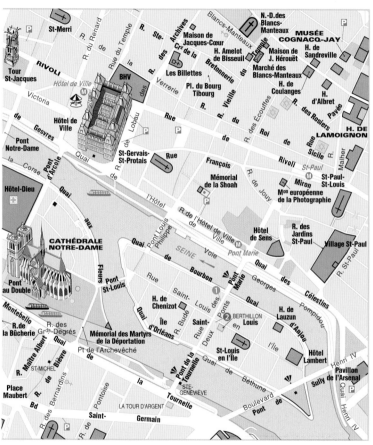

25 Dec - €10 (-26 years free) - free 1st of the month (Nov-March). Narrow and high bays add lightness to the towers. The right tower holds the famous great bell, Emmanuel, which weights 13t. Magnificent **view**★★★.

Crypte archéologique★ – *1 pl. Jean-Paul-II - 𝄞 01 55 42 50 10 - www.crypte. paris.fr - 10am-6pm- closed Mon, 1 Jan & 25 Dec- possibility of guided tour (1hr30min) - €8 (€15 combined ticket with the Catacombs - €5 audioguide.*

Under the 118m/387ft Parvis, the remnants of 3C and 19C monuments have been excavated. Highlights include the remains of two Gallo-Roman rooms heated by hypocaust (to the left on entering); the foundations of a Late Emipre rampart; the cellars of the houses of the former rue Neuve-Notre-Dame, some dating from the Middle Ages; the foundations of the Hôpital des Enfants-Trouvés and some from the église Ste Geneviève-des-Ardents. There are also regular temporary exhibitions.

Around Notre-Dame: Though it has undergone significant renovation, the old quarter of the Chapitre (rue Chanoinesse and rue de la Colombe), remains the last vestige of the medieval character of the Cité .To see the cathedral in its full splendour, head to Pont de la Tournelle (see p.20), on the other side of the Seine, or to Pont de l'Archevêché.

To go to the Ste-Chapelle, enclosed in the Palace of Justice, make a detour by the Flower market, which becomes a bird market on Sundays.

SAINTE-CHAPELLE★★★

E5 M° Cité. Enter on the left of the central gate of the Palais de Justice.8 bd du Palais - 🕾 01 53 40 60 80 - http://sainte-chapelle. monuments-nationaux.fr - Apr-Sept 9am-7pm; rest of the year: 9am-5pm-possibility of guided tour (45min) - €10 - ticket gives access to the Conciergerie; €4.50 audioguide.
This sublime architectural jewel was built by St Louis in the 13C in the heart of the Cité, to house the relics of the Passion. Designed as a giant reliquary in stone and glass, it is a masterpiece of the "Rayonnant" Gothic style, built on request of the king and attached to his royal palace; it is 33m/108ft high and took only six years to construct. The lower chapel is small but beautiful (7m/23ft tall). The **stained-glass★★★** of the upper chapel, which has recently been restored, is the oldest in Paris. The windows display 1,134 scenes, based upon the exaltation of the Passion, its announcement by the great prophets and John the Baptist, and the biblical scenes that precede it. The western rose window, dating from 15C, depicts the Apocalypse of St John. Contemplating the sun streaming through the stained glass at sunset is an unforgettable experience.

CONCIERGERIE★★

E5 M° Cité - 2 bd du Palais - 🕾 01 53 40 60 97 - www.paris-conciergerie.fr - 9am-6pm - closed 1 Jan, 25 Dec - guided tours available (45min) - €9 - €15 combined ticket with the Sainte-Chapelle - free 1st Sun of the month (Nov-March).
The best view of the Conciergerie is from Quai de la Mégisserie, on the Right Bank, where you will see its four towers reflected in the Seine, which originally flowed right up to their base. This was the first palace of the kings of France, before the Louvre; a judiciary function was added in the 14C, as well as a prison.

The twin towers in the centre of the façade once flanked the entrance of the royal palace, while the tower on the right housed the crown jewels,

18

© Pascal Ducept/hemis.fr

19

Conciergerie and Palais de Justice on Île de la Cité

hence the name la **Tour d'Argent** (the tower of silver/money). The square tower on the corner of boulevard du Palais – known as Tour de l'Horloge – received Paris's first public clock in 1370, which still functions today. Inside, the magnificent Gothic rooms are full of revolutionary history: many of those condemned by the Revolutionary Tribunal spent their last moments in the **Salle des Gens d'armes**★★and the cell where Marie Antoinette spent her last nights was converted to an expiatory chapel during the Restoration. Between January 1793 and July 1794, more than 2600 people were transported in by cart from the Conciergerie to Place de la Concorde to meet their fate at the guillotine. Large-scale **projects** are underway

for Ile de la Cité and its buildings (www.missioniledelacite.paris). The construction of a new **Palais de Justice** in the Clichy-Batignolles district in the 17th was completed in 2017 and 4000 magistrates and government employees will move there in Spring 2018. The current Palais de Justice can be visited by the public: the Salle des Pas Perdus was formerly the Gothic Grande Salle of Philippe le Bel, while the Première Chambre Civile was once the apartment of Louis IX (St Louis). *10 bd du Palais - ✆ 01 44 32 52 52 - www.ca-paris. justice.fr - 8am-6pm closed w/e and bank holidays - the public may attend criminal hearings – the children's court is not open to the public.*

PLACE DAUPHINE★

E5 *M° Pont-Neuf.*
For a long time the western tip of the island gave way to a muddy marsh area, broken down by the currents of the Seine In 1607, **Henri IV** organised the construction of a triangular square surrounded by uniform townhouses. The square was divided into lots and sold to traders, in particular to gold and silversmiths (Orfèvres), who lent their name to the quai on the south of the square (though the judicial police replaced the jewellers in the 17C and 18C).

PONT-NEUF★

E5 *M° Pont-Neuf.*
It is the oldest of Paris's bridges, completed in 1604. It was the first bridge to be built without houses on it and the first road in Paris to benefit from pavements separating pedestrians and traffic. The half-moons of the bridge once accommodated street sellers, teeth pullers, comic street entertainers as well as a whole cast of gawkers and thieves.
In the middle of Pont-Neuf, above the Square du Vert-Galant, we find the central pillar around which Paris was constructed: the Right Bank with the Louvre and the Left Bank with the Hôtel de la Monnaie and Institut de France.

QUAI SAINT-MICHEL

E6 The sweep of the bouquinistes lining this quai between St-Michel and Notre-Dame is one of the loveliest sights in Paris. The legendary vendors sell rare and antique books, paintings and etchings as well as old journals and magazines; there are around 217 bouquinistes along the Seine and 900 green boxes containing some 300,000 books and documents.

PONT DE LA TOURNELLE

F6 *M° Pont-Marie.*
Bordered by old houses, the pont (bridge) and the Quai de la Tournelle offer, along with the **Pont de l'Archevêché,** magnificent **views★★★** of Notre-Dame.

ÎLE SAINT-LOUIS★★

F6 *M° Cité ou Sully-Morland.*
Today, this island in the Seine is popular with Parisians for Sunday strolls among the fine stone mansion blocks and picnics on the quais Béthune and Orléans. In medieval Paris there were two smaller islands, the Île aux Vaches and the Île Notre-Dame. In the 16C, contractor Christophe Marie was charged by Louis XIII and the chapter of Notre-Dame with joining the islets and building two stone bridges for access. In exchange for his work, he was given permission to divide the island into lots and build residences, which he sold to nobles, businessmen, bankers and magistrates: the island is

chequered with exquisite townhouses featuring picturesque facades and elegant wrought iron balconies.

Église St-Louis-en-l'Île★ – Finished in 1725, this beautiful church is well worth a look. Its **interior★** is a museum in its own right with an abundance of paintings and sculptures spanning 15-18C.

Quai de Bourbon – With its chain-linked stone posts, 18C canted medallions and view of the Saint Gervais St-Protais church, this tip of the island is an impressive **sight★**.

Pont de Sully – This bridge, which crosses the island, dates from 1876. The north section looks out over the Quai d'Anjou and Hôtel Lambert, the Port des Célestins, **Pont Marie★** and the bell tower of St-Gervais; the south section offers a beautiful view★ of Notre-Dame and the Cité.

© Bertrand Gardel/hemis.fr

21

Parc des Rives de Seine

PONT MARIE★

F6 M° Pont-Marie.
It's the oldest bridge in Paris after Pont-Neuf and in its simplicity, perhaps one of the most beautiful. Its builder Christophe Marie completed it in 1635, but it had to be reconstructed in 1670 after partial collapse. Since then, it has not suffered even a crack.

PARC DES RIVES DE SEINE

Inaugurated in Spring 2017, this park links the 4.5 km (2.8mi) of quais on the Right Bank with the 2.5 km (1.5mi) on the Left Bank (see p. 64). The transformation of the former Georges Pompidou dual carriageway into pedestrian and cyclable spaces was not without controversies, but the park has nonetheless been embraced by Parisians (and visitors). On the Right Bank, the footpath and cycle route stretch from the Tuileries to the Bassin de l'Arsenal, which means that by combining with the park on the Left Bank, it is possible to get to the Eiffel Tower from Bastille without passing a single car. There are a number of facilities along the way including playgrounds, fitness equipment, picnic lawns, deckchairs, concert areas and restaurants.

The Louvre★★★

It is easy to forget that from the time of Philippe Auguste at the end of 12C until the reign of Louis XIV, when the latter moved the court to Versailles, the Louvre was the residence of the kings of France. It was only in 1791 that the palace became a museum bringing together "all the sciences and arts", as decreed by the Assemblée Nationale. Its collection has been growing ever since, and today it houses one of the most significant art collections in the world.

▶**Access:** M° Louvre-Rivoli (line 1) or Palais-Royal-Musée-du-Louvre (lines 1, 7).
Detachable map DE4-5.
▶**Tips:** The museum is so vast that is not possible for all the rooms to be open at the same time: consult the information point under the Pyramid or the Louvre's website to check which are closed on the day of your visit. It is impossible to see everything in one day, so you need to choose which parts you most want to see and prioritise them.

22

A PALACE-MUSEUM

Located between the Palais Royal, the Tuileries Gardens and the Seine, the Louvre occupies a central position both in the city of Paris itself and the history of the capital. For eight centuries, it was the seat of the kings and emperors of France and some of the country's most famous architects worked on its construction, including Pierre Lescot, Philibert Delorme, Jacques II Androuet du Cerceau, Le Vau, Percier and Fontaine, Visconti and Lefuel. Successive expansions of the edifice have made it a monument to the architectural history of the past centuries and have made it the largest palace in the world. It owes its worldly renown to its museum, housing masterpieces including the Mona Lisa and Venus de Milo. The **main entrance** can be found at the Pyramid.
Don't miss: the **Cour carrée**★★★; the **Colonnade**★★, masterpiece of 18C architecture; the **medieval rooms**★★★,

---

Practical info

Up-to-date information ✆ 01 40 20 53 17 - www.louvre.fr - 9am-6pm, Wed amd Fri 9am-9.45pm - closed Tuesdays, 1 Jan, 1 May, 25 Dec - 15 € (permanent collections and Hall Napoléon temporary exhibition) - free: under 18 years and for EU countries under 26, 1st Sun of month Oct-March and 14 Jul.

vestiges of Charles V's palace

Maps – In the Hall Napoléon entrance you will find free maps, essential for finding your way round the museum's three wings: Sully, Denon, Richelieu.

Themed circuits – Visitors may pick up maps for self-guided themed circuits around the museum at the information desk; each takes in around a dozen works.

Audioguide – ✆ 01 40 20 53 17 - www. louvre.fr - Visits with described works are available for adults, children and people with disabilities; tours in French, English, Spanish, German, Italian, Japanese and Korean. Tours in French sign language, for lip readers or Cued Speech can also be organised on the mezzanine level at the entrances of the Richelieu, Sully et Denon wings - €5.

Guided tours – ✆01 40 20 53 17 - www.louvre.fr - €12 - every day except Mondays and 1st Sunday of the month. "Welcome to the Louvre" guided tour (1.5hr) in French or English. Tickets bought at the group entrance under the Pyramid.

THE GREAT WORKS

The Seated Scribe, 1st floor, room 22- Amenophis IV, 1st floor, room 25- *Le Bain Turc* by Ingres, 2nd floor, room 60- *Le Tricheur*, by Georges de LaTour, 2nd floor, room 28- *Le Verrou*, by Fragonard, 2nd floor, room 49.

Denon Wing- *Mona Lisa*, **by Leonardo da Vinci,** Mona Lisa room, 1st floor, room 6- The *Victory of Samothrace*, 1st floor, at the top of the Daru staircase- *Cycladic idol*, mezzanine, room 1- *Gladiator Borghese*, ground

Must-see rooms

- *The medieval Louvre: moat and dungeons*
- *Cour Marly, Cour Puget*
- *Cour Khorsabad*
- *Salle des Caryatides*
- *Galerie d'Apollon*
- *Napoleon III Apartments*

floor, room B- *Psyche Revived by Cupid's Kiss*, by Canova, ground floor, room 4- *Slaves*, by Michelangelo, ground floor, room 4- *The Rite of Napoleon*, by David, 1st floor, room 75- The *Raft of the Medusa*, by Géricault, 1st floor, room 77- *Crown of Louis XV*, Gallery of Apollo- *The Marriage of Cana*, by Veronese, 1st floor, Mona Lisa room.

Richelieu wing- Winged bull, palace of King Sargon II, ground floor**,** Khorsabad courtyard- *Marly horses*, by Guillaume Coustou, mezzanine, Cour Marly- *Tomb of Philippe Pot*, ground floor, courtyard Marly- *Portrait of Erasmus*, by Holbein, 2nd floor, room 8- *Gabrielle d'Estrées and One of Her Sisters*, Fontainebleau school, 2nd floor, room 10- *Bathsheba*, by Rembrandt, 2nd floor, room 31- *La Dentellière*, by Vermeer, 2nd floor, room 38.

Islamic Art - Pyxis of al-Mughira - Baptistery of St. Louis of Monzon - Ewer with a cock-shaped spout.

24

The Marais★★★ *and Les Halles*★

Le Marais is one of the few areas in Paris untouched by Haussmann's renovation, meaning it has retained its narrow medieval roads, little squares and fine mansions, dating from the 17th and 18th centuries. These days it's a hip and buzzy neighbourhood, packed with art galleries, boutiques, quirky cafés and popular gay bars. Shops open on Sunday and the streets are full of locals and visitors shopping in the boutiques, getting brunch and soaking in the atmosphere. Nearby Les Halles is the biggest pedestrianised area in Paris and is a favourite with teens and young people: there's no shortage of fast-food restaurants and clothes shops.

▶ **Access:** The Marais stretches from the section of the Rivoli-St-Antoine thoroughfare between Bastille and Hôtel de Ville to République in the north. The "Haut Marais" (Upper Marais) comprises the triangle between rue Pastourelle, rue du Temple and boulevard du Temple. M° St-Paul (line 1), Rambuteau (line 11).
Detachable map. *28-29. EG4-6*.

▶ **Tips:** The Marais is busy in the day: visit in the morning for a calmer experience.

ÉGLISE SAINT-PAUL-SAINT-LOUIS★★

G5-6 *M° St-Paul. 99 r. St-Antoine - ☎ 01 42 72 30 32 - www.spsl.fr - 8am-8pm - guided tours.*
The layout of this Jesuit church, built between 1627 and 1641, is inspired by the Church of the Gesù in Rome, a perfect example of baroque architecture. You will see classical columns on the facade that hides the dome. Inside the church, don't miss Delacroix's *Le Christ au jardin des Oliviers*★★.

VILLAGE SAINT-PAUL

G6 *M° St-Paul.*
Tucked discreetly between rue des Jardins-St-Paul, rue Charlemagne, rue St-Paul and rue de l'Ave-Maria, this charming little cluster of courtyards is dotted with old houses and antique shops. The longest surviving part of the **Philippe Auguste Wall**★, punctuated by two raised towers, can be found on the rue des Jardins-St-Paul. It once linked Tour Barbeau, located at 32 quai des Célestins, to the St-Paul postern.
Hôtel de Sens★ *(1 r. du Figuier)* Constructed between 1475 and 1507 as a residence for the archbishops of Sens, the Hôtel de Sens is one of the few surviving grand medieval

residences in Paris. The Flamboyant Gothic porch leads into the courtyard where a square battlemented tower encloses a spiral staircase. Turrets and striking dormer windows adorn the house's exterior. The Forney Library, specialising in fine arts, decorative arts and industrial techniques is housed inside.

MAISON EUROPÉENNE DE LA PHOTOGRAPHIE★

F5 M° St-Paul - 5-7 r. de Fourcy - ℘ 01 44 78 75 00 - www.mep-fr.org - ♿ - guided tours on request (1hr30min) 11am-7.45pm - closed Mon, Tue and bank holidays - €8 (under 26 years free).
This prestigious centre for photography was opened in the former Hôtel Hénault de Cantobre (built 1704) in 1966 after restoration and expansion by architect Yves Lion. The museum hosts a changing programme of photographic art exhibitions and has a permanent collection of around 20,000 works, which are rotated depending on the temporary exhibits. The impressive multi-media library and auditorium on the lower ground level is well worth a stop,

PLACE DU MARCHÉ-SAINTE-CATHERINE★

G5 M° St-Paul.
This pedestrianised square is lined by large houses, harmonious in style. With its abundant café terraces, it is one of the prettiest little squares in Paris and a good spot to take a breather after exploring Le Marais.

26

RUE SAINT-ANTOINE

G5-6 M° St-Paul.
Rue St-Antoine was often used by the kings of France to head east out of the city. In the 14C it was one of the widest roads of the city and became a popular spot for promenades and celebrations. In the 17C it was considered the most beautiful road in Paris.

HÔTEL DE SULLY★★

G6 M° St-Paul. 62 r. St-Antoine - ℘ 01 44 61 21 50 - www.hotel-de-sully.fr - courtyard and garden 9am-7pm - bookshop 1pm-7pm -closed Mon - headquarters of the Centre des monuments nationaux. - expert guided tours of the Duchess's apartment (1hr30min) Sept-June: 2nd Sat of month (€10).
Constructed in 1625 and bought in 1634 by **Sully**, a minister of Henri IV, this grand mansion connects to Place des Vosges via the orangerie at the back of the garden. Its **courtyard★★** is a fine Louis XIII architectural composition featuring grand pediments, sculpted dormer windows and allegorical figures representing the Elements and Seasons.

PLACE DES VOSGES★★★

G5 M° St-Paul.
Known as "the most beautiful square in Paris", the Place des Vosges is hemmed in by 36 uniform houses, which present a stunning harmony with their stone and faux-brick facades. Each house comprises an arcade bottom level, two upper floors and a roof featuring dormer windows.

WHERE TO EAT

WHERE TO DRINK

SHOPPING

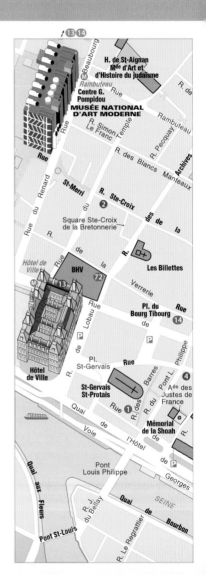

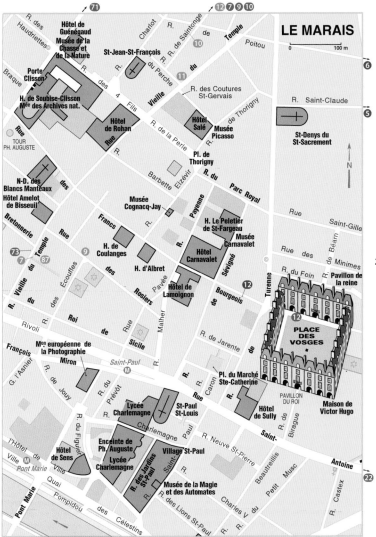

LE MARAIS

71

12 7 9 10

R. des Haudriettes

Hôtel de Guénégaud
Musée de la Chasse et de la Nature

Chariot

R. de Saintonge

de

Temple

Poitou

St-Jean-St-François

du Perche

10

0   100 m

6

Porte Clisson

Braque

R. des 4 Fils

Vieille

11

H. de Soubise-Clisson
Mée des Archives nat.

R. des Coutures St-Gervais

de Thorigny

R. Saint-Claude

5

Hôtel de Rohan

R. de la Perle

Hôtel Salé

Musée Picasso

St-Denys du St-Sacrement

TOUR PH. AUGUSTE

Hôtel Rue

Pl. de Thorigny

N

N-D. des Blancs Manteaux

des

Rue

Barbette

Elzévir

R. du

Parc Royal

Rue

Saint-Gille

Hôtel Amelot de Bisseuil

Musée Cognacq-Jay

Payenne

H. Le Peletier de St-Fargeau

Rue des

de Béarn

Bretonnerie

Rue

Francs

R.

Musée Carnavalet

Minimes

73

Temple

du

7

87

9

H. de Coulanges

des

H. d'Albret

Hôtel Carnavalet

Sévigné

Rue de

Turenne

R. du Foin

Pavillon de la reine

29

Vieille

R.

du

des Écouffes

Pavée

Hôtel de Lamoignon

Bourgeois

12

12

Rivoli

Roi

Rosiers

Malher

de

PLACE DES VOSGES

François

Mon européenne de la Photographie
Miron

Rue

Sicile

R. de Jarente

de

PAVILLON DU ROI

G. l'Asnier

R. de Jouy

R. du Prévôt

Saint-Paul

Pl. du Marché Ste-Catherine

R. Caron

Hôtel de Sully

Maison de Victor Hugo

l'Hôtel

R. du Figuier

Lycée Charlemagne

R.

St-Paul St-Louis

R.

Rue

Saint-

de

Birague

Antoine

22

Hôtel de Sens

de

Ville

Charlemagne

Paul

R. Neuve St-Pierre

Beautreillis

R. Castex

Pont Marie

Ville

Enceinte de Ph./Auguste
Lycée Charlemagne

Village St-Paul

Saint-

Petit Musc

Pont Marie

Quai

R. des Jardins St-Paul

Musée de la Magie et des Automates

Charles V du

R. des Lions St-Paul

R.

Pompidou

des

Célestins

The Pavillon du Roi on the south of the square and the Pavillon de la Reine on the north face each other across the square.

The square was built by Henri IV between 1605 and 1612. He wished to create a beautiful hub for his capital and before long the *place* became a centre of elegance, equestrian displays and courtly festivities. Famous residents of the square include Mme de Sévigné (at no 1 bis), Bossuet (at no 17), Richelieu (at no 21), Théophile Gautier et Alphonse Daudet (at no 8) and Victor Hugo (at no 6). The square's current name dates from 1800 and honours the Vosges *department*, the first to pay its taxes to Napoleon Bonaparte's Empire. Today, visitors may wander the

arcades, admiring the independent art galleries and boutiques or stop for a drink under their arches, where small orchestras play on Sundays.
Maison de Victor-Hugo★ - *6 pl. des Vosges - ℰ 01 42 72 10 16 - www. maisonsvictorhugo.paris.fr - ♿ - 10am-6pm - closed Mon and public holidays- guided tours available (1hr30min) - audioguide and audiodescription available*

RUE DES FRANCS-BOURGEOIS★

FG5 Mᵒ St-Paul et Rambuteau.
This historical axis through the Marais, which stretches from the Place des Vosges to the Centre Pompidou, is now a bustling seam lined with fashion boutiques, perfumeries and jewellers. There are also a number of *hôtels particuliers* dating from the 16C and 17C including **Hôtel d'Albret** at no 31, **Hôtel de Sandreville** at no 36 or au Hôtel d'Alméras at no 30. At no 16, **Hôtel Carnavalet** and **Hôtel Le Peletier de St-Fargeau** house the **Musée Carnavalet**, dedicated to the history of Paris. It is closed for renovation until 2020, but the museum is still organising outdoor walking tours (www.carnavalet.paris.fr).

MUSÉE PICASSO★★

G5 Mᵒ St-Sébastien-Froissart. Hôtel Salé - 5 r. de Thorigny - 75003 Paris - ℰ 01 85 56 00 36 - www.musee picassoparis.fr - weekend, school holidays & public holidays: 9.30am-6pm; rest of the year: 10.30am-6pm -closed Mondays, 1 Jan, 1 May, 25 Dec - guided tours on request (1hr15min) - €12.50 (under 26 years

Staircase, Musée Picasso

© Yoshimi Kanazawa/Michelin

free) - audioguide €5.
The Hôtel Salé was constructed between 1656 and 1659 for Pierre Aubert, lord of Fontenay, an important financier and a salt tax collector, hence the name of the house. It was restored in 1985 and retains the original magnificent **staircase★** with wrought iron railing and intricate sculpted ceiling; the museum reopened its doors in 2014 following five years of renovations. The permanent collection comprises 300 Picasso paintings (1881-1973) and more than 250 sculptures (including the famous Guenon et son petit, 1951) as well as collages, reliefs and more than 4,000 drawings and stamps. There is also a rotating calendar of temporary exhibitions.

THE UPPER MARAIS★

M° Filles du Calvaire. The fine architectural features and hip credentials of the 4th arrondissement continue into the Upper Marais, which is packed with meticulously curated "concept stores", trendy bars and health-centric restaurants.**Le Carreau du Temple** (*2 r. Perrée - 𝒫 01 83 81 93 30 - www.carreaudutemple.eu - guided tours with prior booking) is* a veritable cultural hub hosting diverse activities and events centered round sport and art, as well as salons and concerts. The building was originally a covered market, built in 1860; it has been threatened with demolition several times but has always been saved by locals.

The Marais district - rue des Barres and Église Saint-Gervais-Saint-Protais

© Bertrand Gardel/hemis.fr

Le marché des Enfants-Rouges (*37 r. de Bretagne*) is well worth a look, especially on a Saturday morning. Officially the oldest market in Paris (built in 1615), Enfants-Rouges offers a high concentration of fine food stalls and delicatessens, as well as some restaurants. (♿ *p. 105*). It takes its name from the colour of the clothing worn by the children from the orphanage that neighboured the market in the 17C.

HÔTEL DE SOUBISE-CLISSON★★ AND HÔTEL DE ROHAN★★

F5 M° Rambuteau.
These two *hôtels particuliers* are joined by **beautiful gardens★★**, which are open to the public and have recently been refurbished. Today these buildings are home to the French public archives of the Middle Ages and Anien Régime, as well as the **Musée des Archives nationales★** - *58 r. des Archives (entrance 60 r. des Francs-Bourgeois) - ℘ 01 40 27 60 96 - www.archives-nationales. culture.gouv.fr - 10am-5.30pm, w/end 2pm-5.30pm - closed Tue and public holidays. - €6 (under 26 years free).* The Hôtel de Soubise is the oldest of the *hôtels particuliers* in the Marais (14C) The gateway, known as **Porte Clisson★**, is flanked by a pair of corbelled turrets, the last vestige of 14C private architecture in Paris. The majestic horseshoe shaped **courtyard★★** was remodelled in the 18C and is bordered by an elegant peristyle and balustrade. The **apartments★★** were decorated from 1732 by the best painters and sculptors of the era.

The **Hôtel de Rohan** (*87 r. Vieille-du-Temple - ℘ 01 75 47 20 06 - www. archivesnationales.culture.gouv.fr - closed for renovation),* was built in 1705 for the son of the prince and princess of Soubise, the Bishop of Strasbourg, who later became Cardinal de Rohan. Major works are underway to renovate the house and install magnificent décor from the Hôtel de la chancellerie d'Orléans on the ground floor.

HÔTELS DE GUÉNÉGAUD AMD DE MONGELAS★★

F4 M° Rambuteau. 60 et 62 r. des Archives.
One of the most beautiful residences in the Marais. Constructed by François Mansart around 1650 and reworked in the 18C, the Hôtel de Guénégaud is remarkable in its simple and harmonious lines, with a small French style garden. It houses the **Musée de la Chasse et de la Nature★★** – *62 r. des Archives - ℘ 01 53 01 92 40 - www. chassenature.org - 11am-6pm, Wed 11am-9.30pm - closed Mon and public holidays - guided tours on requests (1hr30min) - €8 (under 18 years free) - free 1st Sun of month.* This unusual, fancy-filled museum is a favourite with children and parents alike (and you don't need to be a hunting enthusiast!).

MUSÉE D'ART ET D'HISTOIRE DU JUDAÏSME★★

F4 M° Rambuteau. 71 r. du Temple - ℘ 01 53 01 86 53 - www.mahj.org - ♿ - 11am-6pm, Wed 11am-9pm, Sun 10am-6pm - closed Saturdays, 1 Jan, 1 May, Rosh Hashanah and Yom Kippur - guided tours on request

© Sylvain Sonnet/hemis.fr

33

Musée d'Art et d'Histoire du Judaïsme

(1hr30min) - €9 - €10 combined ticket with temporary exhibitions.
This ultra-modern museum, set within the historical **Hôtel de St-Aignan★,** presents both artefacts and contemporary works, which help tell the story of Jewish culture; highlights include reconstructions of synagogues and rooms dedicated to the Jewish influence on 20C art and the contemporary Jewish world.

MUSÉE COGNACQ-JAY★★

FG5 Mᵒ Chemin-Vert. 8 r. Elzévir - ℘ 01 40 27 07 21 - www.musee cognacqjay.paris.fr - 10am-6pm - closed Mon and public holidays - guided tours on request

(1hr30min) - €6/8 temporary exhibitions. In a 16C mansion, a collection of 18C European art brought together by the founders of la Samaritaine. Presenting drawings and paintings along with precious *objects* and furniture, the whole collection evokes the refined life of the Century of Light. Watteau cartoons, Rembrandt paintings, Largillière, Chardin, sculptures by Houdon and Clodion, Venetian paintings.

QUARTIER BEAUBOURG

F4-5
The plateau of Beaubourg, which was until the late 1960s the site of old, insalubrious housing, has been a lively

spot since the opening of **Centre Pompidou★★**. The gallery's courtyard attracts street entertainers of all kinds including fire breathers, jugglers, painters and caricaturists, guitarists and organ grinders. Big-name exhibitions attract an international crowd, creating a joyful and colourful atmosphere. To the right of the building, the **Fontaine Stravinski★** is decorated with black sculptures by Tinguely and multi-coloured creations by Niki de Saint Phalle.

CENTRE POMPIDOU★★

F4-5 Mᵒ *Rambuteau - Pl. Georges-Pompidou -* 𝄞 *01 44 78 12 33 - www.centrepompidou.fr - museum and exhibitions 11am-9pm, Thur. 11am-11pm (exhibitions galleries 1 and 2) - closed Tuesdays, 1 May - guided tours available (1hr15min) - €14 - museum and exhibitions- €5 "View of Paris" ticket (access to 6th floor w/o access to museums and exhibitions).*

Richard Rogers and Renzo Piano caused a stir with their "inside-out" design when the gallery opened in 1977. The steel and glass behemoth, with its bright primary colours, criss-crossing pipes, diagonal external escalator, and distinctive glass tubing stands out against the Paris skyline. The sixth floor offers a magnificent **view★★** of the rooftops of Paris and the hill of Montmartre.

Le musée national d'Art moderne★★★

(Levels 4 and 5 of the Georges Pompidou Center). Among the richest modern art museums in the world, its collections cover every artistic wave from 1905 to 1960, in painting, architecture, photography, cinema, new media, sculpture and design.

Modern art- Modern artists can be found on level 5: Fauvism (Derain, Matisse, Dufy), Cubism (Braque, Picasso), the Dada movement with Marcel Duchamp, Abstraction (Kandinsky, Klee, Mondrian), the Surrealists (Dalí, Magritte, Ernst, Miró), then the abstract painters of the 1950s (Hartung, deStaël, Soulages), the American avant-garde (Pollock, Newman), the sculptures of Brancusi and, on the terraces, the monumental works of Miró, Ernst, Calder and Takis.

34

Going on strike to find work at Les Halles

Flanked by a sand and gravel beach (grève) suitable for docking, the right bank of the Seine became a hub for fluvial trade in Medieval Paris. Indeed, Paris became a key location in the economic development of the West in the 12C, thanks to the quality of its wheat lands, its strategic position at the crossroads of northern and southern Europe and its wine production. It was therefore unsurprising that when Les Halles was built at the start of the 13C it would be close to this natural port, Place de Grève (today's Place de l'Hôtel-de-Ville), where workers would go "en grève" looking for a job.

The meaning of the word "grève" changed over the years, eventually coming to signify an important practice in French culture, going on strike.

Contemporary art - Level 4 of the museum exhibits outstanding works of contemporary art from the 1960s onwards: Beuys, Boltanski, Bourgeois, Hantaï, Mitchell, Soulages, Twombly, Warhol. The display is refreshed every two years.

LES HALLES★

EF4-5

Les Halles became (and still is) a huge transport hub with 750,000 people passing through every day, and there were often problems. Architects Patrick Berger and Jacques Anziutti were commissioned to transform their designs after winning an open contest. The result is the Canopée, a vast glass structure with a striking rippling sheet roof; the complex houses more than 6,000 boutiques. Thanks to clever design, the Centre Pompidou is now visible from the patio of Les Halles. The 4ha/9.8ac gardens, Le jardin Nelson-Mandela invite visitors to take a break surrounded by greenery. On the western edge, the former grain hall, which later became la Bourse du commerce (commodities exchange) is now being transformed into a private gallery, housing the collection of French billionaire François Pinault.

Eglise St-Eustache★★ was built between 1532 and 1640 and its current façade was added in 1754. On the north side, the façade du Croisillona retains its Renaissance composition with its two staircase turrets topped by cupolas: rue de Montmartre offers a fine view of the flying buttresses of the chevet and the restored spire.

From there, head to rue Montorgueuil, which still retains old houses adorned with picturesque signs (nos. 15, 17, 23, 25) and connects, via rue Tiquetonne, to the 19C charm of the Grand-Cerf covered passage.

The passage comes out onto rue St-Denis, one of the oldest streets in Paris, opened in the 8C. Once a rich commercial hub, today the street is the eclectic home to a number of bars, as well as sex shops, which in recent years have replaced brothels in this historical red-light district.

Head south to discover the rue de la Grande-Truanderie, the site of one Paris's "courts of miracles", which served as refuges for Paris's thieves, criminals and outcasts (as featured in *The Hunchback of Notre Dame*) until the reign of Louis XIV. Nearby rue des Lombards, a spot where Italian money-lenders once sold their silver for the price of gold, is a great example of a narrow medieval road; today it is dotted with lively terraces and jazz clubs. On the way, you will come across the Fontaine des Innocents, a Renaissance masterpiece designed by Pierre Lescot and sculpted by Jean Goujon and inaugurated to mark the grand entry of Henri II to Paris in 1549. It was formerly a centrepiece of the Cimetière des Innocents, Paris's largest cemetery until 1786, when two million skeletons were transferred to the Catacombs (*see p.58*). Nearby rue de Ferronerie (no 11) is the site of Henry IV's assassination by Ravaillac on May 14 1610.

Not far away, on the other side of boulevard de Sébastopol, you will find 15th-century Gothic Flamboyant church Église St-Merri.

Le Quartier Latin

This historical corner of Paris is dominated by the Panthéon and descends gently down to the Seine, with the rue St-Jacques – Paris's oldest Roman road – running through the area from north to south. The Latin Quarter has been the seat of universities and a centre of learning since the Middle Ages and there are still many prestigious schools in the area around the Sorbonne, while the lively student atmosphere remains. These days, many of the former bookshops may have gone, but students still meet on Place St-Michel and stroll the Luxembourg Gardens.

▶ **Access:** Mᵒ St-Michel (line 4), Cluny-la-Sorbonne (line 10), RER St-Michel-Notre-Dame (lines B and C).

Area map p. 40-41. Detachable map EG6-8.

▶ **Tip:** Avoid restaurants in the ultra-touristy area around rue de la Huchette.

PLACE SAINT-MICHEL

E6 Mᵒ St-Michel.
A meeting place for young people from all over the world. The fountain and square date from 19C. From here, wander the charming medieval streets nearby (rues de la Harpe, de la Parcheminerie, de la Huchette and St-Séverin); go early in the morning to avoid the tourist throngs. These streets are full of fast-food restaurants and souvenir shops and are lively at night.

ÉGLISE SAINT-SÉVERIN ★★

E6 Mᵒ Cluny-la-Sorbonne. 1 r. des Prêtres-St-Séverin.
The church grew laterally as a result of a lack of room during building work in the 14C and 15C and it is now almost as wide as it is tall. The bays pass from Rayonnant Gothic style to Flamboyant; the **ambulatory★★** is also in Flamboyant style, with its superstructure falling in spirals around columns cased in marble and wood. The **stained glass★** in the upper windows is 15C; modern glass in the chevet is by Bazaine.

Follow rue Galande, taking in its medieval houses before stopping at St-Julien-le-Pauvre church, built at the same time as Notre-Dame (1165-1220); the church was given to the Greek Melkite Catholic community in 1889. Next, follow la rue de la Bûcherie to rue des Grands-Degré, admiring the charming old houses and little bookshops.

MUSÉE NATIONAL DU MOYEN ÂGE - THERMES DE CLUNY ★★

E6 Mᵒ Cluny-la-Sorbonne. 6 pl. Paul-Painlevé - ✆ 01 53 73 78 16 - www. musee-moyenage.fr - 9.15am-5.45pm - closed Tuesdays, 1 Jan, 1 May, 25 Dec - guided tours on request (1hr) - €9 - Under renovation until 2020.

38

40

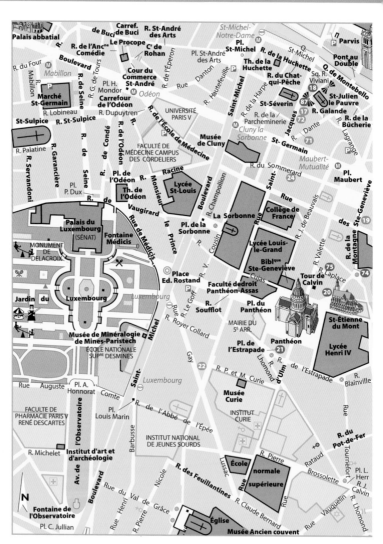

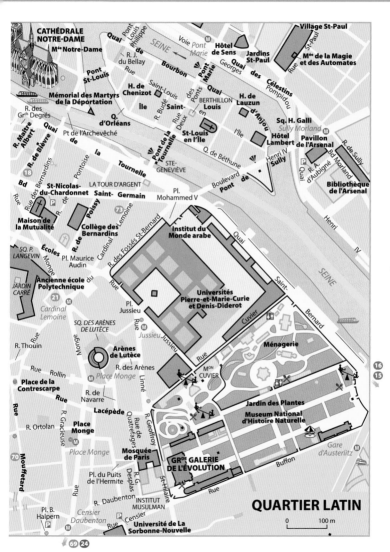

QUARTIER LATIN

0   100 m

The museum is open, but some rooms will be closed or partially closed while new exhibits are installed. Consult the website. The museum brings together two exceptional sites: the Gallo-Roman baths of Lutecia and the **residence of the Cluny abbot**.

Along with the Hôtel de Sens in the Marais, Cluny is one of two remaining large private 15th century residences in Paris and features medieval elements such as decorative niches and turrets.

Thermal baths★ – this vast Gallo-Roman construction, of which only a third remains, was built in the 2C and 3C. It was once a public bath, ransacked and burned by the Barbarians at the end of the Roman Empire.

Museum★★ – The themed rooms tell the story of daily life and art in the Middle Ages. The fine collections include tapestries, fabrics, gold and silver work, iron work, ivory, sculptures and paintings; together, they give us an idea of the sophistication of medieval society. The six hangings of the *Lady and the Unicorn*★★★ are a stunning example of weaving from Holland (15-16C).

LA SORBONNE★

E7 M° Cluny-La Sorbonne.
The bookshops that once lined it have now been replaced by fashion boutiques, but the Place de la Sorbonne still serves as the courtyard for the illustrious university, founded in the 13C. The buildings were originally rebuilt under Richelieu between 1624 and 1632, before being significantly expanded at the end of the 19C. The complex accommodates 22 lecture theatres, two museums, 240 laboratories, a library, a physics tower and an astronomy tower. The rooms, halls and lecture theatres are decorated with historical and allegorical tableaux. The **church★**, built in the Jesuit style, is made up of only two superposed orders (instead of three) on the façade, which serves to lighten the otherwise heavy proportions of the building (1635-1642). The tomb of Cardinal Richelieu (Girardon, 1694) and cupola pendentives painted by Philippe de Champaigne embellish the interior. Other prestigious educational institutions can be found in the area including le Collège de France, lycées St-Louis and Henri-IV and the École Normale Supérieure.

JARDIN DU LUXEMBOURG★★

E6-7 *RER Luxembourg.*
This stretch of green space near to La Sorbonne, Odéon and Montparnasse never fails to delight with its classical beauty
In 1612, Marie de'Medici purchased the residence of the Duke of Luxembourg and its grounds, which would later become a vast park. The garden was designed in the French garden style, characterised by symmetrical lines and harmonious perspectives. The charm of the space is enhanced by the octagonal basin, where children float miniature sailing boats. Italian influences can be seen in the **Medici fountain★**, placed at the end of a picturesque pool; it is surely the most beautiful vestige of Marie de'Medici's garden. Swings, merry-go-rounds and puppet shows can be found on the rue Guynemer edge of the park.
Luxembourg Palace★★ – This palace was completed in 1615 on the commission of Marie de Medici, who wished to escape living in the Louvre, which she hated. Today it houses France's second house of parliament, the Sénat.

PANTHÉON★★

E7 *RER Luxembourg. Pl. du Panthéon - ☎ 01 44 32 18 00 - http://paris-pantheon.fr - Apr-Sep: 10am-6.30pm; rest of the year: 10am-6pm - closed 1 Jan, 1 May, 25 Dec - guided tours (45min) - €9 (under 18 years free)- dome visit €2 (Apr-Oct), accompanied every day at fixed times.*
The restauration of the **Dome★★** of the Pantheon was completed in 2016 and visitors can now climb to the top of the monument (206 steps); 35m/114 feet above Paris, the dome offers a magnificent 360° view of the city.
When **Louis XV** fell gravely ill in 1744, he swore that he would replace the dilapidated church of Ste-Geneviève if he recovered: sure enough, he got better, and charged the architect Soufflot with the construction of a grand church on the highest point of the Rive Gauche. Soufflot designed a huge structure measuring 110 m/360ft long, 84m/275 ft wide and 83m/270ft high. In April 1791, the Revolutionary Assemblée constituante deconsecrated the church and turned it into the Panthéon, a receptacle for the "ashes of the great men of the era of French liberty". Throughout the 19th century it alternately became a church again under the Empire, a necropolis under Louis-Philippe then a church again under Napoleon III, before being used as a general headquarters during the Commune; finally it definitively became a secular temple in 1885, with the reception of Victor Hugo's ashes. Today, more than 70 French cultural figures are buried in the crypt of the Panthéon including Voltaire, Jean Moulin, Louis Braille and Marie Curie. On the front of the church, the peristyle aligns its Corinthian and ribbed columns, which support the triangular pediment, the first of its kind in Paris. Inside, the walls are adorned with paintings undertaken from 1877; the most famous, by Puvis de Chavannes, depict the story of Ste- Geneviève.

ÉGLISE SAINT-ÉTIENNE-DU-MONT★★

E7 RER Luxembourg. 1 pl. Ste-Geneviève - ℘ 01 43 54 11 79 - www.saintetiennedumont.fr - school holidays: *10am-12pm, 4pm-7.45pm, Sun 10am-12.45pm, 4pm-6.45pm (apart from during special masses); rest of the year: 8.45am-7.45pm, Sat 8.45am-12pm, 2pm-7.45pm, Sun 8.45am-12.15pm, 2pm-7.45pm - closed Mondays, 11 Nov - for guided tours, info. on* ℘ 01 43 25 38 49.

This 13C church, reconstructed between the 15C and 17C, is known for its **jube**★★, its organ (the oldest in Paris) and for Ste-Geneviève, who was venerated there. The **façade**★★ is very unusual: three overlaid pediments occupy its centre. Its bell tower softens this imposing frontage. Its Gothic structure explains the luminosity of the church, with large bays on the side aisles; there is also a Flamboyant style choir, ambulatory and a Renaissance window in the nave. The cloister of Charniers bordering the church (it was once bordered by two cemeteries) has beautiful coloured **stained glass**★ evoking biblical sermons (17C).

QUARTIER MOUFFETARD★

F7-8

Don't miss **rue Mouffetard**★, its daily market *(except Mondays.)* and its little shops (À la Bonne Source at n° 122 dates from the 17C); the **place de la Contrescarpe**★ is always well worth an a visit with its lively café terraces. Rabelais held court at le Cabaret de la Pomme de Pin at n° 1.

JARDIN DES PLANTES★★

FG7 M° Gare-d'Austerlitz or Monge. Pl. Valhubert - ℘ 01 40 79 56 01 - www.jardindesplantes.net - summer: 7.30am-8pm; rest of the year: 8am-5.30pm (hours vary dpending on sunrise and sunset) - guided tours available on request (1hr30min) - free. An extraordinary nature reserve, the Jardin des Plantes, offers a dose of oxygen and culture. Visitors may explore the **greenhouses**, the first of their size in the world, constructed in glass and metal (1834-1836). *(* ℘ 01 40 79 56 01 - www.mnhn.fr - guided tours on request - summer: 10am-6pm, Sundays and public holidays 10am-6.30pm; rest of the year: 10am-5pm - closed Tue- €7 (under 4 years free) - ticket gives access to the galerie botanique).* Visitors may also explore the **jardin alpin** *(* ℘ 01 40 79 56 01 - www.jardindesplantes.net - guided tours on request (1hr30min) summer: 7.30am-8pm; rest of the year: 8am-5.30pm - closed Dec.-March - €2 on weekends and public holidays, free during the week. - tickets on sale at the zoo kiosk.),* or visit the animals at the **zoo** opened in 1794. Here, we see small- and medium-sized species, some threatened with extinction, including red pandas and orangutans. *(37 r. Cuvier -* ℘ 01 40 79 56 01 - www.jardindesplantes.net - March-Sept: 9am-6pm, Sun and public holidays. 9am-6.30pm; rest of the year: 9am-5.30pm - guided tours on request (1hr30min) - €13 (under 3 years free),*

44

The garden in a few dates

In 1626, Jean Héroard et Guy de La Brosse, doctors and apothecaries of Louis XIII, obtained the authorisation to install the Royal garden of medicinal plants in Faubourg St-Victor. They turned it into a school of botany, natural history and pharmacy. In 1640, the garden opened to the public. The botanist Tournefort and the three Jussieu brothers travelled the world to enrich its collections. It was under the leadership of Buffon, intendant between 1739-1788, assisted by Daubenton and Antoine Laurent de Jussieu (nephew of the previous), that the botanical garden would reach its apogee. A statue of Buffon was erected during his lifetime, such was his success.

MUSÉUM NATIONAL D'HISTOIRE NATURELLE★★

Grande Galerie de l'évolution★★★

F7 M° Gare-d'Austerlitz. 36 r. Geoffroy-St-Hilaire - ✆ 01 40 79 54 79 - www.mnhn.fr - ♿ - 10am-6pm - closed Tue 1 Jan, 1 May, 25 Dec - guided tours on request (1hr) - €9 (under 26 years free) - €11 combined ticket with temporary exhibitions - ticket gives access to the Children's Gallery- guided tours on request on Saturdays. Info: ✆ 0 826 104 200.

This splendid museum in the heart of the Jardin des Plantes retraces the key stages of evolution through three themes.

The diversity of the living – The museum starts with a marine exhibit on the ground floor, followed by a captivating display of stuffed animals including zebras, giraffes, buffaloes, antelopes and polar bears. The monkeys and birds in the elevator shaft come from tropical rainforest.

Man and evolution – This exhibit looks at man's impact on the natural world, with the most harmful effects on display in the **room of endangered and extinct species★★**.

The evolution of life – Information panels and films explain the theories of the first naturalists (Lamarck, Darwin) up to the most recent discoveries about DNA.

INSTITUT DU MONDE ARABE★

F6 M° Jussieu ou Cardinal-Lemoine. 1 r. des Fossés-St-Bernard - ✆ 01 40 51 38 38 - www.imarabe.org - 10am-6pm, weekend and public holidays 10am-7pm - Closed Mondays, 1 May - guided tours on request (1hr30min) - €8 (under 26 years free).

Architecture – The glass and aluminium building, conceived by Jean Nouvel, synthesises Eastern and Western architectural forms. The south face employs the traditional geometry found in Arabic countries: the 240 panels that open and close each hour evoke moucharabies. To the west, the Book tower is reminiscent of the Great Mosque of Samarra in Iraq. Beautiful **view★★** from the 9th floor terrace (rooftop bar and restaurant).

Museum – The museum presents the many facets of the Arab world and Islam through religion, languages, culture and history; there are exhibitions of contemporary art from Arabic countries.

Muséum national d'histoire naturelle

ARÈNES DE LUTÈCE★

F7 *M° Place-Monge.*
This Gallo-Roman amphitheatre was built in the 2C, before being destroyed by the Barbarians in 280. For 15 centuries it was hidden underground with only the name of the area (clos des Arènes) hinting at its existence. The digging of rue Monge in 1869 would reveal the ancient arena and it was given its current finish in 1910. Today, pétanque and football players share the space.

ÉGLISE DU VAL-DE-GRÂCE★★

E8 *RER Port-Royal. 1 pl. Alphonse-Laveran - ℘ 01 40 51 51 92 - 12pm-6pm - closed Mondays and Fridays, August - €5 (-18 years €2,50) - ticket gives access to the Musée du Service de santé des armées. The church can only be visited via the museum.*

This church was born of Anne of Austria's promise to build a church if she had a son; her wish was granted 21 years later, in 1638, when she gave birth to the future Louis XIV. François Mansart then Lemercier directed the construction. The decoration on the dome is unusual featuring statues, fairies, medallions and cooking pots. The interior is in Baroque style with multicoloured tiling, while the fresco inside the **dome★★** painted by Mignard represents *La Gloire des Bonheureux.*

Saint-Germain-des-Prés★★★ - Montparnasse★

St-Germain, Odéon and Montparnasse are at the heart of the Rive Gauche. Her you walk the footsteps of the intellectuals, activists and writers of post-war Paris, whose haunts were in these legendary districts. It is impossible to resist the charms of St-Germain with its narrow streets lined with galleries, its 17C and 18C hôtels particuliers, grand Haussmannian facades and exquisite window displays. The distinctive atmosphere is completed by the fine art, medicine and architecture schools in the area.

▶ **Access:** M° St-Germain-des-Prés (line 4), Mabillon (line 10), Odéon (lines 4 and 10), St-Sulpice (line 4).

Area map p. 50-51. Detachable map CE5-8.

▶ **Tip:** You'll find most galleries are open on Saturdays.

In post-WW2 Paris, St-Germain-des-Prés became known for its nightlife, jazz cellars and cafés frequented by artists and intellectuals, from Juliette Gréco to Sartre.

On the **Boulevard St-Germain**, which leads to the Odéon district, **Brasserie Lipp** *(151 bd St-Germain - ℘ 01 45 48 53 91 - www.brasserielipp.fr - 11.45am-2am)* was the meeting place of literary and political characters such as Proust, Gide and Malraux, who held salons here; Hemingway also wrote A Farewell to Arms at the café. This era may be over, but walking the streets of St-Germain still offers many delights: the art galleries of rue de Seine, the antique dealers on Quai Voltaire, the bookshops (even

if they are increasingly replaced by fashion boutiques), narrow roads and legendary cafés.

Opened during the Second Empire, the **Café de Flore** *(172 bd St-Germain - ℘ 01 45 48 55 26 - www.cafedeflore.fr - 7am-1.30am.)* is one of the most prestigious, partially because it was a favourite with Apollinaire, Breton, Sartre and Simone de Beauvoir, Camus and Prévert.

Les Deux Magots *(6 pl. St-Germain-des-Prés - ℘ 01 45 48 55 25 - www.lesdeuxmagots.fr - 7.30am-1am)* continues the literary tradition by awarding le prix des Deux Magots each year (started 1933).

Terrasse of Café des Deux Magots

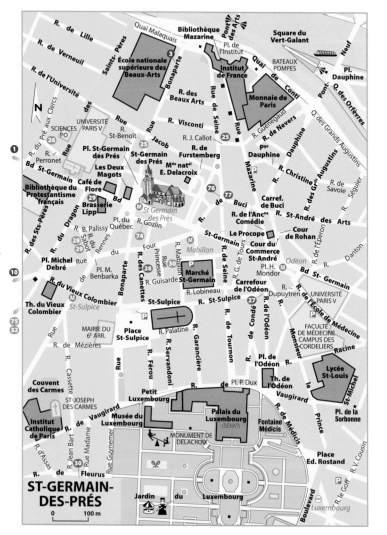

ÉGLISE SAINT-GERMAIN-DES-PRÉS★★

DE6 M° St-Germain-des-Prés.
1 pl. St-Germain-des-Prés - 8am-8pm,
w/e 8.30am-8pm - guided tours on
request (1hr). Major renovation works
underway in the chancel.

Founded in the 6C by Merovingian king Childebert I, son of Clovis, in the 8C this Benedictine abbey became part of the prodigious Benedictine foundation, which comprised 17,000 abbeys and priories, and supplied 24 popes. Despite being destroyed by repeated Norman invasions, the abbey was reconstructed each time. From 1674 it served as a state prison and it was officially declared as such in 1789: its tombs and rich library were removed and replaced by a saltpetre refinery. The 12C architecture has remained largely intact and the huge tower at the front of the church dates from the 11C, while the spire was added in the 19C. The original portal is hidden by an outer portal added in 1607.

RUE DE FURSTENBERG★

E6 M° St-Germain-des-Prés.
A quiet little road with a Paulownia plant-lined square. The **Musée Delacroix★** *(6 r. de Furstenberg - ☎ 01 44 41 86 50 - www. museedelacroix.fr - 9.30am-5.30pm - closed Tuesdays, 1 Jan, 1 May, 25 Dec - guided tours (45min) - €7 (under 26 years free) - €15 combined ticket with the Louvre)* has been established in the workshop occupied by the painter between 1858 and 1863. Major works include, *la Madeleine au désert*, exhibited at the Salon of 1845, and *L'Éducation de la Vierge*. Beautiful gardens in the courtyard.

PLACE SAINT-SULPICE★★

D6 M° St-Sulpice.
Initiated in 1754, the square was designed as semi-circular space defined by uniform façades of the type at **n° 6** (at the corner of rue des Canettes), designed by Servandoni, but the plan's implementation did not materialise.

The central fountain, erected by Visconti in 1844, features sculpted portraits of the great Christian orators of the 17C: Bossuet, Massillon, Fléchier and Fénelon. The district was long famous for selling religious trinkets in specialist shops that surrounded the church. These notoriously kitsch objects, known as "St-Sulpice art", were still very popular until 1960s when fashion boutiques began to

51

New artistic directions

In 1977, 40 antique dealers and gallerists joined together to form the Carré Rive Gauche (www.carrerivegauche.com). Today the association has 120 members concentrated around the Quai Voltaire, rue du Bac, rue des Sts-Pères and rue de l'Université. The group's well-deserved reputation attracts the biggest collectors and museum buyers.

The association Art (www.artsaintgermaindespres.com) was created at the end of the 1990s on a similar model, with galleries on rue de Seine, rue Mazarine and rue Dauphine.

Photo Saint Germain festival Germain (www.photosaintgermain.com), held in November, brings together fifty venues and institutions around a unifying theme such as literature or travel.

replace them: today famous names such as Christian Lacroix and Yves Saint Laurent can be found on the square.

ÉGLISE SAINT-SULPICE★★

D6 *M° St-Sulpice. Pl. St-Sulpice - 8.30am-7.30pm; 8.30am-8pm - guided tour (1hr).*
Founded by the abbey of St-Germain-des-Prés, the church has been rebuilt serveral times and expanded in the 16C and 17C (six architects would work on the project over 134 years). The proportions of the interior are impressive. Delacroix's magnificent **murals★**, painted between 1849 and 1861, decorate the Chapel of Sts-Anges (first on the right): *Saint Michel terrassant le démon* on the vault; *Héliodore chassé du Temple* and *Le Combat de Jacob avec l'Ange* on the walls. The **Chapel of the Virgin★** *(in the chevet)* was decorated under the direction of Servandoni. The Virgin and Child In the niche of the altar is by Pigalle. The **organ case★** is the work of Chalgrin (1776). Reconstructed by Aristide Cavaillé-Coll in 1862, it

is the largest instrument in France (102 manuals distributed across five keyboards) and one of the most impressive.
The little roads to the right of the church lead up towards the Luxembourg Gardens and are full of charm (**rues Férou★, Servandoni★ and Garancière.**)

INSTITUT DE FRANCE★★

E5 *M° St-Germain-des-Prés. 23 quai de Conti - ☏ 01 44 41 44 41 - www.institut-de-france.fr - visits of the dome, salons and courtyard on European Heritage days.*
This majestic edifice sits in harmony with its neighbour across the river, the Louvre. The building seen today came into being thanks to a bequest by **Cardinal Mazarin** for a college of 60 students from France's new provinces acquired from the treaty of the Pyrenees (Piémont, Alsace, Artois and Roussillon). Napoleon transferred the Institute into the buildings of Mazarin's college; it constitutes five Academies: the **Académie française** (created by Richelieu in 1635), the Académie

© Jon Arnold Images/hemis.fr

Pont des Arts and Institut de France

des inscriptions et belles-lettres (established by Colbert in 1663), the Académie des sciences (1666), the Académie des beaux-arts (1816) and the Académie des sciences morales et politiques (1832).

The **bibliothèque Mazarine★** is also the oldest public library in France *(23 quai de Conti - ℘ 01 44 41 44 06 - www.bibliotheque-mazarine.fr - ♿ - grande galerie 10am-6pm - closed w/e,beginning-mid August - guided tours available on request).*

MONNAIE DE PARIS★

***E5** M° St-Germain-des-Prés. 11 quai de Conti - ℘ 01 40 46 57 57 - www.monnaiedeparis.fr - ♿ - 11am-7pm, Thur. 11am-10pm - closed*

Jan 1, 25 Dec. - guided tour on request (1hr) - price varies depending on exhibit. Constructed between 1768 and 1775, the Monnaie de Paris comprises a Neoclassical palace and a minting factory, created by architect Jacques-Denis Antoine. The main body of the palace stretches across 117m/384ft of the quai de Conti, and is remarkable for the simplicity of its lines. The Monnaie de Paris was subject to a huge renovation, named **MétaLmorphoses**: the results were unveiled in autumn 2017, after 7 years of building works. The whole 1.2 ha/2.9ac of the site can now be visited and have been transformed into exhibition spaces and a museum. As well as the museum and collections, workshops are now open to visitors, as well as the garden and internal roads of the complex. The 1st floor has hosted contemporary art exhibitions since 2014. The three Michelin-starred Restaurant Guy Savoy can be found on the first floor (West wing).

QUARTIER DE L'ODÉON★★

E6 M° Odéon.

The crossroads of the Odéon is dominated by a 19C statue of Danton, erected on the site of the tribune house where he was arrested in 1794. It is a lively hub between St-Germain and the Sorbonne packed with cinemas, cafés, old bookshops, galleries and fashion boutiques.

Cour du Commerce-St-André★

Access by n° 130 bd St-Germain, opposite the Danton statue. In 1790 Dr. Guillotin carried out the first test of his guillotine here (on some unfortunate sheep). Marat also printed his Revolutionary journal, *L'Ami du peuple* on this street.

Rue de l'Ancienne-Comédie

Its theatre staged the first performances of plays by Racine and Molière. In 1770, the troop moved to the theatre of the palais des Tuileries before taking over the Odéon. At n° 13, **le Procope** (1686) is the oldest café in Paris, a historical favourite of the elite of Paris's literary scene, from La Fontaine to Verlaine.

La **rue St-André-des-Arts,** which leads to place St-Michel, is lined with fashion boutiques and cafés; fine wrought iron balconies adorn the buildings. **Rue de l'École-de-Médecine**, the Cordeliers Convent was invested in 1791 by the revolutionary club lead by Danton.

The **rue Monsieur-le-Prince** runs alongside the faculty of medicine and lycée St-Louis, towards the Luxembourg Gardens. The restaurant Polidor (n° 41) and le Bouillon Racine (3 r. Racine), are both Art Nouveau addresses , created by the Chartier brothers in 1906. These days they attract plenty of tourists thanks to their eye-catching décor. At n° 4 the beautiful carriage entrance of the former Hôtel de Bacq (mid 18C) can be found. At n° 10, the 2nd floor apartment where philosopher **Auguste Comte** died in 1857 is open to the public. *℘ 01 43 26 08 56 - www.augustecomte.org - Tue 6pm-9pm, Wed 2pm-5pm, Sat 2pm and 3.30pm - closed Aug, public holidays- €4 (under 26 years €2).*

Place★ and Théâtre de l'Odéon

This semicircular plaza, lined with elegant concave buildings, has remained essentially unchanged since its creation in 1779. At n° 1, the café Voltaire was frequented by the Encyclopedists. The **theatre**, created by architects Peyre and de Wailly (1782), was inaugurated by Marie-Antoinette. Ravaged by fire in 1807, Chalgrin (architect of St-Sulpice and the Arc de Triomphe) reproduced the original building. It was renovated in 20C and a magnificent ceiling fresque by André Masson (1965) was added. First performances at Théâtre de l'Odéon include Beaumarchais's *Le Mariage de Figaro*, *Rhinocéros* by Ionesco and *Waiting for Godot* by Samuel Beckett. The Théâtre de l'Odéon was, with the lecture halls of the Sorbonne, one of the sites occupied by students during the unrest of May '68. (& *p. 181*).

LE BON MARCHÉ

D6 M° *Sèvres-Babylone. On the corner of rues du Bac et de Babylone.*
Paris's first department store opened in **Faubourg St-Germain** in 1852. The store's immediate and phenomenal success created many imitators and inspired Zola's novel *The Ladies' Paradise*; its reputation has not diminished since. Today, luxury products are exquisitely displayed amid the original Belle Époque décor. Don't leave without visiting La Grande Épicerie de Paris, a veritable paradise for food-lovers.

MONTPARNASSE★

CD7-8
Follow rue de Rennes, to arrive at Montparnasse.
The area is known for its cinemas and crêperies (Bretons leaving their province for Paris would arrive at Gare Montparnasse) and its legendary brasseries. The latter were made famous by the bohemian intellectuals and artists of the early 20C, who left Montmartre for the south of the city: famous patrons included Modigliani, Salmon, Chagall, Léger, Kisling, Picasso, Apollinaire, Stravinsky and Satie and, in the 1920s, American writers such as Ezra Pound and Ernest Hemingway.

Le Dôme – *108 bd du Montparnasse - ✆ 01 43 35 25 81 - www.restaurant-ledome.com - 12pm-2.45pm, 7pm-11.30pm - closed Sun-Mon (summer).* Created around 1906, this was the favourite haunt of American bohemians.

La Coupole – *102 bd du Montparnasse - ✆ 01 43 20 14 20 - www.lacoupole-paris.com - 8am-11pm, Sat 8am-12am.* Famous dancing spot at the start of the 20C, this brasserie has retained its splendid décor with its frescos, bar and long bay windows.

Le Sélect – *99 bd du Montparnasse - ✆ 01 45 48 38 24 - www.leselect montparnasse.fr - ♿ - 7am-2am, Fri-Sat 7am-3am - closed 25 Dec* The fine Art Deco backdrop of this famous brasserie, inaugurated in 1925, hosted Max Jacob, Apollinaire, Picasso, Modigliani, Cocteau, Zadkine, Henry Miller, Miró, Soutine and Breton.

La Rotonde – *105 bd du Montparnasse - ✆ 01 43 26 48 26 - www.rotondemontparnasse.com - ♿ - 7.30am-2am.* Opened in 1903, this establishment continues the tradition of the Parisian brasserie with aplomb. Its retro environs were once the stomping ground of, among others, Lenin, Trotsky, Picasso, Chagall, Modigliani and Matisse.

The theatres, bars and restaurants of **Rue de la Gaîté** add to the nighttime atmosphere of the area. The Théâtre Montparnasse (n° 31),Théâtre Gaîté-Montparnasse (n° 26), Bobino (n° 20) and the Théâtre Rive-Gauche (n° 6) maintain the artistic reputation of the district.

Tour Montparnasse★

D7 M° *Montparnasse-Bienvenüe. 33 av. du Maine - ✆ 01 45 38 52 56 - www. tourmontparnasse56.com - Apr-Sept: 9.30am-11.30pm; rest of the year: 9.30am-10.30pm, Fri-Sat and the eve of public holidays 9.30am-11pm -*

€15 (under 7 years free. Atop its 209 m/685ft tower (59 floors), the 360° **view**★★★ of Paris is exceptional. The former artists' workshops of the **école de Paris** have been transformed into charming museums.

Musée Zadkine★

100 bis r. d'Assas - ☎ 01 55 42 77 20 - www.zadkine.paris.fr - ♿ - 10am-6pm - closed Mon and public holidays - guided tours on request (1hr) - free - €5/12 temporary exhibitions. The workshop and grand gardens occupied by the Russian sculptor are now a tucked-away museum with a delightful atmosphere.

Musée Bourdelle★

18 r. Antoine-Bourdelle - ☎ 01 49 54 73 73 - www.bourdelle.paris.fr -
10am-6pm - closed Sun and public holidays - guided tour (1hr) bookable Tues-Wed Booking: ☎ 01 49 54 73 91 - €5/9 temporary exhibitions - €5 audioguide. Housed in the former home and workshop of sculptor Antoine Bourdelle (1861-1929), just the site in itself is well worth a visit. Bourdelle, a one-time student of Rodin, was responsible for, among other projects, the decoration of the Théâtre des Champs-Élysées.

Cimetière du Montparnasse

***D8** M° Edgar-Quinet. 3 bd Edgar-Quinet - 8am-6pm (opening hours vary depending on season).* This cemetery, founded in 1824 is the resting place of artists, writers and intellectuels: Baudelaire, Proudhon, Saint-Saëns, Maupassant, Sartre,

Musée Bourdelle

Simone de Beauvoir, Samuel Beckett, Jean Seberg, Marguerite Duras and Serge Gainsbourg, among others. At 19ha/47ac, it is the second biggest burial ground in the city of Paris after Père-Lachaise.

Fondation Cartier pour l'art contemporain★

D8 M° Raspail. 261 bd Raspail - ☎ 01 42 18 56 50 - www.fondation. cartier.com - ♿ - 11am-8pm, Tue 11am-10pm - closed Mondays - guided tours on request (1hr) - €10.50 (under 25 years €7). This "building of images" created by Jean Nouvel plays with perceptions of the real and virtual with a glass wall-cum-screen that elongates the perspective of Boulevard Raspail. The exhibitions span the most varied domains of creation: arts naïf , contemporary art and high-tech arts.

The nearby **rue Campagne-Première** saw many artists pass through in the 1920s and '30s. Man Ray rented a studio at nos 31-31 bis between 1922 and 1940, where all the big names of the Paris art and fashion world came to be photographed; the building is easily recognisable with its floor-to-ceiling glass windows and multicoloured tile and sandstone façade. At no 17, you'll find a passage lined with little buildings housing artists' studios.

Fondation Henri Cartier-Bresson

D8 M° Gaîté. 2 imp. Lebouis - ☎ 01 56 80 27 00 - www.henricartierbresson. org - 1pm-6.30pm, Wed 1pm-8.30pm, Sat 11am-6.45pm - closed Mon - guided tours on request (1hr) - €8 - free Wed (6.30pm-8.30pm) - open only *during exhibitions.* Housed in a bright, airy studio arranged over several levels, the foundation is a hotspot for photography lovers. It contains the works of Cartier-Bresson (1908-2004).

Catacombes★

Out of map M° Denfert-Rochereau. *1 r. du col.-Henri-Rol-Tanguy - ☎ 01 43 22 47 63 - www.catacombes.paris.fr - 10am-8pm - closed Mon, 1 May - guided tours (1hr30min) €12 - €16 combined ticket with the Crypte archéologique of Notre-Dame - €5 audioguide. No toilets or cloakrooms - visit not recommended for those with heart or breathing difficulties; mobility constraints; young children (130 steps to climb down, 83 to climb back up, temperature: 14 °C).* These former Gallo-Roman lime quarries, converted into a vast ossuary between 1785 and 1810, brought together skeletons from the different parishes of Paris. Shivers guaranteed in front of the arrangements of skulls and femurs! The entrance to the Catacombs is found on Place Denfert-Rochereau, with the Lion of Belfort at its centre (bronze sculpture by Auguste Bartholdi) evoking Colonel Denfert-Rochereau who defended the town of Belfort, in 1870-1871, during the Franco-Prussian war. You will find little shops at the pedestrianised rue Daguerre nearby; this colourful little street is a favourite of legendary director Agnès Varda. It is a great spot for food vendors and fruit and vegetable sellers.

Invalides★★★ - Eiffel Tower★★★

The tree-lined avenues of the 7th arrondissement are home to ministries, embassies and hôtels particuliers with grand gardens. Walk the district and you'll be treated to glimpses of the Eiffel Tower and the dazzling dome of the Invalides complex. The Musée du Quai-Branly adds a touch of modernity in otherwise formal surroundings with its exhibits of global art spanning four continents.

▶**Access: Invalides:** M° Invalides (lines 8and 13), Varenne (line 13), La Tour-Maubourg (line 8). RER Invalides (line C).
Tour Eiffel: M° Bir-Hakeim (line 6), École-Militaire (line 8), Trocadéro (lines 6 and 9). RER Champ-de-Mars-Tour-Eiffel (line C). You can also get to the area on Batobus (Tour-Eiffel and Musée-d'Orsay station).
Detachable map AD4-6.
▶**Tip:** If you're taking a break between sights, opt for the Rives de Seine park or the gardens of the Musée Rodin. For shopping, fairly hard to come by in this neighbourhood, head for the place de l'École-Militaire and rue Cler (a lively cobbled street, packed with bars, restaurants and quality shopping spots).

PONT ALEXANDRE-III★★

C4
This majestic bridge was built for the 1900 World Fair. The first stone was laid on 7 October 1896 by Tsar Nicolas II and the bridge has since symbolised the secular bond between France and Russia. The 109m/357ft single-span bridge was a technical marvel at the time of its inauguration and it still dazzles with its fine decoration (vaulting, candelabras) and burnished details, matching the dome of the Invalides; two golden Pegasus statues on the Left Bank represent War and two on the Right Bank represent peace.

LES INVALIDES★★★

From the bridge, walk or cycle across the Esplanade des Invalides, constructed between 1704 and 1720 by Robert de Cotte, brother-in-law of Mansart. Take a minute to contemplate the view of the majestic dome of the Hôtel des Invalides and its tree-lined lawns.

The Hôtel des Invalides

C5 M° Varenne. 129 r. de Grenelle - ℘ 01 44 42 51 73 - www.musee-armee.fr - ♿ - Apr-Oct: 10am-6pm; rest of the year: 10am-5pm, Christmas holidays 5.30pm - closed 1st Mon of month (except Jul-Sept), 1 Jan, 1 May, 25 Dec - guided tour (1hr45min) - €11 *(under 25 years free) - ticket gives access to permenant collections, Musée de l'Armée, Eglise du Dôme, Napoleon I's tomb, Historial Charles de Gaulle, Musée des Plans-Reliefs, Musée de l'Ordre de la Libération.*

The Invalides was originally commissioned by Louis XIV as a retirement home for destitute war veterans. Later it would become a barracks then a monastery before coming back to its first use at the start of the 20C, when it was once more used as a place to tend to the war wounded. It houses various military administrations and several museums, including the Musée de l'Armée. The 196m/643ft **façade★**, designed by Libéral Bruant, is impressive to look upon: its vast central portal (the only example of its kind in France) is reminiscent of the Arc de Triomphe and gives acess to the **cour d'honneur★★**. The austere beauty of the site is striking; Napoleon often passed through here to inspect his veterans. A statue called the *Petit Caporal*, by Seurre, occupies the middle of the courtyard

Église St-Louis des Invalides★

The construction of the "soldiers' church" was the work of Jules Hardouin-Mansart, who was inspired by the designs of Libéral Bruant. Inside, flags seized from enemy forces are the only decoration. Behind the high altar, the baldachin of the Eglise du Dôme can be seen through a large glass pane.

Église du Dôme★★★

C5 This majestic church in French Classical style was constructed between 1677 and 1706 by Jules Hardouin-Mansart. The ribbed and hemispherical dome corresponds with the vertical thrust of the base, constructed on the model of the Greek cross. It was renovated to magnificent effect on the bicentenary of the French Revolution, when 555,000 sheets of gold (weighing 12.65 kg) were added to the dome. **Napoleon's tomb**, comprised of a sarcophagus made of porphyry rock, can be found at the end of the crypt. Two large bronze statues stand guard, one holding a globe and the other holding a sceptre and the imperial crown, surrounded by twelve figures of Victory, sculpted by Pradier.

Musée de l'Armée★★★

C5 *Entry via the cour d'honneur on the Esplanade. For practical details, see Hôtel des Invalides.*
Dedicated to military history and technique, this is one of the world's richest army museums. Its exceptional collection comprises arms and armour from the 13C to 17C including the sword and armour of Francois I, uniforms and battle models from the time of Louis XIV to Napoleon III, as well as musical instruments and military decorations. The dedicated **World Wars I and II** sections tell the story of the conflicts, from defeat at the end of the Franco-Prussian war to the Libération and surrender of Germany and Japan in 1945. The **Historial Charles-de-Gaulle★** traces the career of the general via more than 500,000 pieces, with a particular focus on images. In the **Musée des Plans-Reliefs★★** we find extraordinary models of towns, ports and strongholds, used for the study of military strategy.

MUSÉE RODIN★★

C5 M° Varenne. Hôtel Biron - 79 r. de Varenne - ℰ 01 44 18 61 10 - www. musee-rodin.fr - ፟ - 10am-5.15pm - closed Mondays, 1 Jan, 1 May, 25 Dec - guided tours on request (1hr30min) - €10.

The Musée Rodin occupies the stunning **Hôtel Biron★★** and its garden, dating originally from the 18C; **Auguste Rodin** (1840-1917) installed his workshop here in 1908. Recently reopened after a total renovation, this secluded site has been completely reimagined and offers a chronological and thematic exploration of Rodin's work, displayed across 18 beautiful wood-panelled rooms. Most works are in bronze or marble and marked by a vigour of expression and energy and their powerful content. The "Rodin at Hôtel Biron" room has been reconstructed, with the help of photographs from the time, to look as it would have when the sculptor occupied the space and features his restored furniture. The "Rodin and Antiquity" room displays more than 100 fragments of Greek, Roman and Egyptian sculptures, bought and collected by Rodin.

There are also superb **gardens**, dotted with some of the sculptor's major works (Le Penseur, Les Bourgeois de Calais, La Porte de l'Enfer, the Ugolin group), plus a chapel with a 12m/40ft-high glass ceiling.

Visitors may also discover the creations of **Camille Claudel** (sister of playwright Paul Claudel and Rodin's mistress), including *La Vague*, as well as three Van Gogh canvasses (*Le Père Tanguy, Vue du Viaduc d'Arles* and *Les Moissonneurs*), from the personal collection of the master.

ÉCOLE MILITAIRE★

B6 M° École-Militaire.
The building is made up of a central pavilion (designed by Jacques-Ange Gabriel) decorated with ten Corinthian columns topped with a ribbed pediment. The wings flanking the pavilion date from the Second Empire. The school was created to train 500 young gentlemen without means to become officers. Today the building still houses the School of Advanced War Studies and the School of National Defence.

JARDINS DU CHAMP-DE-MARS★

B5-6 M° École-Militaire ou RER C Champ-de-Mars-Tour-Eiffel.
At the time of the construction of the École Militaire, the market gardens that stretched from the buildings to the Seine were transformed into a military manoeuvres ground, named the Champ-de-Mars. It also became a place of patriotic celebrations: the first anniversary of the seizing of the Bastille was celebrated there on 14 July 1790 and Napoleon would use the site to distribute military decoration. It later became an exhibition site for Paris's successive World's Fairs during the Belle Époque. At the southern tip of the park we find the **Wall of Peace**, created by artist Clara Halter and built in 2000 by architect Jean-Michel Wilmotte to mark the millennium. It is inspired in a good part by the Wailing Wall in Jerusalem. Today this vast open park welcomes large crowds on special

occasions, like the firework display on France's National Day, July 14. On sunny days, this is a popular picnic spot for tourists and Parisians with its expansive lawns and fine view of the Eiffel Tower and Palais de Chaillot.

TOUR EIFFEL★★★

A5 RER C Champ-de-Mars-Tour-Eiffel. Champ-de-Mars - ℘ 0 892 70 12 39 - www.toureiffel.fr - from mid-June to end of Aug. 9am-12am; rest of the year: 9.30am-11pm - €17 -summit access by elevator; €11 access 2nd level by elevator; €7 access 2nd level by stairs - tickets can be purchased online.

😊 The summit can be reached by climbing 1,652 steps or in the elevators. Buy tickets online to save time or arrive 15-30 min. before opening to minimise queuing; there's no rule for the wait later in the day and crowds vary depending on the day. You cannot go directly to the 3rd level, instead you must go to the 2nd level and take another lift (the wait is between 5 and 45min depending on the day). Between October and April, be sure to wrap up warm as the queue for the summer is an exposed spot and it can be very windy and cold.

A viewing tower over the whole capital, the Eiffel Tower is indisputably the most famous silhouette in the world. Its interlacing metal beams and lifts are the work of engineer **Gustave Eiffel** (1832-1923). Between 1887 and 1889, 300 acrobatic construction workers assembled two and a half million rivets. Total height: 324m/1062ft; weight: 7300t and 60t of paint, renewed every seven years.

On the ground floor, the elaborate machinery of the elevator can be visited. On the 1st floor (57m/187ft), there is a glass floor extending the internal edge of the level: a must for thrill-seekers. There is also an outdoor area on this level, displaying photographs and information about the history and construction of the tower. On the second level, (115m/377ft) the monuments of Paris

The tower saved by the radio

Gustave Eiffel's project for the Exposition Universelle of 1889, launched in 1884, was initially a very controversial undertaking. The tower was originally meant to stand for twenty years, which was already too much for a group of writers, painters and pre-eminent artists who called themselves "the 300" in mocking reference to the height of the tower (300m). They published a public letter of protest, which was signed by such cultural luminaries as Guy de Maupassant and Charles Garnier. Luckily, many other artists were impressed and inspired by the "Iron Lady", seeing it as symbol of modernity and the new artistic style of the coming century. Cocteau and Apollinaire celebrated it, while Pissarro, Duffy, Utrillo, Seurat and Delaunay notably featured it in their works. In 1909 it was threatened with destruction, but was saved by its utility for the TSF (wireless telegraph): an aerial was placed at its summit and it was from here that the first radio telephone tests were carried out at the start of the 20th century.

can be observed through porthole windows or the open-air viewing platform; animated panels explain the construction of the tower. Restaurants and shops can be found on the upper level of the second floor. On the third floor, at 276m/905.5ft, the **view★★★** can extend across 67km/42mi in ideal conditions. View information displayed on every level.

Lovers of Japanese culture may visit **Maison de la culture du Japon à Paris**, just next to the tower (*101 bis quai Branly - ℘ 01 44 37 95 00 - www. mcjp.fr - ♿ - Tue-Sat 12pm-8pm - closed August, some public and school holidays.*)

MUSÉE DU QUAI-BRANLY★★

B4-5 *RER C Pont-de-l'Alma. 37 quai Branly - ℘ 01 56 61 70 00 - www. quaibranly.fr - ♿ - 11am-7pm, Thu-Sat 11am-9pm - closed Mondays, 1 May, 25 Dec - guided visits on request (1hr) - €10.*

The north facade of the museum is covered with a vast **vegetation wall★** created by botanist Patrick Blanc. It is made up of 15 000 plants spanning 150 species from across the world. Conceived by Jean Nouvel, the museum was created in 2006 with the amalgamation of collections from the Musée de l'Homme and the Musée national des Arts d'Afrique et d'Océanie. Organised in four geographic zones (Oceania, Asia, Africa, America, each continent with its own colour-coded floor), the collection exhibits almost 3,600 works (from a collection of 270,000 pieces). The subdued light and the large, dark volume of the space without

walls or rooms superbly highlight the **collections★★★** contextualised by various visual and sound documents. The sheer volume of masterpieces is astounding. The garden-savannah that surrounds the museum, created by Gilles Clément, is the setting for cultural activities in summer (see website for details).

Next to the museum, you will see the five golden domes of the new Orthodox cathedral of Paris *(corner of Av. Rapp-Quai Branly)*, which houses the **Russian Orthodox Spiritual and Cultural Center**.

PARC RIVES DE SEINE, RIVE GAUCHE

BD4-5 *Entre le RER Pont-de-l'Alma et Musée-d'Orsay.* ☺ *For information on the programme for the Berges de la Seine, see www.paris.fr/rivesdeseine or go to the information point at Port de Solférino (Tue-Sun 12pm-7.30pm).* You can buy picnic food on rue de l'Université (between Pont de l'Alma and Invalides) or rue St-Dominique (behind the Musée d'Orsay).

All supermarkets sell prepared foods good for picnics.

This 2.5km/1.5mi pedestrian walkway, integrated into the Rives de Seine Park (p.21), stretches along the Left Bank of the Seine, between the Musée du quai Branly (Pont de l'Alma) and the Musée d'Orsay (Pont Royal). It's a popular relaxation and leisure space and you'll find floating gardens, chill-out spaces, bars, restaurants, pop-up installations and a stage.

Musée d'Orsay ★★★

Located along the Seine in the heart of Faubourg St-Germain, the Orsay was inaugurated in 1986 in the former Gare d'Orsay. It houses the most beautiful collection of Impressionist art in the world. It is a short stroll or cycle ride along the Seine from the Musée du Quai-Branly.

▶**Access:** RER Musée-d'Orsay (line C), M° Solférino or Assemblée nationale (line 12).

Detachable map **D5.**

▶**Tip:** Take advantage of the late opening hours on Thursday, when the museum is less busy.

The gallery covers all the innovative and avant-garde artistic movements of the period between 1848-1914 (Neoclassicism, Romanticism, the Barbizon school, Eclecticism, Academic art, Symbolism, Impressionism, Naturalism, school of Pont-Aven, neo and post-Impressionism and the Nabis) in a collection that spans painting, sculpture, architecture, decorative arts, graphic art and photography. It makes an excellent bridge between the collections of the Louvre and the Centre Pompidou. The works are presented chronologically, by artists and/or movements and the museum is constantly working on ways to better display the works and make them accessible to the wider public. Temporary displays of more fragile pieces that can't be exhibited for long periods (drawings, pastels, photographs) are interspersed around the space.

KEY WORKS

Among the **paintings**, don't miss *La Chasse aux lions* by Eugène Delacroix, l'*Angélus du soir* by Jean-François Millet, *Un enterrement à Ornans* by Gustave Courbet, *La Famille Bellelli* by Edgar Degas, *Orphée* by Gustave Moreau, *Le Déjeuner sur l'herbe* and *Olympia* by Édouard Manet, the *Cathédrale de Rouen* series by Claude Monet, *Les Raboteurs de parquet* by Gustave Caillebotte,

Practical info.

📞 01 40 49 48 14 - www.musee-orsay.fr - 9.30am-6pm, Thu 9.30am-9.45pm - closed Mon, 1 May, 25 Dec - €12-€16 combined ticket with the Musée de l'Orangerie - €5 audioguide - €6 guided tour .

Palace, station, museum

In 1910, Orsay was a palace used for State administration. It was destroyed by fire during the Paris Commune in 1871 and the Orléans Railway Company acquired its burnt-out ruins. In the lead-up to the 1900 World's Fair, the company made plans to transform it into a prestigious station, aesthetically worthy of the elegant neighbourhood close to the Louvre and Tuileries. Victor Laloux (1850-1937) oversaw the project. The industrial glass and metal of the main structure would be hidden by a monumental facade, inspired by the Louvre and a stucco ceiling on the inside. The station was inaugurated on 14 July 1900.

the *Bal du moulin de la Galette* by Auguste Renoir, *Pommes et Oranges* by Paul Cézanne, *La Toilette* by Henri de Toulouse-Lautrec, *Les Nourrices* by Édouard Vuillard, l'*Autoportrait au Christ jaune* by Paul Gauguin, l'*Église d'Auvers-sur-Oise* by Vincent Van Gogh, *Le Cirque* by Georges Seurat, and *La Dame au jardin clos* by Maurice Denis, acquired in 2012, *Danseuses*, also called *Le Ballet* by Pierre Bonnard, acquired in 2013 and *Le Toast* by Félix Valloton, acquired in 2014.

Sculptures: la *Danse* by Carpeaux, *Honoré de Balzac* by Rodin, *Petite Danseuse* by Degas and *L'Âge mûr* by Camille Claudel.

In the **decorative arts** section (1850-1880) the workd on show demonstrate the 'eclecticism of an era marked by colonisation, travel, World's Fairs: the dressing tables of the Duchesses of Parma, by the maison Froment-Meurice, made in 1851; grand wood panelling (1900-1906) created by Jean Dampt for the Countess of Béarn, Gallé's Vitrine aux libellules; the Nénuphar lamp by Majorelle and the Daum brothers. The **photographic** collection (on the ground floor and mezzanine level, on rue de Lille side) featuring works from well-known figures— Le Gray, Bayard, Nègre, Nadar — and anonymous artists (50,000 prints in total), charts the history of photography from Nicéphore Niépce in 1839 until the 1920s.

The **graphic arts** collection is comprised of more than 10,000 drawings, with some exceptional examples such as *Le Nœud noir* by Georges Seurat and *L'Autoportrait dit aux masques* by Léon Spilliaert.

The **architecture** section (at the back of the main hall on the ground floor) focuses on the Second Empire (1852-1870) and Haussmann's urbanisation of Paris. The display features scale models and examples of décor, including a very interesting model of the Opéra district displayed under a glass panel in the floor.

67

After your visit

Take a stroll in the Parc Rives de Seine (📞 see p.64). The Solférino footbridge connects to the Tuileries Gardens on the Right Bank (📞 see p.74).

Trocadéro - Chaillot★★ - Alma

The hill of Chaillot, located in a quiet and elegant district, offers a magnificent uninterrupted view of the Eiffel Tower and museums to suit every taste (ethnography, architecture, Asian art, modern and contemporary art, fashion). This well-heeled part of town is also home to the luxury stores that make Paris the fashion capital of the world: Chanel, Dior, Vuitton and Givenchy can be found along the opulent Avenue Montaigne.

▶**Access:** M° Trocadéro (lines 6 and 9). RER Champ-de-Mars-Tour-Eiffel (line C). M° Alma-Marceau or Iéna (line 9).
Detachable map AC3-4.
▶**Tip:** The Cité de l'Architecture et du Patrimoine has a great café with floor-to-ceiling windows and terrace offering an uninterrupted view of the Eiffel Tower and Champs-de-Mars; Café Lucy on the 2nd floor of the Musée de l'Homme also offers fine views.

PALAIS DE CHAILLOT★★

A4 M° Trocadéro. This palace was erected for the World's Fair of 1937, as is the case for most of the Trocadéro buildings. Its courtyard of the Droits de l'homme leads to a vast **terrace★★★** with an uninterrupted view of the Eiffel Tower. The **Jardins du Trocadéro** spread out below, also designed for the World's Fair. Two buildings flank the *parvis.*

Musée de l'Homme★★

17 pl. du Trocadéro - ☎ 01 44 05 72 72 - www.museedelhomme.fr - ♿ - guided tours on advance booking (1hr30mins) 10am-6pm - closed Tue, 1 Jan, 1 May, 25 Dec - €10 - Resource Centre open to all. Festival of ethnographic film. Bookshop. Café Lucy and Café de l'Homme. Bringing together diverse scientific disciplines – biology, philosophy, anthropology and history – the Musée de l'Homme reopened in October 2015 after six years of renovations. Exhibition spaces feature fascinating displays and innovative mueseography including audio-visual installations using screens, sounds and documentary film. The museum aims to respond to three key questions: Who are we? Where do we come from? And where are we going?

The richness of human nature is examined via eclectic exhibits: from the brain of the Cro-Magnon man to the brain of Descartes; from the Venus de Lespugue sculpted in mammoth ivory over 20,000 years ago, via the curious display (19m/62ft long and 11m/36ft high) of busts in plaster and bronze from throughout the 19C. The planisphere wall is well worth seeing:

Parvis des droits de l'homme, Palais de Chaillot and the Eiffel Tower

the visitor is invited to "pull" tongues to activate recordings of 30 languages from around the world. Another exhibit allows visitors to virtually transform their face from homo sapiens to Neanderthal.

Next door, the **Musée national de la Marine** retraces the history of the French navy from the 17C. via some 350 model boats, a collection of naval sculptures and various displays. The museum will be closed for renovation until 2021.

Chaillot Théâtre National de la Danse

1 pl. du Trocadéro - ☎ 01 53 65 30 00 - www.theatre-chaillot.fr - closed 1 Jan, 1 May, 14 Jul, 15 Aug - price varies depending on show. A vast theatre can

be found under the palace's terrace. Firmin Gémier created the TNP (Théâtre National Populaire) here in 1920, which Jean Vilar directed from 1951 to 1963. Today, "Chaillot" offers an excellent programme of contemporary dance and theatre.

Cité de l'architecture et du patrimoine★★

1 pl. du Trocadéro-et-du-11-Novembre - ☎ 01 58 51 52 00 - www.citechaillot. fr - ♿ -guided tours; book in advance (2hr) 11am-7pm, Thu. 11am-9pm -closed Tuesdays, 1 Jan, 1 May, 15 Aug, 25 Dec - €8 - €12 combined ticket with contemporary exhibitions. Founded in 1879 on the initiative of architect Viollet-le-Duc, this tastefully modernised museum presents the key monuments of France from the Middle Ages to the 18C. You will find casts, models and life-sized replicas housed in a huge gallery with Pompeian red walls. A room dedicated to murals can be found on the second floor.

MUSÉE NATIONAL DES ARTS ASIATIQUES - GUIMET★★★

A4 M° Iéna. 6 pl. d'Iéna - ☏ 01 56 52 53 00 - www.guimet.fr - 10am-6pm - closed Tuesdays, 1 Jan, 1 May, 25 Dec - €7.50-€9.50 combined ticket with temporary exhibitions.

This temple of Asian culture was built by the Lyonnais collector Émile Guimet (1836-1919) in 1889 and was renovated in the 1990s by the architects Henri and Bruno Gaudin, creating a bright exhibition space. Its collection of Asian art is reputed to be the richest in the world. Highlights include: the **treasures of Khmer art★★**, sumptuous burnished bronze Buddhas, Nepalese portable paintings, Tibetan statuettes and ritual objects, **spirit objects★★** from the northern Chinese provinces and **Ming porcelain★** (1368-1644) in colourful enamel or decorated in sumptuous blues and whites. The collection also features lacquered furniture, gilded and inlaid with dazzling mother-of-pearl, as well as beautiful prints signed by Utamaro (18C), Sharaku (late 18C), Hiroshige (19C) and Hokusai, including the famous **The Great Wave off Kanagawa★★**.

MUSÉE D'ART MODERNE DE LA VILLE DE PARIS★★

B4 M° Iéna. 11 av. du Prés.-Wilson - ☏ 01 53 67 40 00 - www.mam.paris.fr - 10am-6pm, Thu 10am-10pm - closed Mondays, some public holidays - guided tours (1hr) - free - permanent collection, €5/12 temporary exhibitions.

All the major waves of 20C painting are exhibited in this wing of the Palais de Tokyo, built for the Exposition Internationale des Arts et Techniques of 1937 and since redesigned. Presented chronologically, the collections comprise the avant-garde movements of the 20C (Fauvism, Cubism, Surrealism, including Fernand Léger). Next comes post-War abstraction and the Expressionism of the 1920s (École de Paris: Modigliani, Soutine, Pascin, Blanchard).

For the second half of the 20C, the emphasis is on French and European movements, represented by, among others: Louise Bourgeois, Daniel Buren, Christian Boltanski, Bertrand Lavier and Annette Messager.

Among the major works of the century: Les Disques by Léger (1918), L'Équipe de Cardiff by Robert Delaunay (1912-1913), the Pastorale and the magnificent **Danse de Paris★** by Matisse (1932), the Évocation by Picasso, Rêve by Chagall. **La Fée Électricité★** (1937) by Raoul Dufy, which is among the biggest canvasses in the world (600 m², 1968 ft² ; 250 juxtaposed panels), sets Antiquity against its transformation by philosophers and scholars who studied and harnessed its energy.

70

The Master of Impressionism

The **Musée Marmottan-Monet★★** hosts what is probably the most important body of work of the Master of Impressionism. Sixty-five paintings are exhibited, bequeathed by his son Michel Monet, including "Impression, soleil levant" (1872), the canvass that would give the Impressionist movement its name. Many of the works were painted at Monet's Normandy home at Giverny, while other pieces show the artist's preoccupation with light (Rouen Cathedral). The collection also features paintings by his contemporaries and friends, including Renoir, Caillebotte and Berthe Morisot. The gallery hosts temporary exhibitions too, usually themed around Impressionism.

B4 Mᵒ La Muette - 2 r. Louis-Boilly - ☎ 01 44 96 50 33 - www.marmottan.fr - ♿ - 10am-6pm, Thu 10am-9pm - closed Mondays, 1 Jan, 1 May, 25 Dec - €11 - €20.50 combined ticket with the Fondation Monet in Giverny.

PALAIS DE TOKYO - SITE OF CONTEMPORARY CREATION★

B4 Mᵒ Iéna. 13 av. du Prés.-Wilson - ☎ 01 81 97 35 88 - www.palaisdetokyo.com - ♿ - 12pm-12am - closed Tue 1 Jan, 1 May, 25 Dec - guided tour (1hr30mins) - €12 (under 18s free). Entirely reorganised in 2012, this fully modular 22,000m²/ 72,178ft² space is an irreverent hub for new artistic practices and experiments across the domains of art, design, fashion, photography, video, film, literature and dance. With a packed programme of exhibitions, artistic performances, conferences, screenings, concerts and interactive children's workshops, there is always something to see or do at the Palais de Tokyo.

PALAIS GALLIERA - MUSÉE DE LA MODE DE LA VILLE DE PARIS

B4 Mᵒ Iéna ou Alma-Marceau. 10 av. Pierre-1ᵉʳ-de-Serbie - ☎ 01 56 52 86 00 - http://palaisgalliera.paris.fr - ♿ - 10am-6pm, Thu 10am-9pm - closed Mondays, some public holidays- guided tours (1hr30min) - €12 - only open during temporary exhibitions. This pretty mansion was built by Léon Ginain between 1878 and 1894 at the request of Marie Brignole-Sale, Duchess of Galliera, to house her rich collection of art. Today it is the site of the **Musée de la mode de la Ville de Paris**, which hosts temporary exhibitions on themes of fashion and costume, drawn from a vast collection from 1735 to the present day.

MUSÉE YVES SAINT LAURENT PARIS

B4 Mᵒ Alma-Marceau. 5 Avenue Marceau - ☎ 01 44 31 64 00 - https://museeyslparis.com- ♿ - 11am-6pm, Sun 11am-4.30pm - closed Mon. For almost 30 years this grand mansion was the couture house of Yves Saint Laurent. In October 2017 it reopened as a museum dedicated to the legendary Parisian designer's work, displaying a rotating selection from a vast archive of 5,000 garments

Palais Galliera

and 15,000 accessories. There are also original notes and sketches, visual installations and voiceovers. Among the exquisite sartorial creations, the intimate recreation of YSL's studio is a highlight.

AVENUE MONTAIGNE

B4-C3

Lined with prestigious **fashion boutiques** (Armani, Valentino, Chanel, Christian Dior, Céline, Nina Ricci), it is on this street (at n° 30) that Christian Dior presented his first collection in 1947, soon followed by Yves Saint Laurent. Once known as "Widows' Alley", this avenue has changed drastically since the time of Eugène Sue, who chronicled its bad reputation *Les Mystères de Paris*.
The **Théâtre des Champs-Élysées★** (n° 15) is the work of the Perret brothers (1912). Antoine Bourdelle designed the façade, while Maurice Denis was responsible for the décor of the ceiling and *grande salle*. Diaghilev, Joséphine Baker and Rudolf Noureïev all at one time graced the iconic stage.

Champs-Élysées★★★ and the West

The "Voie Triomphale" or Triumphal Way, which extends 7km/4.3mi across the city, is the most iconic vista in Paris. From the Louvre to modern arch at La Défense, its architecture takes in close to nine centuries of history. The Voie Triomphale is peppered with some of France's greatest monuments including seats of high power, two magnificent palaces built for the 1900 World's Fair, famous museums and magnificent gardens.

▶ **Access:** M° Tuileries (line 1), Concorde (lines 1, 8 and 12), Champs-Élysées-Clemenceau (lines 1 and 13), Franklin-D.-Roosevelt (lines 1 and 9), George-V (line 1) and Charles-de-Gaulle-Étoile (lines 1, 2 and 6). RER Charles-de-Gaulle-Étoile (line A). Batobus Champs-Élysées station.
Detachable map AD1-4.
▶ **Tip:** Walk the exceptional route between the Louvre and the Arc de Triomphe, stopping at the Tuileries Gardens or further down the Seine at the Port des Champs-Élysées (on the Right Bank, between the Passerelle Solférino and Pont des Invalides). Here, you will find an enchanting riverside village, hidden in plain sight in the heart of Paris.

PLACE DE LA CONCORDE★★★

CD4 M° Concorde.
The **Obelisk★**, given to France in 1831 by Muhammad Ali, viceroy of Egypt, was erected in its current position in 1836. Made of pink granite, covered in hieroglyphics, with a lead and gold tip, it is 23m/75ft high and weighs almost 220t. The Obelisk provides the best spot from which to appreciate the famous vistas: the Chevaux de Marly (the work of Coustou, originals at the Louvre) guide the gaze towards the Champs-Élysées; the winged horses of Coysevox (originals in the Louvre) point towards the Tuileries and the Louvre. The immense pediment and high columns of the **Madeleine★** are visible at the end of **rue Royale★**,

mirroring the **Palais-Bourbon★** (Assemblée Nationale) on the other end of the **Pont de la Concorde**.

JARDIN DES TUILERIES★

D4 M° Concorde ou Tuileries. R. de Rivoli - ☏ 01 40 20 53 17 - June-Aug: 7am-11pm; March-May and Sep: 7am-9pm; rest of the year: 7am-7pm - the Louvre Museum offers guided visits of the garden and its sculptures, Apr-Oct: weekends and public holidays 3pm (free), meeting point: foot of the Arc de Triomphe du Carrousel du Louvre.
To embellish her future Château des Tuileries, Catherine de'Medici drew up Italian-style gardens. She installed fountains, a labyrinth, a menagerie, and even a grotto. Henri IV added

an orangery and a greenhouse and this park subsequently became a fashionable walkway. In 1664, Colbert entrusted its improvement to Le Nôtre. To catch the slope of the land, he raised two longitudinal terraces, creating the magnificent perspective of the central alley; he dug grand ponds and landscaped parterres, staggered rows of plants and elegant ramps. The Orangerie was built in 1853 and the Jeu de Paume in 1861. The terrace of the Bord-de-l'eau offers a beautiful view of the Seine and the gardens, adorned with statues and chestnut and plane trees: a perfect spot to appreciate the magnificent architectural composition of the site.

MUSÉE DE L'ORANGERIE★★

Jardin des Tuileries (Seine side) - ☎ 01 44 50 43 00 - www.musee-orangerie.fr - 9am-5.45pm - closed Tuesdays, 1 May, 14 Jul (morning), 25 Dec - guided visits (1hr30min) - €9 - €16 combined ticket with Musée d'Orsay - €6 expert guided visits - €5 audioguide - €4.50 stories, mimes and family visits - €7 workshops.
Since 1927 the Orangerie has housed Claude Monet's famous **Water Lilies ★★★** series. Since 1927 the Orangerie has housed Claude Monet's famous Water Lilies series. This Impressionist masterpiece is displayed in natural light, as Monet wished it to be. The Orangerie also exhibits the fine collection of Walter-Guillaume, which includes paintings by Cézanne, Sisley, Monet, Renoir, Gauguin, Marie Laurencin, Picasso, Modigliani, Utrillo, Matisse and Soutine.

GALERIE DU JEU DE PAUME

1 pl. de la Concorde - ☎ 01 47 03 12 50 - www.jeudepaume.org - 11am-7pm, Tue 11am-9pm - closed Mondays, 1 Jan, 1 May, 25 Dec - guided visits (1hr) - €10 - free last Tuesday of the month. Only open during exhibitions.
Jeu de Paume hosts temporary exhibitions centred around the image as explored through photography (from its origins to the present day), video and multimedia.

LES CHAMPS-ÉLYSÉES★★★

BC3-4 *Mᵒ Champs-Élysées-Clemenceau, Condorde et Charles-de-Gaulle-Étoile.*
This iconic thoroughfare is the longest avenue in Paris, stretching 2km/1.2mi across the west of the city, between the Place de la Concorde and the Arc de Triomphe; it is 71m/234ft wide. It is also the emblematic site of public celebrations, including the annual military parade on Bastille Day, the end of the Tour de France and New Year's Eve festivities. Starting at Place de la Concorde, cross the English-style gardens to arrive at the Champs-Élysées roundabout. Here you will be able to appreciate the magnificent **Grand Palais★** and **Petit Palais★★**, masterpieces of stone, metal and glass, constructed for the World's Fair of 1900.
The **Grand Palais★** *(3 av. du Gén.-Eisenhower - ☎ 01 44 13 17 17 - www.grandpalais.fr - 🚫 - 10am-8pm, Wed and Fri-Sat 10am-10pm - closed Tue - guided tour (1hr30min) - €13)* hosts world-beating temporary exhibitions and organises events

Modern masterpiece

Dans la partie nord du **bois de Boulogne★**, *la* **fondation Louis-Vuitton★★**, *designed by Frank Gehry and inaugurated in 2014, is an innovative addition to the architecture of Paris, featuring twelve "sails" which are immense, but manage to give the impression of lightness. The American-Canadian architect was initially inspired by the image of a transparent cloud. The Fondation is a gallery and cultural centre, which hosts a diverse and prestigious programme of exhibitions. Children love the neighbouring Jardin d'Acclimatation with its rides, games and activites.*

M° Les Sablons - Carrefour des Sablons - bois de Boulogne - ✆ 01 40 67 90 85 - www.jardinacclimatation.fr - School holidays and Jul-Aug: 10am-8pm; rest of the year: 11am-6pm, weekends and public holidays 10am-7pm - 3.50 € (under 3 years free).

under ita sumptuous glass dome. The west part of the building houses the **Palais de la Découverte★★** *(Av. Franklin-Roosevelt - ✆ 01 56 43 20 25 - www.palais-decouverte.fr - 9.30am-6pm, Sun and public holidays 10am-7pm - closed Mon, 1 Jan, 1 May, 14 Jul, 25 Dec - €9 + €3 planetarium.),* a museum dedicated to science and applied science, whic offers various workshops. The **Petit Palais★★** *(Av. Winston-Churchill - ✆ 01 53 43 40 00 - www.petitpalais.paris.fr - 10am-6pm - closed Mondays, some public holidays- guided visits (1hr30min) - 7/12 €temporary exhibitions, 5€ audioguide.)* houses the rich collection of the Musée des Beaux-Arts de la Ville de Paris, focussing particularly on the waves of French art between 1880 and 1914. With **Pont Alexandre-III★★**, the palaces form a vast architectural ensemble, built in 1900. On the corner of Avenue George-V is the famous **Fouquet's**, which has historical monument status: this was the restaurant *de préférence* of the great and good of 20C Paris.

ARC DE TRIOMPHE★★★

AB2-3 RER A et M° 1, 2 et 6 Charles-de-Gaulle-Étoile. Pl. Charles-de-Gaulle - ✆ 01 55 37 73 77 - www.arc-de-triomphe.monuments-nationaux.fr - Apr-Sep: 10am-11pm; rest of the year: 10am-10.30pm - closed 1 Jan, 1 May, 8 May (morning), 14 Jul (morning), 11 Nov (morning), 25 Dec - guided tours on request (1hr30min) - €12.

At the top of the Champs-Élysées, the Arc de Triomphe, inspired by Antiquity, is colossal in proportions, measuring 50m/164ft tall and 45m/147ft wide. Celebrating the glory of the Grande Armée, it stands imperiously over the centre of the former Place de l'Étoile—renamed Place Charles-de-Gaulle in 1970—which opens onto 12 grand avenues radiating out in a star shape (hence the name). Commissioned in 1806 by Napoleon and Jean-François Chalgrin (1739-1811), the monument had only reached a paltry 5m/16ft at the time of Napoleon's death. The construction was finished under Louis-Philippe, in 1836. Since 1921, the arch has housed the **Tomb of the Unknown Soldier**.

The **Flame of Remembrance** has been burning since November 11, 1923 and is relit every evening at 6.30pm. The **view★★★** from the top of the Arc de Triomphe is spectacular.

QUARTIER MONCEAU★

C1-2 I

In the 19C, sumptuous mansions were built on "Monceau plaines". Some of these would later be turned into museums. Today, roads lined with grand Haussmannian facades meet at the splendid park. The area is quiet, family-orientated and bourgeois.

Parc Monceau★

BC2 M° *Monceau.* This exceedingly elegant park has an enchanting array or rare and unusual trees: you'll find sycamore maple, oriental plane and gingko. By the entrance you'll find the Ledoux Rotunda, one of the 47 toll booths along the Fermiers Généraux Wall. Three others remain at Denfert-Rochereau, Stalingrad and Nation.

Musée Nissim-de-Camondo★★

C2 M° *Monceau. 63 r. de Monceau - ℘ 01 53 89 06 50 - www.lesarts decoratifs.fr - & - 10am-5.30pm - closed Mon, Tue - guided tours (1hr30min) - €9 - €10 combined ticket with Musée des Arts décoratifs.*This museum, located in a beautiful *hôtel particulier*, exhibits sumptuous décor and furnishings chosen by its former owner, the Count of Camondo; expect delightful Belle Époque atmosphere.

Musée Cernuschi★

C2 M° *Monceau. 7 av. Vélasquez - ℘ 01 53 96 21 50 - www.cernuschi.paris.fr - & - 10am-6pm - closed Mondays and public holidays - guided tours (1hr30min) - €8 - conferences, activities can be booked online. Brings together collections of Asian art collected at the end of the 19C by banker Henri Cernuschi.*

Musée Jacquemart-André★★

C2 M° *Miromesnil - 158 bd Haussmann - ℘ 01 45 62 11 59 - www.musee-jacquemart-andre.com - & - 10am-6pm, Mon (when exhibitions on) 10am-8.30pm - guided tours on request (1hr) - €13.50.* A prestigious collection of decorative art from the 18C and French paintings (from the école du Nord and Italian Renaissance school) is exquisitely laid-out in this mansion constructed in 1869. Artists include: Boucher, Chardin, Canaletto, Fragonard, David, Rembrandt, Hals, Van Dick and Tiepolo. Be sure to stop at the sumptuous Salon de Thé and the garden (no reservations and the queue can sometimes be long).

LES BATIGNOLLES★

D1 M° Rome

You'll find plenty of "bobos"—Paris's famous "bourgeois bohemians"—in this neighbourhood, which has a distinct country feel with its bucolic **Ste-Marie-des-Batignolles church** and English-style square lined with trendy bistros and boutiques. In the north of the district, abandoned railway lines have been transformed as part of a huge urban development project. The first phase saw the inauguration of handsome **Parc Martin-Luther-King**, which covers 10ha/24.7ac. The emblematic 160m/525ft tower, designed by Renzo Piano houses new Palais de Justice de Paris (formerly at Île de la Cité).

Opéra★★ - Palais-Royal★★

In the daytime, the Opéra district is abuzz with activity and saturated with traffic jams: tourists marvel at the window displays of the department stores and business people hurry to meetings at the banks. At night, it becomes a culture-lover's paradise, host to world-class dance, music and theatre performances. The Palais-Royal area, characterised by independent boutiques and secret passageways, is a pocket of secluded quiet.

▶**Access:** Mᵒ Opéra (lines 3, 7 and 8), Pyramides (lines 7 and 14), Palais-Royal-Musée-du-Louvre (lines 1 and 7), Quatre-Septembre (line 3).
*Area map **p. 83**. Detachable map **DF3-4**.*
▶**Tips:** The department stores are very busy at the weekend: go on weekdays or opt for late-night shopping on Thursday evening.

PALAIS GARNIER - OPÉRA NATIONAL DE PARIS★★

D3 Mᵒ Opéra. Pl. de l'Opéra (entrance on the corner of r. Scribe et Auber) - ☎ 0 892 89 90 90 - www. operadeparis.fr - ♿ - from mid-July to end-Aug: 10am-6pm, matinée days 10am-2pm; rest of the year: 10am-5pm, matinée days 10am-1pm - closed 1 Jan, 1 May 25 Dec, days of some special performances - guided tour (1hr30min) - €12 - ticket gives access to exhibition.

An undeniable triumph of the Second Empire, this edifice, designed in 1860 by then-35-year-old Charles Garnier, dominates the Place de l'Opéra with its gargantuan façade. The front of the building shows a series of sculpted figures including La Danse on the arcade and at the top of the façade, Apollo, raising his lyre to the sky,

recalling the vocation of the building. On the **interior★★★** of the building, Garnier's use of multicoloured marble (white, blue, pink, red, green), quarried in different parts of France, is testament to his originality. The **Great Staircase** and the **Grand Foyer** are theatrical masterpieces, designed for pageantry.

AVENUE DE L'OPÉRA★

DE3-4

The **Place de l'Opéra★★** opens onto boulevard des Capucines, which leads to the **Madeleine★** and rue de la Paix. Drawn up between 1854 and 1878, Avenue de l'Opéra quickly became a prestigious thoroughfare. This commercial district is a favourite with international tourists with its duty-free shops and grand department stores. Printemps, opened in 1865, and Galeries Lafayette, originally a

79

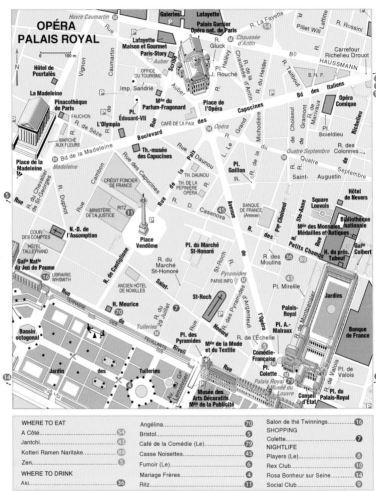

WHERE TO EAT		Angélina	70	Salon de thé Twinings	16
A Côté	54	Bristol	5	SHOPPING	
Jantchi	43	Café de la Comédie (Le)	79	Colette	7
Kotteri Ramen Naritake	89	Casse Noisettes	45	NIGHTLIFE	
Zen	5	Fumoir (Le)	6	Players (Le)	8
WHERE TO DRINK		Mariage Frères	4	Rex Club	10
Aki	36	Ritz	11	Rosa Bonheur sur Seine	14
				Social Club	9

The Opéra in numbers

The Palais Garnier has a vast surface area of 11,237m2 (36,866ft2) but only has space for a relatively modest 2,200 in the audience: a great deal of room is taken up by practical functions (the Opéra employs roughly 1100 people) and the stage, which can accommodate 450 performers! The guided tour is fascinating and includes a visit to the Grande Salle with its ornate ceiling painted by Chagall.

small haberdashery created in 1895 by Alphonse Kahn, are imitated around the world. Galeries Lafayette is uniquely charming with its century-old dome and balustrades; it also offers a fine view of the back of the Opéra from its terrace. Expect beautiful illuminations and gorgeous window displays during holiday season.

PLACE VENDÔME★★

D3
Undoubtedly one of the most beautiful squares from the latter part of Louis XIV's reign, arranged around a monumental statue of the Sun King. It was designed by Jules Hardouin-Mansart in a distinctive octagonal shape. The equestrian statue of the monarch (by François Girardon), was inaugurated in 1699, but construction of the square began in 1702. In 1720 the octagon was finally lined with its intended facades with their fine avant-corps and colossal Corinthian pilasters. The royal statue was destroyed during the Revolution. In 1810, Napoleon Bonaparte ordered the construction of a column, inspired by Trajan's Column in Rome. The 44m/144ft monument is covered in a spiralling bronze design, made of 1250 melted-down canons, seized from the enemy at the Battle of Austerlitz; a classical-style statue of the emperor sits atop the column. The recently renovated Hôtel Ritz can be found at no 15. On each end of the square you'll find **Rue de la Paix** (to the north) and **Rue St-Honoré★** (to the south), known for their sumptuous window displays and high concentration of luxury jewellers (Cartier, Van Cleef & Arpels, Boucheron).

MUSÉE DES ARTS DÉCORATIFS★★

D4 M° Palais-Royal-Musée-du-Louvre. *107 r. de Rivoli - ℘ 01 44 55 57 50 - www.artsdecoratifs.fr - 11am-6pm, Thu. 11am-9pm - closed Mondays, 1 Jan, 1 May, 15 Aug, 25 Dec - guided tours booked in advance (1hr30min) - €11 - €13 combined ticket with the Musée Nissim de Camondo.*
This charming museum, located in a wing of the Louvre palace, presents a complete cross-section of decorative arts from the Middle Ages to the present day. The works span ceramics, furnishings, gold and silver, jewellery and glass and key names such as Boulle, Sèvres, Aubusson, Christofle, Lalique, Guimard and Mallet-Stevens. The remarkable interiors have been artfully renovated. Highlights include the private apartment of Jeanne Lanvin and

the dining room by Eugène Grasset. The building also houses the **Musée de la Mode et du Textile**★.

The long gallery of arcades opposite the Louvre is a busy section of the **rue de Rivoli**★ with a high concentration of low-cost souvenir shops.

LA MADELEINE★

D3 M⁰ Madeleine.
A grand colonnade and an immense sculpted pediment make up the striking facade of this church, consecrated in 1842. From the imposing front steps, take in the impressive **view**★ across rue Royale, the Obelisk, the Palais-Bourbon and the dome of the Invalides.

PALAIS-ROYAL★★

E4 M⁰ Palais-Royal-Musée-du-Louvre.
Just by the Musée du Louvre and the Place des Victoires, is the Palais-Royal (modern-day seat of the Conseil Constitutionnel) and its superb courtyard **gardens**★. In 1624, **Richelieu** constructed a vast and striking palace here: the Palais-Cardinal, which later became Palais-Royal when of Austria lived here with her son, the young Louis XIV. In 1780, the palace passed into the hands of Louis-Philippe d'Orléans, cousin of the monarch, who undertook significant building works. On three sides of the garden, he constructed matching houses with uniform facades. He added arcaded galleries lined with commercial spaces,

Galerie Vivienne

© Dr. Wilfried Bahnmüller/imageBROKER/age fotostock

The "maison de Molière"

*Founded in 1680 by Louis XIV, the Comédie-Française is one of Paris's largest theatres. Though the repertoire performed here is largely classical, the oldest troop in the world has slowly opened itself to contemporary writing. The famous statue of Voltaire by Houdon decorates the interior of the theatre, as well as the chair on which, on February 17 1673, **Molière** was seized by a fatal coughing fit while acting in the title role of his last play,* The Imaginary Invalid.

which became gambling houses and brothels, and were very popular until they were banned in 1836. The creator of this remarkable architecture was Victor Louis. In 1786, Philippe Égalité commissioned Louis to build the Salle du Théâtre-Français, now **Comédie-Française★**, and the **Théâtre du Palais-Royal★**.

Artist Daniel Buren's 1986 installation of 260 striped black and white columns of various sizes creates a harmonious contrast with the 19C colonnades of the courtyard garden, though its addition was controversial at the time. Today the arcades house old-fashioned shops, elegant designer fashion boutiques and art galleries and the Palais-Royal has become a hotspot for fashionistas. Perhaps the most charming element of this area is the network of little passageways that surround the galleries.

Over the last few years, **rue Ste-Anne**, has been transformed into a Japanese enclave in the heart of Paris, filled with restaurants, food shops and a few bookshops. Explore the roads around it to discover 17C architecture, quirky and luxurious independent boutiques and covered passages, constructed in the 19C, such as the **Galerie Véro-Dodat★★** and its beautiful Neoclassical décor.

GALERIE VIVIENNE AND GALERIE COLBERT ★★

E4 M° Pyramides.

The Galerie Vivienne (1823), lit by long glass windows, retains its original décor featuring nymphs and goddesses. N° 13 was once the home of legendary French criminal Eugène François Vidocq, who went on to become a detective and inspire writers such as Victor Hugo and Edgar Allen Poe. The Galerie Colbert, restored to its original Pompeian décor, is an annex of the **Bibliothèque Nationale** (*Richelieu site, 58 r. de Richelieu*) conserving only specialist collections of manuscripts, prints and photographs, cards and sheet music. Be sure to have a peek at the Salle de Lecture des Imprimés, as well as the magnificent **Galerie Mazarine★**, constructed by Mansart.

PLACE DES VICTOIRES ★

E4 M° Bourse.

Its construction was initiated by Marshall La Feuillade, courtier of Louis XIV, who wanted to demonstrate his admiration to the monarch. Decorated with an equestrian statue of the Sun King, the Jules Hardouin-Mansart-designed square is beautifully laid out.

LES GRANDS BOULEVARDS

DEF3

The Grands Boulevards were constructed on the site of the city walls that once hemmed in a smaller Paris (♿ *p. 175*). Fast-food restaurants and low-cost souvenir shops have largely replaced the elegant cafés of the 19C. The main tourist draws are the **Musée Grévin**, iconic cinema the **Grand Rex**, and the various charming **covered passages** you'll find around the area. The nearby **Hôtel des ventes Drouot-Richelieu** is an auction house and veritable cabinet of curiosities (*9 r. Drouot - ☏ 01 48 00 20 20 - www.drouot.com - 11am-6pm, Thu 11am-9pm - closed Sundays and. public holidays, from mid-July to mid-Sept - guided tours booked in advance (1hr30min) - free - programme online.*). The **passages Jouffroy** (n° 10 bd Montmartre) and **des Panoramas** (at n° 11) are worth visiting for their idiosyncratic atmosphere, at once retro and trendy: old-fashioned shops have closed and been replaced by chic eateries, fine dining spots and organic restaurants. The area is thrumming with new life. Continue to the more tucked-away **Passage Verdeau,** which still retains much of its original charm. On the boulevard des Italiens (n° 5), the **Passage des Princes** has been completely renovated.

Musée Grévin★ – M° Grands-Boulevards. 10 bd Montmartre - ☏ 01 47 70 85 05 - www.grevin-paris.com - 10am-6.30pm - closed 5 days in October (check before.) - guided tours on request (1hr30min) - €24.50.

In 1881, Arthur Meyer, director of daily newspaper *Le Gaulois*, decided to present the celebrities who graced his front pages in the form of life-size wax models. He enlisted Alfred Grévin, a multi-skilled sculptor, humourist and costume designer: the success was instant. More than 2,000 wax personalities have followed since. Situated at the very start of Boulevard Poissonnière, Art Deco cinema the **Grand Rex★**, (1932), complete with 2 650 seats across three levels and sumptuous period décor, has been classed as a historical monument since 1981.

And for a journey through the history of cinema, **Les Étoiles du Rex** showcases a 50-minute behind-the-scenes visit of the Rex, from filming to projection (*1 bd Poissonnière - ☏ 01 45 08 93 58 - www.legrandrex.com - school holidays: every day except Monday morning. 10am-6pm ; rest of the year: Wed-Sun and public holidays 10am-6pm, Sat 10am-6.30pm - closed 1 Jan, 25 Dec - €11 - guided tour on reservation ☏ 08 25 05 44 05 - tour of the Grand Rex and Étoiles du Rex*).

Finally, stop off at the tranquil **Cité Bergère**, where Chopin and Henrich Heine once lived, at 6 rue du Faubourg-Montmartre. At no. 7, admire the décor of the legendary **Bouillon Chartier restaurant**, opened at the end of the 19C. Stop for a meal and a thoroughly charming experience: the archetypal French waiters, dressed in white shirts and black waistcoats, careen from one side of the immense room to the other, balancing plates of grated carrot, bœuf bourguignon and chocolate mousse (*see p. 115*). Head north to discover the **Cité de Trévise**, a quiet and timelessly beautiful enclave in neo-Renaissance style.

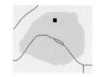

Montmartre★★★ - Pigalle

With its iconic church and rich artistic heritage, Montmartre a very popular spot indeed. However, despite gentrification and an abundance of tourists, "la butte" is still packed with bucolic charm: you'll find winding cobbled streets, enchanting old houses, secret passageways and even a vineyard. The area at the bottom of the hill around rue des Martyrs, known as South Pigalle ("SoPi"), has become ultra-trendy in recent years and there is always a new bar or restaurant to be tried.

▶**Access:** M° Abbesses (line 12) or Pigalle (lines 2 and 12), the Sacré-Cœur funicular, the Montmartrobus and the «petit train» of Montmartre.
Area map p. 88-89. Detachable map E1.
▶**Tips:** Crowds generally congregate around Place du Tertre, rue Norvins and around Abbesses: for a calmer experience, come early in the morning and consider exploring the less tourist-trodden north side of the hill. In order to fully appreciate the unique layout of the "butte", climb (at least) one its iconic steep staircases. If you're tired, the Montmartrobus, a little electric bus that weaves the steep streets, follows a very pretty route between Pigalle and the Mairie (town hall) of the 18th arrondissement. Don't miss a chance to attend the Fête des Vendanges (Harvest Festival) in the second weekend of October (www.fetedesvendangesdemontmartre.com).

WALKING "LA BUTTE MONTMARTRE"★★★

This walking route will show you the most iconic sights of the area.
From Blanche metro station (*line 2*), take **rue Lepic★**, which will take you past the Café des Deux-Moulins, made famous by Amélie. Follow the road up to the **Moulin de la Galette**, which has stood in this spot for six centuries six centuries. The ball here was all the rage in 19C Paris. It inspired Renoir (his *Bal du moulin de la Galette* hangs in the Orsay), as well as Van Gogh and

Willette. Its real name is *le Blute-Fin*. At **Place Marcel-Aymé**, you may be surprised to see a gentleman passing through the wall, an homage to the author of *Passe-Muraille*. Head up the hill via the quiet **Avenue Junot**, where you wil see the workshops and pavilions of **Hameau des Artistes** or the **Villa Léandre★**. Turn back on yourself and cross Square Suzanne-Buisson, where an impressive **statue of Saint Denis** holding his decapitated head in hands placed above a water basin. The miraculous preacher was said to have washed his head in this spot before heading north to the place he eventually fell, which would become suburb St-Denis. To the north-east of the square, between the rue Girardon and Allée des Brouillards, you'll find a romantic edifice dating from the 18C, which would later become a public ballroom, **Château des Brouillards**. Leave the square and head in the direction of the cemetery, where you will meet legendary singer Dalida, who lived in this neighbourhood for 25 years; her bust overlooks the square that takes her name (she lived at 11 bis rue d'Orchampt). At the crossroads of rue des Saules and **rue St-Vincent**, you'll discover what is indisputably the most bucolic spot in Paris with its little staircase, steep slope, abundant greenery and the famous Lapin Agile cabaret, hidden by an old acacia tree.

St-Vincent cemetery is the resting place of Émile Goudeau, Maurice Utrillo, Dorgelès, Gabrielo and Marcel Carné.

Stop to inspect the charming **vineyard** (rue des Saules), planted at the start of the 20C; the grape harvests are occasions of great celebration.

Musée de Montmartre★ – *12 r. Cortot - ℘ 01 49 25 89 39 - www. museedemontmartre.fr - & - Apr-Sept: 10am-7pm; rest of the year: 10am-6pm - guided tours on request (1hr30min) - €11 - audio guide available (included in ticket). Lovely tearoom backing on to the garden.* Surrounded by three delightful gardens, the museum is housed in the Maison du Bel Air, which was once the haunt of famous artists such as Auguste Renoir, Suzanne Valadon, Émile Bernard, Émile Othon Friesz and Raoul Dufy.

The bohemian history of Montmartre is told via posters, paintings, drawings, a recreation of the Café de l'Abreuvoir and the studio-cum-apartment of Suzanne Valadon and her son, Maurice Utrillo. It is a charming immersion in the history of *la Butte*, its spirit of liberty, its communards and its artistic exuberance. Next door, the Hôtel Demarne hosts temporary exhibitions themed around Montmartre.

Église St-Pierre-de-Montmartre★ - *2 r. du Mont-Cenis - ℘ 01 46 06 57 63 - www.saintpierredemontmartre.net - 9.30am-7.30pm, Fri 9am-6pm - guided tours (20 min).* The last remaining vestige of Montmartre Abbey, this is one of the oldest churches in Paris (11C.), built in the place of a former basilica dedicated to Saint Denis. The vaults of the nave were constructed in the 15C, the west façade dates from the 18C. The simple grace of the church's belltower contrasts with the imposing aspect of the domes of the Sacré-Cœur. The very old **Cimetière du Calvaire** *(open only on Nov 1)*, joined to the north of the church, is the smallest cemetery in Paris; it can be seen through a beautiful bronze gate.

Place du Tertre★ - This quaint little square is full of tiny houses and pretty trees, but you may not notice the bucolic atmosphere amid the throngs of tourists and the dozens of artists vying to sketch you. It's best explored early in the morning.

Place Émile-Goudeau★ – A square made famous by painters (Picasso, Braque and Juan Gris developed Cubism here) and poets (Max Jacob, Apollinaire, Marc Orlan). This artistic set all congregated at the

88

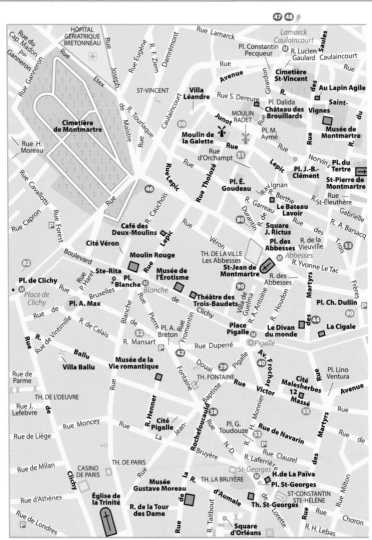

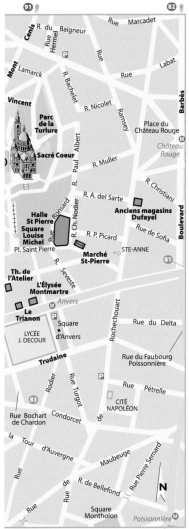

MONTMARTRE PIGALLE

0   200 m

WHERE TO EAT

Atelier St Georges	53
Bijou	90
Brasserie Barbès	81
Coq Rico (Le)	51
Flesh	52
Jeanne B.	50
Khaosan (Le)	83
Pantruche (Le)	55
Wepler (Le)	82

89

WHERE TO DRINK

Albion	37
Bâton Rouge (Le)	38
Carmen	42
Comestibles et Marchands de Vins	91
Dirty Dick (Le)	40
Divette de Montmartre (La)	48
Étoile de Montmartre (L')	47
Fourmi (La)	44
Guêpe (La)	53
Marlusse et Lapin	90
Persifleur (Le)	80
Recyclerie (La)	82
Sans-Souci (Le)	39
Vingt Heures Vin	46

Bateau-Lavoir (nº 13).
Place des Abbesses★ -Abbesses metro is perhaps the most iconic stop of the whole network: created by **Hector Guimard**, the Art Nouveau entrance is one of only two surviving originals from 1900 (the other is Porte Dauphine). Lined by cafés and restaurants, artisanal boutiques and shops of all kinds, the square and its narrow surrounding roads are lively at any time of the day. It is dominated in the south by the **Église St-Jean-de-Montmartre**, the first religious building to be constructed in reinforced concrete (1904), quite a shock at the time. Montmartre locals have nicknamed it St-Jean-des-Briques (St-John of the Bricks) after its striking facade. In the north of Place des Abbesses, the Square Jehan-Rictus houses the **Wall of "Je t'aime"**, a mural of enamel tiles covered with "Je t'aime" ("I love you") written in multiple languages.

SACRÉ-CŒUR★★

Mº Anvers et funiculaire de Montmartre. Pl. du Parvis-du-Sacré-Cœur - ℘ 01 53 41 89 00 - www.sacre-coeur-montmartre.fr - &. - 6am-10.30pm - access for people with reduced mobility 35 r. du Chevalier-de-la-Barre (9.30am-5.30pm). This Byzantine-style basilica (1876-1914) is the work of architect Paul Abadie (1812-1884). Since before its consecration in 1919, the faithful have assured, day and night, uninterrupted adoration of the Blessed Sacrament. The **dome** is accessed from the crypt (*left side aisle - ℘ 01 53 41 89 00 - www.sacre-coeur-montmartre.com -*

€6 - €8 combined ticket with the crypt- the dome can be closed and opening hours changed according to the weather.) . You will be rewarded for the fairly steep 300-step climb with a sweeping view of Paris from the outdoor viewing gallery. On a clear day, the **view★★★** stretches over 30 km/18mii. The crypt contains treasures and an audio-visual exhibition presents the history of the basilica and the Cult of the Sacred Heart.

HALLE SAINT-PIERRE★

Mº Anvers. 2 r. Ronsard - ℘ 01 42 58 72 89 - www.hallesaintpierre.org - &. - August: daily except weekeneds 12pm-6pm; rest of the year: 11am-6pm, Sat 11am-7pm, Sun 12pm-6pm, 24 and 31 Dec 11am-4pm - closed 1 Jan, 1 May, 14 Jul, 15 Aug, 25 Dec - guided tours on request (1hr) - €9 - pleasant café and bookshop.
Built by a student of Baltard in 1868, this former covered market has retained its beautiful iron architecture and vast windows. For the last twenty years the space has been dedicated to arts brut (outsider art). The large temporary exhibitions are unusual and unpretentious, eschewing the academic trends of contemporary art.

PIGALLE

A1 *Mº Pigalle.*
Thanks to the proliferation of hip bars and trendy boutique hotels, this once-bawdy district has become one of Paris's hottest going-out spots with an atmosphere that is at once ultra-fashionable and transgressive.

Parisians have taken to calling the southern part of the district "SoPi" (South Pigalle) in reference to SoHo (South of Houston Street) in New York, which gives you an idea of the vibe.

The stretch of Boulevard de Clichy between Place Blanche and Place Pigalle attracts all manner of revellers. In the midst of the sex shops, don't miss Cité Véron at no. 94, dotted with houses with little gardens (where Boris Vian and Jacques Prévert once lived) or the Cité du Midi, where you'll find the preserved tiled façade of a former public bath house at no. 48.

Place Blanche, or "White Square", owes its name to the former gypsum quarries that surrounded this area. Here you will see the legendary **Moulin Rouge**, founded in 1889. It was a "caf'conc'" (café-concert) where the bourgeois and bohemians of Montmartre would come to watch stars Yvette Guilbert, Valentin le Désossé and la Goulue dance the famous French-Cancan; these scenes were immortalised by Toulouse-Lautrec.

In the ultra-hip area around rue des Martyrs, rue Henri-Monnier and rue Rochechouart in the **south of Pigalle**, you'll notice a high concentration of bars, restaurants, organic shops and vintage boutiques. The chic **Nouvelle-Athènes** enclave can be found in the heart of this area, characterised by Neoclassical architecture and grand *hôtels particuliers*. **Place St-Georges** was the hub of this neighbourhood in the 19C when it was frequented by artistic types like Chopin and George Sand. On rue Notre-Dame-de-Lorette, the **Hôtel de la Païva**

(1840) is worth stopping at with its stunning Neoclassical architecture and elaborate facade featuring cherubs and busts of Diana and Apollo. This was the home of Thérèse Lachmann, Marquise of Païva, a famous demi-mondaine.

Musée Gustave-Moreau★

M° St-Georges. 14 r. de la Rochefoucauld - ℘ 01 48 74 38 50 - www.musee-moreau.fr - 10am-12.45pm, 2pm-5pm, Fri-Sun 10am-5pm - closed Tuesdays, 1 Jan, 1 May, 25 Dec - €6 - free 1st Sun of the month. In 1895, Gustave Moreau (1826-1898) installed his pieces in his family house. The museum brings together his finest copies of the masters (Raphaël, Carpaccio, Botticelli) and more than 6,000 of his creations (paintings, sketches, drawings, sculptures).

Musée de la Vie romantique★

M° Pigalle. 16 r. Chaptal - ℘ 01 55 31 95 67 - http://parismusees.paris.fr - 10am-6pm - closed Mondays, some public holidays - guided tours on request (1hr30min) - €8 - permanent collections, temporary exhibitions, get information first. The narrow tree-lined alley leading to this charming bucolic building sets the tone. The painter **Ary Scheffer** (1795-1858), received her literary artistic friends , appreciated by Louis Philippe, received her literary and artistic friends here, including Delacroix, Liszt and Renan. The museum exhibits memorabilia belonging to George Sand and works by Ary Scheffer. The little garden is particularly charming, as well as the tearoom, a great spot for lunch on a warm day.

91

Canal Saint-Martin★ - *La Villette*★★

The history of this traditionally working-class district is anchored in the industrial activity of 19th century Paris. Today, it is a popular spot with locals, and in summer you'll find students and trendy young people hanging out, eating and drinking all along the canal, while local bistros put tables out onto the pavement. Strolling northwards from Canal Saint-Martin to Parc de La Villette is a great way to soak up the atmosphere of the area. At La Villette you'll find an innovative space combining nature and scientific discovery, as well as leisure activities and music. Conclude your tour of the area with a wander round the beautiful Parc des Buttes-Chaumont.

▶**Access:** M° République (lines 3, 5, 8, 9 amd 11), Jacques-Bonsergent (line 5), Goncourt (line 11) et Jaurès (lines2, 5 and 7b).
La Villette: M° Porte-de-la-Villette (line 7 - entrance at Cité des sciences et de l'industrie), Porte-de-Pantin (M° line 5 and T3b- entrance at La Philarmonie).
Area map p. 96. Detachable map G1-3.
▶**Tip:** On Sundays and public holidays, the canal is car-free from rue de la Grange-aux-Belles (Quai de Jemmapes, at the swing bridge) to Place Stalingrad. Take advantage of the quiet by strolling or cycling ride along Canal St-Martin (there are cycle routes all the way up to Canal de l'Ourcq). In summer, relax on the grass at La Villette and watch an open-air film as part of the Festival de Cinéma en Plein Air. ♿*Cultural agenda, p. 166.*

CANAL SAINT-MARTIN★

♿ *Boat tours, p. 162. G1-3*
With its new **locks**, iron footbridges, cobblestones and pretty lines of trees, the Canal St-Martin is a charming spot, where the spirit of French cultural legends (Arletty, Balzac) linger. At

102 Quai de Jemmapes, the facade of the **Hôtel du Nord**, evokes one of the most famous lines from French cinema, uttered by Arletty to Louis Jouvet—"Atmosphère, atmosphere" —from the eponymous film by Marcel Carné (1938). Today, chic boutiques and vintage stores, restaurants and hip

From the Nile to the Ourcq

The construction of Canal St-Martin was ordered by Napoleon I in 1802 in order to join the river Ourcq to the Seine. The project would be overseen by Pierre-Simon Girard, an engineer who had studied the level of the Nile on expedition in Egypt. The formidable task would not be finished until 1825, though a first section of the canal was inaugurated in 1808. Dug in order to provide fresh, clean water for Parisians and to supply fountains, the canal has nine locks with a total lowered water level of 25m/82ft and is 4.5km/2.8ft long. It is covered between Bastille and rue du Faubourg-du-Temple.

cafés pepper the banks of the canal. At the foot of the embankment, before Stalingrad, **Point Éphémère** is a centre of artistic dynamism. (♿*Addresses, p. 131*).

Rotonde de La Villette★ – One of Ledoux's toll booths, an access point to Paris along the Farmers General Wall. La Rotonde now houses a restaurant and bar.

Bassin de La Villette★

GH1 M° *Jaurès ou Stalingrad.*
The bassin extends the canal to the north. It's a lovely place to relax, full of cyclists, and leisurely walkers on sunny days: it's a great day for a picnic, a coffee *en terrasse* or a game of pétanque. Housed in the warehouse of a former food market, mixing brick and the Eiffel girders from the 1878 World's Fair, the MK2 Quai-de-Loire cinema links to its twin across the water by a little boat *(free shuttle)*. At the other end of the basin, don't miss the sight of the **rue de Crimée bridge** rising. Head to the **104** by rue Riquet.

LE 104

Off map G1 M° *Riquet. 5 r. Curial -*
℘ 01 53 35 50 00 - www.104.fr - ♿ -
12pm-7pm, w/e 11am-7pm - closed Mon,
7-25 Aug, 1 Jan, 25 Dec- ticket prices
vary depending on exhibition.
This vast cultural space opened in 2008 in a former undertaker's building. Its aim is to open contemporary arts to the public, inviting artists in residence. The centre is a favourite with the inhabitants of this diverse working-class neighbourhood. There is always something to see or do. Young people come here to dance and families visit the free exhibitions.

PARC DE LA VILLETTE★

Off map H1
Between Canal St-Denis and Canal de l'Ourcq, on the former site of the **abattoirs of Paris**, this vast contemporary park, packed with playgrounds, houses the **Cité des Sciences et de l'Industrie**, the **Philarmonie**, the **Grande Halle** and Zénith. With a combination of modern architecture and greenery, it's a great place to soak in culture or relax.

Grande Halle, Parc de La Villette

Cité des sciences et de l'industrie★★

M° Porte-de-la-Villette. 30 av. Corentin-Cariou - ☏ 01 40 05 80 00 - www.cite-sciences.fr - 10am-6pm, Sun 10am-7pm - closed Mondays, 1 Jan, 1 May, 25 Dec - guided tours on request (45min) - €12 - €16 combined ticket with the Cité des Enfants, €24 with the Cité des Enfants and la Géode. The aim of this museum is to make science accessible to the public. Interactive scenography uses cutting edge technology.

Explora and the Planetarium – Levels 1 and 2. Interactive exhibits explore the world of today and tomorrow. The **Planetarium** takes the viewer on a visit through the Milky Way, exploring constellations and galaxies (hours vary depending on programme).

La **Cité des Enfants★★** – *30 av. Corentin-Cariou - ♿ - 10am-6pm, Sun 10am-7pm - Closed Mondays, 1 Jan, 1 May, 25 Dec - €12-€18.50 combined ticket with the Géode - reservation recommended - www.cite-sciences.fr - ☏ 0 892 697 072 (€0.34/mn).* Two spaces (2-7 years and 5-12 years) offer different interactive educational activities.

La Géode★★ – *30 av. Corentin-Cariou - ☏ 01 40 05 80 00 - www.lageode.fr - 10.30am-8.30pm - closed 1 Jan, 1 May, 25 Dec - €12.* Films and documentaries are shown on the gigantic Hemisphere Screen (26m/85ft in diameter) in this

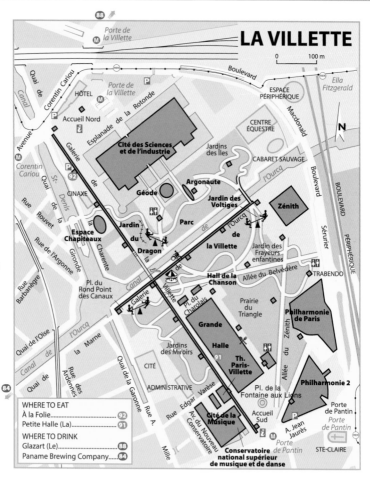

LA VILLETTE

0   100 m

N

Porte de la Villette
Quai de Corentin Cariou
Canal
HOTEL
Accueil Nord
Esplanade de la Rotonde
Porte de la Villette
Avenue
Corentin Cariou
Quai de St. Denis
CINAXE
Rue Rouvet
Rue de la Gironde
Espace Chapiteaux
Rue de l'Argonne
Rue Barbanègre
Pl. du Rond Point des Canaux
Galerie de la Villette
Quai de l'Oise
l'Ourcq
Canal de la Marne
Quai de
Rue des Ardennes
CITÉ
ADMINISTRATIVE
Rue A.
Rue Edgar Varèse
Av. du Nouveau Conservatoire
Mille
Quai de la Garonne

Boulevard
Macdonald
ESPACE PÉRIPHÉRIQUE
Ella Fitzgerald
CENTRE ÉQUESTRE
Cité des Sciences et de l'industrie
Jardins des Iles
CABARET SAUVAGE
Argonaute
Géode
Jardin des Voltiges
Zénith
Jardin du Dragon
Parc de la Villette
l'Ourcq
Jardin des Frayeurs enfantines
Hall de la Chanson
Allée du Belvédère
TRABENDO
Pl. du Charolais
Prairie du Triangle
Philharmonie de Paris
Grande Halle
Jardins des Miroirs
Th. Paris-Villette
Pl. de la Fontaine aux Lions
Allée du Zénith
Philharmonie 2
Porte de Pantin
Cité de la Musique
Accueil Sud
A. Jean Jaurès
Porte de Pantin
Conservatoire national supérieur de musique et de danse
Porte de Pantin
STE-CLAIRE
BOULEVARD
Sérurier
PÉRIPHÉRIQUE
Boulevard

WHERE TO EAT

À la Folie.................................... 92
Petite Halle (La)......................... 91

WHERE TO DRINK

Glazart (Le)................................. 88
Paname Brewing Company...... 84

96

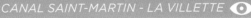

vast steel ball, which has become an iconic symbol of La Villette.

La Philharmonie de Paris★

Mᵒ Porte-de-Pantin, T3b Porte-de-Pantin - 221 av. Jean-Jaurès - ℰ 01 44 84 44 84 - http://philarmoniedeparis.fr - guided tours on prior request (1hr45min) 12pm-6pm, weekends 10am-6pm - closed Mondays, 1 Jan. 1 May, 25 Dec - €13.50. An immense shell lined with mirrors, **Philharmonie 1** is the latest controversial creation from the atelier of Jean Nouvel. Its exceptional 2400-seat auditorium (*free to visit*) welcomes the symphony orchestras from around the world. Temporary exhibitions are also organised.

Musée de la Musique★ – *Mᵒ Porte-de-Pantin - 221 av. Jean-Jaurès - ℰ 01 44 84 44 84 - http://philharmoniedeparis.fr - &. - 12pm-6pm, Sun 10am-6pm - closed Mon, Jan. 1, May 1, 25 Dec - guided tours available (1hr30mins) - €7 (under 26 free) - €10 temporary exhibitions.* The museum is part of the **Cité de la Musique**★ (Philharmonie 2) designed by Christian de Portzamparc, which comprises a concert hall and the museum. The viewer is invited on aural journey exploring music from the 16C to the present day featuring over a thousand instruments. There are also themed temporary exhibitions.

PARC DES BUTTES-CHAUMONT★

H1-2 Mᵒ Buttes-Chaumont ou Botzaris, Danube (libe 7b), Pyrénées, Jourdain, Place-des-Fêtes (line 11). There are park entrances on rue Botzaris, rue Manin, avenue Simon-Bolivar and rue de Crimée. 1 r. Botzaris - ℰ 01 48 03 83 10 - http://equipement.paris.fr - &. - Jul-Aug: 24hr; May-June: 7am-10pm; Apr and Sept: 7am-9pm; rest of the year: 7am-8pm - games, puppet shows, ponies, restaurants.

The 100m/328ft (stripped) hill which forms this park was once known as "bald mount". In the 14C, Philip the Fair ordered every house in Paris to be coated in plaster, for insulation purposes and to protect against fire, leading to the mining of the quarries of Montmartre and the Buttes-Chaumont for gypsum. Over the years the hill became a sinister place frequented by criminals. In the 19C, Haussmann transformed the Buttes into a park, under the direction of Jean-Charles Alphand, who eschewed architectural order of the traditional French garden for a more romantic style, reminiscent of a romantic country garden.

The park is known for its dramatic lakes, cliffs and waterfalls and its giant trees, planted at the end of the 19C (you'll find plane trees, poplars, maples, horse chestnuts and ash trees).

QUARTIER D'AMÉRIQUE OU MOUZAÏA★

Off map by H1

In 1890 250 maisonettes with gardens were built for workers living in the East of Paris. Tucked behind a row of buildings between Place de Rhin-et-Danube and Place des Fêtes, today this is a pretty and thoroughly unusual spot to visit: think cobblestone streets lit by 19C-style street lamps.

97

Bastille★ and the East

The East of Paris is characterised by its diverse population, a charming hodgepodge of architecture, public gardens, artists' studios and trendy bistros. One-time villages Belleville and Ménilmontant, with their charming sloping roads, are well worth a visit for those interested in seeing a less formal side of Paris.

▶**Access:** M° Bastille (lines 1, 5and 8), Ledru-Rollin (line 8). **Père-Lachaise:** M° Père-Lachaise (lines 2 and 3), Gambetta and Porte-de-Bagnolet (line 3), Philippe-Auguste and Alexandre-Dumas (line 2). **Belleville:** M° Belleville (lines 2 and 11), Pyrénées, Jourdain, Place-des-Fêtes, Télégraphe (line 11). **Ménilmontant:** Ménilmontant (line 2) et Gambetta (libes 3 and 3b). ***Detachable map G6 and H3-4.***
▶**Tip:** The artists' studios in Belleville often host open days. Info: www.ateliers-artistes-belleville.fr.

BASTILLE

G6 M° Bastille.
For Parisians, **Place de la Bastille** is the site of political and union protests, parades and large outdoor concerts. Lines of paving stones trace the outline of the old Bastille fortress, a state prison from the 17C and a symbol of the power of the king who only had to sign a letter to lock up anyone he deemed inconvenient, such as the overly frank Voltaire, Diderot or Mirabeau. On July 14, 1789, the prison was attacked by revolutionaries and 800 workers dismantled it stone by stone (⟁ *p. 180*). The July Column (1831-1840) at its centre is in memory of the Parisians killed during the revolutions of 1830 and 1848. Atop the column is the Génie de la Liberté

("Spirit of Freedom") holding the flame of liberty and the broken chains of tyranny.

Opéra Bastille★
120 r. de Lyon - ✆ 0 892 89 90 90 - www.operadeparis.fr - check opening hours. - guided visits on request (1hr15mins) - €15 - prices vary depending on the show. Built in place of the former Gare de la Bastille, the Opera was created by Uruguayan-Canadian architect Carlos Ott between 1983 and 1989. It contains a 2 700-seat concert hall. The immense size of the building is because every person involved in the creation of the opera is housed in the space: 74 different professions, from wig-maker to the electrician, work inside.

Port de plaisance de Paris-Arsenal

You may feel a bit disorientated at this port between Place de la Bastille and the Seine. It is in fact the opening between the Seine and Canal St-Martin *(see p.92)*, which runs beneath the Boulevard Richard Lenoir and resurfaces at République. It is lined by boats and pretty gardens.

Promenade plantée★

Along Avenue Daumesnil *(follow it towards Gare de Lyon)*, the **Viaduc des Arts★** houses under its vaults artisans' studios and contemporary furniture shops. The immense windows contribute to the beauty of the stone and red brick arcades. Above the arcade, the **Promenade Plantée★** *(accessible by lifts and escalators, at the start of Av. Daumesnil)* offers an atypical view over the surrounding architecture. This former railway linked Bastille to the eastern suburbs of Paris for more than a century (1859 to 1969), giving Parisians the chance to breathe the country air in the Bois de Vincennes or along the banks of the Marne. Today it is a 4,5 km/2.7mi pedestrian walkway, lined with lime trees, hazel trees, rosebushes and climbing plants. The nearby **Marché d'Aligre**, on the square of the same name, is very picturesque, with shops selling food, second-hand clothes and antiques).

Rue du Faubourg-St-Antoine – Courtyards, cul-de-sacs, alleys and charming pedestrian passageways with old-world charm form the artisanal heart of the district. Rare cabinetmakers and furniture makers still have their workshops and warehouses here, tucked away in flowery cobblestone courtyards. Steal into cours (courtyards): de l'Ours, de la Maison-Brûlée, des Trois-Frères, de l'Étoile-d'Or.

CIMETIÈRE DU PÈRE-LACHAISE★★

Off map H4 M° Père-Lachaise, Gambetta, Philippe-Auguste. 8 bd de Ménilmontant - ℘ 01 55 25 82 10 - www.paris.fr - from mid-March end of Oct: 8am-6pm, Sat 8.30am-6pm, Sun and public holidays 9am-6pm; rest of the year: 8am-5.30pm, Sat 8.30am-5.30pm - guided visits available - the other entrances are closed as part of "le plan Vigipirate" (heightened security measures). This cemetery, dotted with more than 3000 trees, Is the resting place of an exceptional number of distinguished figures and features many beautiful graves. Created under the Empire by Brongniart, it is an intriguing and moving museum of funeral statuary. Visitors go to pay their respects to different cultural figures, depending on their sympathies and tastes: legendary frontman of The Doors Jim Morrison, spiritualist Allan Kardecm Chopin, Balzac, Proust, Édith Piaf and Oscar Wilde are just some of the famous figures buried here. Perhaps the most moving part of the cemetery is the monument dedicated the members of the French Resistance and those deported during the Second World War (south-east corner). It's also worth seeing the **Mur des Fédérés** (Communards' Wall). It was here on May 28, 1871 that the last bloody episode of the Commune would play out. The insurgents, who had themselves shot their prisoners, took refuge in the cemetery. The "Versaillais" attacked them and a brutal showdown took place. The next day at dawn the survivors were shot against the wall of the cemetery, their bodies thrown into an open grave.

BELLEVILLE

H3 M° Belleville ou Pyrénées.
This diverse working-class district and former village is well worth exploring. Start by climbing the restaurant- and bazaar-lined rue de Belleville, where the legend has it that the great Édith Piaf was born at no 72 (she was in fact born at Hôpital Tenon in nearby Porte de Bagnolet). Take la rue des Pyrénées (on the right) and follow it to no 371, where the little staircase of rue Levert leads to place Henri-Krasucki, the historic heart of Belleville, leading to the picturesque rues des Cascades and rue de la Mare. The rue des Envierges will bring you up to the highest parts of Belleville, where you'll find **Parc de Belleville★** with its spectacular **view★★** over Paris. It was in Belleville Cemetery, the highest summit in Paris, that the first telegraph was tested.
Rue des Cascades – This long, narrow road is full of old-world charm with its short buildings and little bars: in fact, it feels more like a little provincial village than a world capital. From the stairs on rue Fernand-Raynaud you can appreciate a lovely view of Paris. Here, you will also find "regards", little maisonette-type buildings that once let visitors look down at the water in the area's underground spring. At no. 42, the **Regard St-Martin** belonged

to the St-Martin-des-Champs priory: on the beaten insignia on the left you see Saint-Martin the horseman on his steed. At no. 17 (go down the stairs) you will find the Regard des "Messiers" (guards who kept watch over the vines and fields.)

MÉNILMONTANT

H4 At the bottom of rue des Cascades. turn right onto rue de Ménilmontant.
Église Notre-Dame-de-la-Croix was once the centre of the village of Ménilmontant. It has one of the longest naves in Paris, thanks to the metallic structure of its vaults. At the foot of the stairs, make a stop at **Place Maurice-Chevalier** with its shady horse chestnut trees and distinctive smell of hookah pipes. You are in the heart of the **Hameau (hamlet) de Ménilmontant★**, where in the 18C many Parisians came to stroll and to drink cheap wine outside of Farmers General tax wall. It is also worth exploring some of the little roads and passages of the area: the Villa de l'Ermitage (rue de l'Ermitage) is lined with artists' studios and houses punctuated with greenery lovingly maintained by the residents, while adjacent Cité Leroy features pretty wooden facades adorned with climbing plants.

On the corner of rue des Pyrénées and rue de Ménilmontant, take a peek at the Pavillon Carré de Baudouin, a former "folie" dating from the 18C, once a dance hall, holiday resort and "house of pleasure". Today it is one of the major cultural centres of the arrondissement (*exhibition programme at www.carredebaudouin.fr*).

Addresses

Rosa-Bonheur sur Seine, Quai d'Orsay
© Bertrand Gardel/hemis.fr

🍴
Where to eat

❧ Find the addresses on our maps using the numbers in the listing (ex. ①). The coordinates in red (ex. C2) refer to the detachable map (inside the cover).

LA CITÉ AND LES QUAIS

Area map p. 16-17
Picnic idea – *Stop at Square Barye, on the eastern edge of Île Saint-Louis, and you'll feel like you're in the very heart of Paris. Picnic fare can be found at all supermarkets.*

Lunch menu €24
⑥ Sequana – *E5 - 72 quai des Orfèvres - M° Pont-Neuf - ☎01 43 29 78 81- www.sequana.paris - closed Sun and Mon - lunch menu €24/32 - dinner €47.* Ideally located just by the elegant Place Dauphine and on the edge of the Seine, this affordable restaurant offers a small menu of seasonal dishes. The chef, Eugénie, who hails from Senegal, cooks up plates inspired by the family recipes of her childhood. Meanwhile, Philippe excels at bread and pastry. Expect exciting dishes cooked to fresh perfection: think sea snail and artichoke or sole with orange blossom.

Lunch menu €26
① Les Fous de l'Île – *F6 - 33 r. des Deux-Ponts, - M° Pont-Marie - ☎01 43 25 76 67 - www.lesfousdelile.com - ♿ - daily 10am-12am - lunch menu and weekdays €26 - dinner and weekends €30.* A bright neo-bistro in the heart of Île Saint-Louis offering tasty food and a good-humoured welcome. The décor adds to the charm with wooden cabinets displaying an impressive (model) chicken collection. The restaurant is run by Boris and Emilie Bazan (aka Les Fous or "the wild ones").

THE LOUVRE

From €20
⑤ Zen – *E4 - 8 r. de l'Échelle,- M° Palais-Royal - ☎01 42 61 93 99 - www.restaurantzenparis.fr - Mon-Fri 12pm-2.30pm, Sat-Sun and public holidays 12pm-3pm, every evening 7pm*

Changing prices
Prices can vary significantly between lunch and dinner in the same establishment. Even very good restaurants may offer lunch menus for less than €25, while their evening menu starts at €40. Our price ranges are based on the prices of lunch menus at the time of our visits, but they can increase significantly in the evening, in particular for the top-rate restaurants. To make the most of Parisian restaurants, we recommend booking in advance where possible. Bon appétit!

10.30pm. A Japanese canteen serving authentic cuisine in a refreshing setting, the white walls splashed with green.

LE MARAIS AND LES HALLES

Area map p. 28-29
Picnic idea – *There are wooden tables in front of the Hôtel de Ville (in line with the Bateaux-Mouches station) on the Right Bank or take a break under the weeping willows on the riverside.*

From €10

😊 ⑨ **L'As du Fallafel** – *F5* - *34 r. des Rosiers, - M° St-Paul - ☏01 48 87 63 60 - &. - daily 11.30am-12am. Closed Fri eve. and Sat - no reservations.* The signature stuffed pita here, piled high with the tastiest of falafel—plus salad, hummus and hot sauce—is simply divine. For meat-eaters, L'As also serves the best shawarma in Paris. There is a takeaway kiosk if you can't bear to wait.

⑬ **Bob's Kitchen** - *F4* - *74 r. des Gravilliers, - M° Arts-and-Métiers - ☏09 52 55 11 66 - www.bobsjuicebar. com - Mon-Fri. 8am-3pm, weekends 8am-4pm.* This California-style joint serves juice blends, soups, salad and maki. With its veggie and organic fare, Bob's Kitchen is a favourite with the young creatives of the area and a great spot to stop for a healthy lunch.

From €15

⑫ **Marché des Enfants-Rouges** - *G4* - *39 r. de Brandagne, M° St-Sébastien-Froissart - daily 8am-8.30pm and Sun 8.30am-5pm. Closed Sun eve and Mon.* The covered market of choice for the "bobos" (bourgeois bohemians) of Paris offers a mouth-watering range of street food options: Japanese bento, Caribbean accra, tagine and Italian delicacies. Crowds are guaranteed: you'll be eating perched on the corner of a table, at the counter or on the go. Our favourites are the Moroccan couscous stand (arrive early on Sunday to get a seat) and the Estaminet des Enfants rouges (t 01 42 72 28 12 - www. lestaminanddesenfantsrouges.com), which share the prettiest terrace.

Lunch menu €15

⑮ **Big Fernand** – *F4* - *32 r. St-Sauveur, - M° Sentier - ☏09 67 22 40 06 - www. bigfernand.com - daily 12pm-10.30pm (Sat 11pm) - menu 15/18 € - menu 15/18 €.* A hamburger in Paris? Why not! Big Fernand proves that good food doesn't have to be complicated with its signature moist bread, juicy steak and delicate confit onions to finish. There are even vegatarian options.

㊴ **Popolare** – *E3* - *111 r. Réaumur - M° Bourse - ☏01 42 21 30 91 - www.bigmammagroup.com - daily 11.45am -10.45pm.* This scrumptious establishment was opened in early 2017 by the unstoppable Big Mamma Group, which has been delighting Parisians with its gourmet pizzas for some years now. Arrive early to avoid queues: this is a popular spot. The products (and waiters!) are Italian and the pizzas spill enticingly off the plate. You can't go wrong with any of the pizzas, but we highly recommend trying the double truffle topped with fior di latte mozza, Parmigiano Reggiano, truffle cream and fresh grated truffle—cheesy, gluttonous, and delicious!

Lunch menu €18

85 La Marée Jeanne – *E4* -*3 r. Mandar, - M° Sentier - ℘01 42 61 58 34 - www.lamareejeanne.com - & - daily 12pm-2.30pm, 9pm-10.30pm.* Fish and shellfish top the bill at this self-designated "bistronautique" restaurant. The interior charms with its upscale fishmonger vibe. The inventive menu features a lunch special centred around three exquisitely put together small plates. In warm weather, enjoy the small, quiet terrace.

Lunch menu €20

14 Pirouette - *F4* - *5 r. Montdétour - M° Andienne-Marcel - ℘01 40 26 47 81 - www.pirouetteparis.com - daily 12pm-2pm and 7.30pm-10pm. Closed Sundays and August* This chic yet cosy restaurant offers a menu full of surprising delights, serving cheeky reboots of traditional classics, like the lime rum baba. Tasteful contemporary décor.

Lunch menu €18-25

11 Breizh Café – *G5* - *109 r. Vieille-du-Temple, - M° Saint-Paul - ℘01 42 72 13 77 - http://breizhcafe.com - Tue-Sun 11.30am-11pm.* This popular contemporary creperie in the heart of the Marais has inspired many imitators with its chic granite, raw timber and slate décor and dedicated use of only the finest ingredients. Crêpes are imbibed with Beurre Bordier and can be eaten simply: sprinkled with brown sugar or topped with Tatin-style apples, flambé with Calvados. The more adventurous may wish to opt for unusual toppings such as white chocolate mousse, matcha ice cream or poached peach with fresh mint.

7 Les Philosophes – *F5* - *28 r. Vieille-du-Temple- M° St-Paul - ℘01 48 87 49 64 - www.cafeine.com/fr/philosophes - daily 9am-2am - brunch €21, fixed menus from €27.* This large bistro and its pretty corner terrace are hard to miss. The big sister of La Belle Hortense, the restaurant proudly displays the provenance of its (often organic) products, artfully blended together in the dishes. This is classic fare, presented to perfection, served in

© Patrice Hauser/hemis.fr

Pirouette

a relaxed atmosphere: think carrot and ginger soup, wild cod fillet and real tarte tatin.

87 **La Chaise au plafond** - *F5 - 10 r. du Trésor, - M° St-Paul - ☎01 42 76 03 22 - cafeine.com/chaise-au-plafond - daily 9.30am-1.15am - brunch served from 9am (€21) - €18/35.* The little sister of Les Philosophes offers an attractive terrace on the quiet rue du Trésor and a menu that blends the traditional and organic.

From €25

8 **Champeaux** - *F4 - Forum des Halles, La Canopée- M° Les-Halles - ☎01 53 45 84 50 - www.restaurant-champeaux.com - daily 11.30am-12am.* Alain Ducasse is behind this contemporary brasserie, located at the entrance of the Canopée des Halles, close to Saint-Eustache. Its immense floor-to-ceiling windows enclose a bustling restaurant serving traditional mainstays (kidney, calf's liver, farmer's chicken) and signature dishes including sweet and savoury soufflés, marinated fish, knife-cut tartare and a fusion beef sandwich with sweet and sour vegetables. Food and drink are served all day: in the afternoon, pop in for a chocolat liégeois, made from Manufacture Ducasse chocolate, before moving on to evening cocktails prepared by mixologist Marjolaine Arpin, accompanied by a generous sharing platter of charcuterie.

16 **Edgar** - *F3 - 31 r. d'Alexandrie- M° Sentier - ☎01 40 41 05 69 - www.edgarparis.com - &- Mon-Sat 8am-1am, Sun 8am-5pm.* This lovely seafood restaurant is a favourite with regulars and serves a menu

laced through with salt and sea air. Select your seafood of choice from the display, take it to the kitchen and nab a seat on the terrace (very busy in summer). Crunchy fish and chips, zingy seasoning and utterly delighted taste buds guaranteed. €27 brunch at weekends from 12pm-2.30pm.

Around €30

10 **Soma** - *G4 - 13 r. de Saintonge- M° St-Sébastien Froissart - ☎09 81 82 53 51 - lesoma.fr - 12pm-2.30pm and 7.30pm-11pm Closed Sun and Mon.* This recently opened Japanese restaurant in the Marais is never empty thanks to its open kitchen, where the chef cooks vegetables, fish and seafood in front of diners; the warm atmosphere evokes an *izakaya* (Japanese pub). The beef mi-cuit with ponzu sauce is exceptional. Good selection of sake.

86 **Elmer** - *F4 - 30 rue Notre-Dame-de-Nazarandh- M° Temple - ☎01 43 56 22 95 - elmer-restaurant.fr - Tue-Fri 12.15pm-2.15pm and 7.30pm-10.30pm, only evening on Sat-closed Sun-Mon, 1st week of Christmas hols.* This gourmet favourite, presided over by young chef Simon Horwitz, who trained under some of the greats, lets the ingredients do the talking in a sophisticated gastronomic menu. The vegetables and meats are treated with care, evident in the hanging cuts of lamb and pork cooking slowly in the open kitchen. The décor, characterised by raw wood, soft lighting and stylish South American crockery, completes the picture of perfection.

107

🍴

QUARTIER LATIN

Area map p. 40-41

Picnic idea – *The Jardin des Plantes is the perfect spot for a lunch stop.*

Under €10

70 Au p'tit grec – *F7* - *68 r. Mouffandard* - *M° Place Monge* - *☎06 50 24 69 34* - *www.auptitgrec.com* - *daily 10.30am-12.30am.* The almost permanent queue at the counter is testament to the quality of this Greek tavern-Breton creperie hybrid. With only a few stools inside, your best bet is to take away.

Under 15 €

21 Strada Café – *F7* - *24 r. rue Monge-M° Cardinal-Lemoine* - *☎09 72 45 12 87* - *www.stradacafe.fr* - *& - 8am-6.30pm weekends 10am-6.30pm.* This discreet and friendly café offers a slice of New York coffee shop atmosphere in Paris. It's an ideal spot to stop, read a book and, most importantly, try an organic coffee, one of the best in Paris. Excellent lunch menus, homemade pastries and fresh fruit juices are on offer, all served in warm, welcoming atmosphere. Brunch available on weekends.

71 Mexi & Co – *E6* - *10 r. Dante,* - *M° Cluny-la Sorbonne* - *☎01 46 34 14 12* - *daily 9am-11pm.* Order a jug of margarita and snack on the homemade guacamole, or try their famous versions of the classic burritos and nachos. Expect colourful furnishings and a South American soundtrack.

From €15

17 Mirama – *E6* - *17 r. St-Jacques* - *M° Cluny-La Sorbonne* - *☎01 43 54 71 77* - *daily 12pm-10.30pm.* Located just off Bd St-Michel and behind Eglise St-Séverin, Mirama is a hidden treat for lovers of authentic Chinese cuisine. Be sure to try the soup and the Peking duck, both house specials.

19 Lhassa – *F6* - *13 r. de la Montagne-Ste-Geneviève* - *M° Maubert-Mutualité* - *☎01 43 26 22 19* - *& - daily sf Mon 12pm-2pm and 7pm-10.30pm.* Tibetan restaurant with a zen vibe and atmospheric music. The varied menu encompasses steamed dishes, soups made from barley flour, spinach and meat, as well as beef dumplings, all at a fair price.

23 Le Petit Bain – *H8* - *7 port de la Gare* - next to Piscine Joséphine-Baker - *M° Bibliothèque-François-Mitterrand* - *☎01 80 48 49 81* - *www.petitbain. org* - *& - Tue-Sat 4pm-12am, Sun 11.30am-3pm - dishes €12/16.* This 70-cover restaurant, housed on a floating barge at the foot of the National Library of France, offers "market cooking". The menu changes every Wednesday and features fresh products and natural wine; there is also an outdoor "rooftop" with a beautiful view. Au Petit Bain is a floating cultural space and social enterprise, with some staff members drawn from a work rehabilitation scheme.

From €20

24 Le Pré Verre – *E6* - *8 r. Thénard-M° Maubert-Mutualité* - *☎01 43 54 59 47* - *www.lepreverre.com* - *Tue-Sat 12pm-2pm, 7.30pm-10.30pm.* A lively French spot in the heart of the Latin

Quarter featuring warm-toned décor. The bistro fare is well executed and the prices are very reasonable. Dishes include pig's head, puréed dates with vinegar, poultry liver parfait with Madeira sauce, marinated raw tuna dipped in poppy seeds, potato confit and mushroom cappuccino with chestnut foam. For dessert, indulge in a devilishly sour lemon and kaffir lime tart.

72 Piment Thaï – *E6* - *21 r. St-Jacques - Mº Cluny la-Sorbonne – ☏01 56 24 84 88 - www.pimentthai21.com - daily 12.30pm-10.45pm.* Chef Too spent much of her childhood in Thailand in her grandmother's kitchen and brought her family recipes with her when she came to Paris. Helped by only one commis chef, the young chef takes pride in making everything herself. Expect delicate spring rolls, lightly bread-crumbed fried prawns, beef in red curry and an exquisite pad Thai with meltingly soft noodles and marinated beef selected by renowned butcher Hugo Desnoyer. Excellent value for money.

22 Maison Marie – *E7* - *222 r. St-Jacques - RER Luxembourg – ☏01 43 54 78 68 – www.maisonmarie.fr – daily 8am-2am.* This former early 20C greengrocer is now the home of a large brasserie that serves food all day and is ideally situated between the Panthéon and Jardin du Luxembourg. The menu includes burrata, spiced tuna tartare, scallop carpaccio, croques, steak, chicken casserole and old-fashioned blanquette de veau. There is also a south-facing terrace and a family-friendly brunch on Sundays.

Lunch menu. Around €32

18 Aux verres de contact – *F6* - *33 r. de Bièvre - Mº Maubert-Mutualité - ☏01 46 34 58 02 - www.auxverresdecontact.com - ⛔ - daily 12pm-2pm and 7pm-10pm. Closed Sat lunch and Sun.* The team from Jadis (in the 15e) have taken over this friendly contemporary bistro, complete with colourful décor and a fresh and seasonal French menu: soup of the day, veal and vanilla pot de crème. There's also an excellent wine list. Good value for money.

73 Bistro des Gastronomes – *F6* - *10 r. du Cardinal-Lemoine - Mº Cardinal-Lemoine - ☏01 43 54 62 40 - Tue-Sat 12pm-2.30pm and 7pm-11pm.* This restaurant in the heart of the 5th arrondissement is a great find for food-lovers. The young, energetic chef presides over a menu of bistro classics, reproduced with market-fresh ingredients, including celery remoulade and pan-seared steak with grenaille potatoes. The décor is elegant with wood panelling and retro condiment jars.

69 Les Délices d'Aphrodite – *F8* - *4 r. Candolle Mº Censier-Daubenton - ☏01 43 31 40 39 - www.mavrommatis.com - 12pm-2.15pm, 7pm-11pm.* This was the favourite tavern of singer Georges Moustaki. A meal here will transport you from central Paris to sunnier climes. Chef Andreas Mavrommatis's creations stimulate the senses – think grilled octopus, garlic prawns, roast lamb with shallots – without being pretentious.

109

🍴

ST-GERMAIN-DES-PRÉS-MONTPARNASSE

Area map p. 50

Picnic idea: The sumptuous Jardin du Luxembourg, known affectionately among Parisians as "le Luco", is a perfect spot. Pull up a chair by the Grand Bassin.

Under €20

25 Au pied de fouet –*DE5* - *3 r. St-Benoit*- M° St-Germain-des-Prés - ✆*01 42 96 59 10* - *www.aupieddefouet. com* - *Mon-Sat 12pm-2.30pm and 7pm-11pm* - *set menu around 18 €.* This former inn has been given a new lease of life. There are just 20 seats in this restaurant serving authentic French fare, largely to devoted regulars. The food is rustic (gizzard salad, andouillette), washed down with house French wine. The atmosphere is friendly and the prices are from a different era!

Lunch menu €20

29 Blueberry Maki Bar – *D6* - *6 r. du Sabot,* - M° St-Sulpice - ✆*01 42 22 21 56* - *www.blueberrymakibar.com* - *daily except Sun-Mon, Tue-Fri 12pm-2.30pm and 7.30pm-10.30pm, Sat 12.30pm-3pm and 7.30pm-11pm.* There is a certain pop *je-ne-sais-quoi* at Blueberry that makes it an absolute must for maki (and sushi) lovers. The inventively named maki—Rackham le Rouge, Trublion, Iroquois—is king in this establishment and absolute freshness is standard. You'll find eel, skipjack and avocado with prawn. We only have one recommendation: get the maki! (€30-58 à la carte).

74 Tsukizi - *DE6* - *2 bis r. des Ciseaux*- M° Saint-Germain des Prés - ✆*01 43 54 65 19* - *12pm-2.15pm and 7pm-10.30pm - closed midday Sunday and Mon.* A classic sushi bar where patrons watch the chef take his knife to the raw fish. The chirashi is delicious, as is the wide range of fish spanning tuna, salmon, jack mackerel, octopus and cuttlefish.

From €20

32 Mamie Gâteaux - *D6* - *66 r. du Cherche-Midi*- M° St-Placide - ✆*01 42 22 32 15* - *www.mamie-gateaux.com* - *Tue-Sat 11.30am-6pm.* Mamie is full of down-to-earth charm with its wipe-clean tablecloths and well-loved cast iron cooker. Laid on top of checked tablecloths on the counter, you'll find tarts of the day and salad, but the biggest draw here is without a doubt the desserts: think chocolate fondant, pain perdu positively imbibed with butter, and carrot cake washed down with an extremely calorific homemade hot chocolate, topped with chantilly cream. Word to the wise: Ultra-popular, expect a queue.

30 Marcello - *E6* - *8 r. Mabillon* - M° Mabillon - ✆*01 43 26 52 26* - *daily 8am-12am.* Marcello is a slick mix of Turin café and Brooklyn coffee shop, with a gorgeous secluded terrace set back from the hustle and bustle of Saint-Germain. Egg-white omelette and organic Japanese matcha are on the menu for breakfast with truffle arancini and calamari à la plancha with spelt spaghetti to follow. High-class finger food is available throughout the day, with elegant house cocktails served in the evening.

Lunch menu €24/25

28 La Bocca della Verità – **D6** - 2 r. du Sabot M° St-Sulpice - ☏01 45 48 96 65 - www.boccadellaverita.fr - 12pm-3pm, 7.30pm-11pm. La Bocca della Verità means "the mouth of truth", and we're not lying when we say you can rely on this address for Italian elegance, respect of ingredients and indulgence. This restaurant is full of life, thanks in no part to its young (and charming) owners, sisters Marie-Lorna and Florence Vaconsin and its Neapolitan chef Antonio Vassallo. The vegetable plate is enchanting; the burrata is as creamy as those found in Puglia; and the linguine alle vongole is served peppered and al dente, in authentic Napolese style. The menu changes daily to keep the locals on their feet. A ray of Italian sunshine in the heart of St-Germain.

75 Café Trama – **D7** - 83 r. du Cherche-Midi - M° St-Placide - ☏01 45 48 33 71 - Tue-Sat 12pm-2.15pm, 6.30pm-10.15pm. This establishment is presided over by Marion Trama, the daughter of acclaimed chef Alain Trama, who sees her restaurant as a "new-generation" bistro. Patrons can grab a seat at the zinc bar or in the main dining room amid chic wood and marble décor, complete with an immense wall-mounted slate board. The menu is mouth-watering: think mullet ceviche and green asparagus with foie gras.

Lunch menu €28

31 Le Timbre – **D7** - 3 r. Ste-Beuve e - M° N.-D.-des-Champs - ☏01 45 49 10 40 - www.restaurantlandimbre. com - daily 12pm-3pm and 7.30pm-11pm. Closed Sun-Mon. This charming restaurant is as dinky as a postage stamp, hence the name (Le Timbre means "the stamp"). The young chef has held onto the wooden tables, banquettes and lively, informal atmosphere, while offering inventive and tasty "cuisine du marché", packed with fresh ingredients. His partner Agnès advises on the excellent wine menu.

26 Clover – **D5** - 5 r. Perronand- M° St-Germain-des-Prés - ☏01 75 50 00 05 - www.clover-paris.com - daily 12.30pm-2pm and 7.30pm-10pm - Lunch menu: €35, dinner menu: €73 - Closed Sun-Mon, 2nd week of August. The new opening from two-Michelin-starred chef Jean-François Piège and his wife Élodie is a richly deserved success. The décor is well thought-out and St-Germain diners are handsomely fed with fine concoctions such as the sumptuous young lamb with chickpeas and spiced jus.

Around €30

76 Ida – **C7** - 117 r. de Vaugirard-M° Falguière - ☏01 56 58 00 02 - www.restaurant-ida.com - Mon-Sat 12.30pm-2.15pm, 7.30pm-10.30pm. Denny Imbroisi welcomes his customers like friends in a restaurant that's half contemporary bistro and authentic Italian trattoria. The menu is bursting with delicious options—raw fish, ceviche, sublime charcuterie, freshly-arrived from Italy—but if you are going "chez Denny", you cannot leave without trying his spaghetti alla carbonara, consistently voted the best in Paris. Reservations recommended.

🍴

Lunch menu €35

㉝ Le Caméléon d'Arabian – *D7* - *6 r. de Chevreuse, - M° Vavin - ℘01 43 27 43 27 - daily 12pm-2.15pm and 7pm-10.30pm - Closed Sat midday and Sun, 3rd week of August.* Here you'll find the best calf's liver in Paris and an exquisite royal hare. The eponymous chameleon man, Jean-Paul Arabian is an show-off and provides the necessary soul for this discreet restaurant located on a small road right by Montparnasse.

INVALIDES-TOUR EIFFEL

Picnic idea: The Jardin Catherine Labouré (29 r. de Babylone) is an enclave of country charm, complete with vegetable garden and fruit trees. The banks of the Seine and the gardens of the Champ-de-Mars are attractive alternatives.

Lunch menu €19

㊱ Le Café du Marché – *B5* - *38 r. Cler - M° École-Militaire - ℘01 47 05 51 27 - www.cafe-du-marche.fr - ♿ - Mon-Sat 7am-12am, Sun 7am-12am.* A local favourite serving tasty smaller dishes and copious bistro fare. Diners may eat *en terrasse* or in the dining room; either way, expect a friendly atmosphere and a typically Parisian feed.

Around €20

㊞ Marcel – *D6* - *15 r. de Babylone - M° Sèvres-Babylone - ℘01 42 22 62 62 - www.restaurantmarcel.fr - Mon-Fri 10am-11pm, w/end 10am-7pm.* When you enter Chez Marcel, you may momentarily feel as if you've left Paris:

all the dishes are in English and an à la carte brunch is served all day. Options include: eggs Benedict; meatball salad with sucrine lettuce, bulgur wheat and spicy meatballs; and even that famous NYC favourite, kale salad. Finish up with a scrumptiously indulgent key lime pie, a moist carrot cake or apple pie served with cream.

Lunch menu €25

㊆㊆ Plume – *C6* -*24 r. Pierre-Leroux - M° Vaneau - ℘01 43 06 79 85 - www.restaurantplume.com - ♿ - 12pm-2.15pm and 7.30pm-10.15pm. Closed Sun-Mon.* This new opening has got heaps of charm and flavour. Fitting with the trend for "bistronomie", the young chef offers inventive cuisine that lets the produce do the talking, including cheeses from neighbouring Quatrehomme. The space is bright and the décor very current, ticking all the boxes for a trendy new opening. Reservation recommended.

Lunch menu €28

㉟ Les Cocottes – *B5* - *135 r. St-Dominique - M° École-Militaire - ℘01 45 50 10 28 - www. maisonconstant.com - daily 12pm-11pm - Lunch menu weekdays €28 - no reservations.* This is more of a counter, complete with high tables, than a traditional restaurant, though the atmosphere is warm and friendly. An elegant revisit of bistro cuisine is on the menu: think terrine de campagne and côte de veau rôtie, served in individual casserole dishes.

From €30

😊 **37** **Oudino** – **C6** - 17 r. Oudinot - M° Vaneau - ✆01 45 66 05 09 - www.oudino.fr - daily 12pm-2.30pm and 7.30pm-11pm Closed Sun. This is an indulgent culinary pitstop in the heart of government ministry district offering an attractive set menu and bistro-style cuisine (crispy lamb shoulder, duck parmentier).

From €36

34 **Café Constant** – **B5** - 139 r. St-Dominique- M° École-Militaire - ✆01 47 53 73 34 - www.maisonconstant.com - daily. 8am-11pm - breakfast 7am-11am, Sun 8am-11am - 35/60 € - no reservations. This simple and down-to-earth restaurant from the renowned Christian Constant offers gourmet bistro cuisine at affordable prices. Dishes include eggs mimosa, oyster tartare, roasted lamb and rice pudding.

40 **Au bon accueil** – **B5** - 14 r. Monttessu - M° Pont-de-l'Alma - ✆01 47 05 46 11 - www.aubonaccueilparis.com - Mon-Fri 12pm-2pm and 6.30pm-10.30pm - closed weekends and 3rd week of August - set menu €36. This chic yet discreet bistro enjoys an excellent location on a quiet road in sight of the Eiffel Tower. An appetising seasonal menu, using market-fresh ingredients offers dishes such as French smoked and marinated salmon with mashed potato and hazelnut butter or brioche pain perdu topped with caramel and mango and passionfruit sauce. The prices will also leave a good taste in your mouth!

Between €20 and €42

😊 **L'Os à Moelle** – **Off map A7** - 3 r. Vasco-de-Gama - M° Lourmel - ✆01 45 57 27 27 - osamoelle-restaurant.com - Tue-Sat 12pm-2pm and 7.30pm-10.30pm, Sun 12.30pm-2.30pm (closed 3rd week of Aug) - set menu 20 € (weekday lunch)/ 25 €/42 €. Thierry Faudes, one of the pioneers of the "bistronomie" movement, serves up generous dishes in this charming restaurant, with touches of audacious inventiveness in the menu. Across the street, the "cave" (wine shop) of the l'Os à Moelle is a charming spot for a glass of wine and light snack, or a prix fixe dinner.

TROCADÉRO-CHAILLOT

113

Lunch menu €18

😊 **79** **Les Marches** – **B4** - 5 r. de la Manutention - M° Iéna - ✆01 47 23 52 80 - www.lesmarches-restaurant.com - ♿ - Mon-Sat 12pm-2.30pm (Sun 3pm) and 7.30pm-10.30pm. This restaurant is one of three "Les Routiers" listed restaurants in Paris, with a menu reminiscent of France from days gone by: steak with Béarnaise sauce, oeufs meurettes (poached eggs in red wine sauce) and citrons givrés (lemon sorbet served in a hollowed-out lemon). The owner sets the tone for the friendly and welcoming service and is happy to tell the story of how he achieved his dream of opening a "routier", after being fascinated by the roadside restaurants in childhood (à la carte: €28/36).

🍴

Around €20

41 **Schwartz's Deli** – *A4* - *7 av. d'Eylau - M° Trocadéro - ☏01 47 04 73 61 - http://schwartzsdeli.fr - Mon-Fri 12pm-3pm, 7.30pm-11pm; weekends 12pm-3pm, 7pm-11.30pm (Sun 11pm)*. This American diner brings a touch of New York to Paris, all the way down to the checkered tablecloths. There are no less than 14 burgers on the menu, including beef, cod and even duck breast. Macaroni, soup and salads are also on offer.

CHAMPS-ÉLYSÉES AND THE WEST

From €25

80 **Café Latéral** - *B2* - *4 av. Mac-Mahon - M° Charles-de-Gaulle-Étoile - ☏01 43 80 20 96 - www.cafelateral.com - daily 7am-2am, Sun 7.30am-1am.* A typically Parisian café located just a few short steps from the Eiffel Tower. The menu comprises good-quality traditional French fare and the service is attentive and efficient. The terrace attracts the young professionals of the area and is lively at lunch and after work hours.

44 **Ladurée** - *B3* - *75 av. des Champs-Élysées - M° Franklin-Roosevelt - ☏01 40 75 08 75 - www.laduree.com - daily 7.30am-11.30pm (Sat 8.30am-12.30am)* Before gawping at the astounding range of macarons in the boutique, stop upstairs for a salmon club sandwich, the famous croque Ladurée or a traditional dish such as the vol au vent or Normandy plaice with Chardonnay sauce.

From €40

42 **Le Mini Palais** – *C4* - *3 av. Winston-Churchill, - M° Champs-Élysées-Clemenceau - ☏01 42 56 42 42 - www.minipalais.com - ♿ - daily 10am-2am - dishes 19/39 €.* The Mini Palais, housed in a wing of the Grand Palais, occupies an impressive 300m2/984ft2 peristyle. The vibe is, however, not stuffy and you won't need to dress up or wear a tie: all that's required is an appetite in order to appreciate the food created by Stéphane d'Aboville and consulting chef Éric Frechon; perfect service comes courtesy of the always-excellent René Carbonnière. Try the whiting (fish) with almonds or the tetragon (NZ spinach), péquillos and caper salad; or at tea time, treat yourself to the giant rum baba served with light vanilla cream.

OPÉRA-PALAIS-ROYAL

Area map p. 83

Picnic idea: The Palais-Royal gardens make a lovely, quiet place to take a break, surrounded by classical architecture and contemporary art (Buren's columns).

Lunch menu. From 12 €

43 **JanTchi** - *E4* - *6 r. Thérèse - M° Pyramides - ☏01 40 15 91 07 - www.jantchi.com - daily except Sun 12pm-3pm and 7pm-10.30pm - lunch menu €12/14.* Simple but distinctive, this temple of Korean cuisine may surprise you with its mouth-watering blend of flavours and colours. Indulge in the japchae and then famous spiced pork bibimbap, rounded off with homemade green tea ice cream. Allow for a 20-minute queue in the evening.

89 Kotteri Ramen Naritake – *E4 - 31 r. des Petits-Champs - M° Pyramides - 01 42 86 03 83 - daily 11.30am-10pm. Closed Tue.* This tiny Japanese restaurant serves delicious noodle soups (ramen) and tasty gyoza. The often-long queue is testament to the reputation of this popular little spot.

From €15

45 Bouillon Chartier – *E3 - 7 r. du Faubourg-Montmartre - M° Grands-Boulevards - 01 47 70 86 29 - www.bouillon-chartier.com - & - daily 11.30am-12am - menu €18/22 - no reservations.* An ideal place to dine on a budget, but also to experience the authentic old-fashioned atmosphere of this typically Parisian workers' canteen from 1896. The décor hasn't changed since opening, with its glass atrium ceiling, wood panelling and brass luggage racks where the regulars keep their napkin.

Lunch menu from €22

48 L'Office – *F3 - 3 r. Richer - M° Poissonnière - 01 47 70 67 31 - www.office-resto.com - daily except weekends 12pm-2pm and 7.30pm-10.30pm - reservation recommended.* This is one of two bistros, along with le Richier (across the street, opened a year ago), run by Charles Compagnon. Its tiny size means it's a cosy fit. The inventiveness of chef Yosuke Yamaji, trained under Ducasee and Robuchon, is impressive.

115

© René Mattes/hemis.fr

Bouillon Chartier

54 **À Côté** – *E3 - 16 r. La-Fayette - Mº Chaussée-d'Antin - ☏01 48 78 03 68 - www.acote.paris - Mon-Fri 11.30am-11pm.* Boris and Sébastien serve the "platter of their dreams", comprised of a fine prime rib of Limousine beef cooked "black and blue" (or crispy on the surface) with Béarnaise sauce, homemade fries and an enormous marrowbone. Excellent wine.

Lunch menu €30

46 **Les Diables au Thym** – *E3 - 35 r. Bergère- Mº Grands-Boulevards - ☏01 47 70 77 09 - www.lesdiablesauthym.com - daily - Lunch menu €30, dinner menu €40. Closed Sat lunch, Sun and public holidays* Located near Musée Grévin, this is a simple space with a bistro vibe (a few contemporary paintings decorate the walls). Modern, seasonal food is on the menu with a selection of organic wines chalked up on the wall.

Set menu €37

😊 **47** **La Régalade Conservatoire** – *E3 - 9 r. du Conservatoire - Mº Grands-Boulevards - ☏01 44 83 83 60 - www.hoteldenell.com - ♿ - daily 12pm–2.30pm and 7pm–10.30pm - set menu €37 - reservation recommended.* One of the latest additions to the "chic canteens" family (or néobistrot). Our top pick is the slow cooked veal steak with vegetables cooked Nice-style.

MONTMARTRE-PIGALLE

***Area map** p. 88-89*
Picnic idea – *The gardens of the Sacré-Cœur offer a stunning panoramic view over Paris.*

From €15

52 **Flesh** – *D1 - 25 r. de Douai, - Mº Blanche - ☏01 42 81 21 93 - ♿ - 12pm-2.30pm and 7.30pm-10.30pm, Fri-Sat 11pm, Sun 12.30pm-3pm and 10am-10.30pm - Lunch menu/weekdays €15/18.* Meat-lovers will go wild for this carnivorous gem serving meat specials in an industrial-style wood and concrete setting. Think Argentinian red meat and barbecue spare ribs, smothered in house sauce (bourbon or lemon-honey) with a side of traditional fries, courgette marinated in goat's cheese and lemon or grilled corn with parmesan and coriander.

Lunch menu €19

50 **Jeanne B.** – *61 r. Lepic - Mº Lamarck -Caulaincourt - ☏01 42 51 17 53 - www.jeanne-b-comestibles.com - 10am-10.30pm.* The little sister of Jeanne A offers table d'hôte stylings and fine ingredients: everything is homemade and the products undergo a rigorous selection process. Be sure to try the speciality meats, roasted medium rare, accompanied by deliciously creamy gratin dauphinois.

😊 **55** **Le Pantruche** – *E1 - 3 r. Victor-Massé, - Mº Pigalle - ☏01 48 78 55 60 - 1 - 12.30pm-2.30pm and 7.30pm-10.30pm - lunch menu €19 - Closed weekends, 1st week of Christmas hols, 1st week of Easter hols and 3rd week of*

August. The relaxed atmosphere brings people here as much as the inventive food. The experience of the rack of lamb with potatoes grenaille will stay with you long after the meal: simple and delicious.

From €20

81 **Brasserie Barbès** – *F1* - *2 bd Barbès, - M° Barbès* - *☎01 42 64 52 23 - www.brasseriebarbes.com - ⅙ - daily 8am-2am - reservations only possible at lunchtime.* This multi-purpose space (bar, restaurant, club) has established a reputation as the hip hangout of this traditionally working-class neighbourhood. Detox juices and health-focussed cuisine are available as well as more traditional options like the burger and tartare (plat du jour: €13). When the weather is good, the patio is an ideal lunch spot. In the evening the second floor is taken over by dancing.

53 **Atelier Saint-Georges** – *E2* - *16 r. Henry-Monnier - M° St-Georges - ☎01 77 16 18 96 - www.atelier-saint georges.com - 12pm-3pm, 7pm-11pm, Closed Mon, Tue lunchtime and Sun eve.* Each of the burgers makes a nod to French gastronomic tradition, from knife-minced beef, camembert and Granny Smith apples in "Monsieur Gaston" to pan-fried foie gras escalope in the "Monsieur Paul" burger. Table service.

Formule From €26

82 **Le Wepler** – *D1* - *14 pl. Clichy - M° Place de Clichy - ☎01 45 22 53 24 - www.wepler.com - daily 8am-12.30am.* It is hard to walk past this institution without stopping. All the dishes, from the club sandwich to the seafood platter, are excellent in this typically Parisian brasserie. It has happily changed very little over the years.

90 **Bijou** – *E1* - *10 r. Dancourt - M° Anvers - ☎01 42 57 47 29- daily 12pm-2pm, 7pm-11.30pm.* In this pretty pizzeria, next door to the Théâtre de l'Atelier, Gennaro is constantly concocting new recipes. All the ingredients come from Italy and each new pizza is tried and tested by the team. Patrons may choose from classic pizzas à la carte or "gourmettes", like the Antica with old-fashioned ragu, Buffalo mozzarella, basil and extra virgin olive oil.

From €30

83 **Le Khaosan** – *E1* - *52 r. Condorcet- M° Anvers - ☎01 49 70 07 06 - www. khaosan.fr - ⅙ - daily. 12pm-3.30pm and 7.30pm-2am.* Other than the actual dishes on offer (and the name), this is not a typical Thai restaurant. You'll find a relaxed informal atmosphere, an exciting cocktail menu and a kitchen full of flavours. The menu is wide, featuring all the classics, with an excellent *suea rong hai* (steak with chili sauce).

From €48

51 **Le Coq Rico** – *98 r. Lepic - M° Lamarck-Caulaincourt - ☎01 42 59 82 89 - www.lecoqrico.com - ⅙ - daily 12pm-2.30pm and 7pm-10.30pm.* At Coq Rico, chef Antoine Westermann expertly experiments with poultry in all its forms. The result is magic. You can choose between the "coin rotisserie" where you'll while watching the chefs at work or the more select side room

🍴

where subtler chicken dishes are on offer. If you are in a large group, we recommend sharing a Poulette de Racan or a Canette des Dombes. Plat du jour specials (€15) are available at lunch.

CANAL-ST-MARTIN-LA-VILLETTE

***Area map** p. 96*
Picnic idea: The banks of the Canal St-Martin are a very popular picnic and drinking spot among Parisians. The Parc de la Villette is more familial and a good option if you'd like a little more space to stretch out.

Lunch menu from €15

59 **Soya** – *G3* - *20 r. de la Pierre-Levée - M° Goncourt - ☎01 85 15 27 84 - www. soya-cantine-bio.fr - Tue 7pm-11pm, Wed-Sat 12pm-4pm and 7pm-11pm, Sun 11.30am-4pm.* This organic canteen is housed an attractive space with wood detail. Patrons tuck into fresh products such as beetroot tartare, vegetable mezzes and delicious juices. Everything is homemade.

91 **La Petite Halle** – *211 av. Jean-Jaurès - Parc de La Villette - M° Porte de Pantin - ☎09 82 25 81 81 - www.lapetitehalle.com - Mon-Tue 12pm-3pm, Wed-Thur 12pm-3pm and 7pm-11pm, Fri-Sat 12pm-11pm, Sun 12pm-3pm.* With its hip décor, trendy "bistronomie"-style menu and regular cultural events, La Petite Halle is well worth a look-in.

Lunch menu from €20

92 **À la folie** – *26 av. Corentin-Cariou - Parc de La Villette - M° Porte de La Villette - ☎07 76 79 70 66 - www.alafolie.paris - ♿ - summer:*

11.30am-2am. Closed Mon-Tue. With its huge "ginguette"-style terrace, this lively food spot is an ideal place to take in the Parc de La Villette. A paradise for meat-eaters (barbeque is practically a religion here), but veggies are also catered for.

Set menu €32

57 **Le Galopin** – *G2* - *34 r. Ste-Marthe-M° Belleville - ☎01 42 06 05 03 - www.le-galopin.com - Mon-Wed 7.30pm-11pm, Thur-Fri 12pm-2pm and 7.30pm-11pm - Lunch menu. €32, evening tasting menu €54 - closed w/e.* Romain Tischenko, the first winner of Top Chef (a MasterChef equivalent) in 2010 is adored by the media and his customers – and with good reason. Try his Clavisy lamb with herbs and coco de Paimpol beans. The menu changes each day with a different seven-course taster menu on offer every night.

Set menu €70

58 **Le Chateaubriand** – *G3* - *129 av. Parmentier - M° Goncourt - ☎01 43 57 45 95 - www.lechateaubriand.nand - daily 7pm-11pm - set menu €70 - closed Sun lunch and Mon, closed Christmas.* Trendy 30-somethings heap (well-deserved) worship on Inaki Aizpitarte, the brilliant inventor of "bistronomie". The now-famous surprise menu is an exhilaratingly refined affair, attracting a cosmopolitan clientele. Think glistening roasted monkfish, coated in garlic, almonds and tomato sprinkled with tiny crunchy chunks of coffee bean.

BASTILLE AND THE EAST

Picnic idea: Parc de Bercy, faces the Bibliothèque François-Mitterrand and each offers a distinct atmosphere; it's up to you to choose which you prefer!

Lunch menu from €15

64 Ben's – *G6* - 19 r. du Fbg-St-Antoine - M° Bastille - ℘01 43 41 35 - www.bensparis.fr - daily 12pm-12am. Dan and Yoni are behind this American-style diner of which the recipes have been developed with the help of several Meilleurs Ouvriers de France (a prestigious award for France's best craftspeople). The bacon cheeseburger, Argentinian steak and à la carte bagels are all excellent, but you absolutely cannot leave without tasting the incredible carrot cake, undoubtedly the best in Paris.

84 Le Bøti – *H4* - 74 bd de Ménilmontant - M° Père-Lachaise - ℘06 65 49 12 29 - boti.lafourchandte. rest - daily 12pm-2.30pm and 7pm-10pm. Closed Sun and Mon. Located close to Père-Lachaise, le Bøti offers a small set menu (3 starters, 3 mains, 3 desserts), all made with fresh ingredients. In-season vegetables are celebrated and go way beyond mere accompaniment, as the risotto made with various varieties of asparagus shows. The restaurant has a terrace on Boulevard de Ménilmontant, perfect for soaking up the unique buzz of the area.

93 Fric-Frac – *G3* - 79 quai de Valmy-M° République - ℘01 42 85 87 34 - http://fricfrac.fr - daily 12pm-10pm. This is the veritable temple of the croque-monsieur, located on the banks of the Canal Saint-Martin. In a light and modern space, complete with hanging baskets and patterned cushions, you'll discover a total revisit of the famous croque. The "Winnie" is filled with goat's cheese and dried fruit; the "Viking" is salmon gravlax and apples, while the classics are still on the menu, generously topped with Mornay béchamel, emmental grand cru and Prince de Paris ham. The homemade pain perdu is also well worth a try. An excellent option for tight budgets.

62 Dong Huong – *H3* - 14 r. Louis-Bonnand - M° Belleville - ℘01 43 57 42 81 - www.dong-huong.fr/restaurant - daily 12pm-10.30pm - menu €15/20. Closed Tue. A great Belleville Vietnamese canteen: fast and delicious. Think pho, summer rolls and ultra-fresh bo-bun.

Lunch menu from €19

61 Le Baratin – *H3* - 3 r. Jouye-Rouve - M° Pyrénées - ℘01 43 49 39 70 - daily 12pm-2.30pm and 7.30pm-11pm. Closed Sat lunchtime and Sun-Mon. An institution with a capital "I". Even the grumpiness of the owner is a part of its charm. Pâté de tête (head cheese) and pig ears with vinaigrette are on the menu. Raquel is a queen!

Lunch menu around €20

67 Auberge Flora – *G5* - 44 bd Richard-Lenoir - M° Bréguand-Sabin - ℘01 47 00 52 77 - www.aubergeflora.fr - daily 9am-12am - set menu €19 on weekdays. An urban inn with a contemporary feel where you'll eat well from breakfast to supper. The hostess Flora Mikula prepares fabulous delights such as pied de cochon croquettes, scallops roasted in dill butter and mackerel ceviche with shallots. The "tapas tree", made to share, is an excellent choice for the evening.

38 Will - *H6* - *75 r. Crozatier - M° Faidherbe-Chaligny - ☏01 53 17 02 44 - Tue-Sat 12pm-2.30pm, 7.30pm-10.30pm - set menu €21, dinner menu €49.* Chef William Pradeleix has travelled the globe and serves a menu packed with allusions to other world cuisines: think asparagus with dashi mousse, finely-cut tartare served with truffle and gomashio cream or cod with boy choy!

Lunch menu from €22

68 Le Cotte Rôti - *H7* - *1 r. de Cotte, M° Ledru-Rollin - ☏01 43 45 06 37 - daily 12pm-2.30pm and 8pm-11pm. Closed Sat lunch, Sun and Mon, 3rd week of August - reservations recommended.* This gem on rue de Cotte surprises with its inventiveness, attention to detail and respect of seasonal ingredients. Chef Nicolas Michel masters his art with impressive assurance. The only hitch is the price of wine by the bottle (there's nothing at less than €48) – get yours by the glass. The lunch menu is a bargain.

Lunch menu from €32

☺ 65 Septime - *H6* - *80 r. de Charonne - M° Charonne - ☏01 43 67 38 29 - www.septime-charonne.fr - daily except Mon lunch, weekends and 3rd week of Aug - reservation essential.* The Chateaubriand and Septime are the most hyped addresses of the 11th, and the latter was awarded its own star in the 2017 Michelin guide.

Bertrand Grébaut favours simplicity without artifice: think meats and sauce such as Pluma ibérica, reinvented depending on the inclination of the chef. Septime represents the best of this new generation of Paris dining, at once super-trendy and totally epicurean.

Around €30

66 Les Provinces - *H6* - *20 r. d'Aligre - M° Faidherbe-Chaligny - ☏01 43 43 91 64 - www.boucherie-lesprovinces.fr - Tue-Fri 11.30am-2pm (weekends 3pm), Thur-Fri 6.30pm-10pm - closed 2nd week of Aug.* Les Provinces risks turning even the most committed vegetarian into an enthusiastic meat-eater with its slowly matured cuts of beef and spicy chorizo. It's a veritable sensory experience: meats sizzle at the grill and arrive bubbling hot, accompanied by steaming pommes de terre grenailles. A paradise for hungry bellies, just a couple of steps from the famous Marché d'Aligre.

From €35

63 Vingt Heures Vin - *G3* - *2 r. des Goncourt - M° Goncourt - ☏01 49 29 79 56 - www.vingtheuresvin.com - From 6pm, brunch Sun 12pm-4pm.* Set back a little from Belleville proper, this wine bar with its selection stretching across an entire wall, serves delightfully indulgent offerings such as house foie gras with cognac and Italian charcuterie. A recent opening which already has faithful regulars. *See also p.129.*

Where to drink

Lively terraces, buzzy bars, salons de thé and cosy watering holes: Paris is perfectly set up for kicking back, the world capital of "art de vivre".
For brunches, reserving in advance is strongly recommended.

👆**Find the addresses *on our maps using the number in the listing (ex.* ❶ *). The coordinates in red (ex. C2) refer to the detachable map (inside the cover).***

LA CITÉ AND LES QUAIS

Area map *p. 16-17*

Salon de thé

❷ **Berthillon** - *F6 - 29 r. St-Louis-en-l'Île - Mᵒ Pont-Marie - ☎01 43 54 31 61 - www.berthillon.fr - Wed-Sun 10am-8pm - breakfast served from 10am.* Since 1954, the most famous ice cream maker in Paris has retained its reputation. There are countless flavours: on top of the classics you'll find lychee, rhubarb and thyme & lemon sorbets, as well as ice cream flavours like gingerbread, ginger, Tatin and nougat. You can take away or sit in the 20-seat *salon de thé.*

LE LOUVRE

Salons de thé

⓰ **Salon de Thé Twinings** – *D4 - 248 r. de Rivoli - Mᵒ Concorde - ☎01 44 77 88 99 - Mon-Sat 10am-7pm, Sun 10.30am-6.30pm.* Tucked in the first floor of the legendary WH Smith on rue de Rivoli (a favourite of English-speaking luminaries such as Woody Allen) this tea room has just reopened its doors after closing for 30 years. There are over 50 varieties of tea on offer: make your selection and pair it with a buttery shortbread or carrot cake. Porridge is also available, or you can even plump for savoury afternoon tea with pork pies and salmon toast. The view over the Tuileries and the history of the spot (this is the one-time apartment of George Washington) add to the magic of the place.

© Laurene Bourdais/Photononstop

Berthillon

🎁

70 Angelina – *D4* - *226 r. de Rivoli - Mᵒ Tuileries - ☎01 42 60 82 00 - www.angelina-paris.fr - Mon-Fri 7.30am-9pm, weekends 8.30am-7.30pm.* This star of Paris's salons de thé was born in 1903 and quickly became a favourite with aristocracy passing through Paris. Amid beautiful Belle Époque décor, be sure to try one of the house specialities, such as the famous Mont-Blanc soaked in hot chocolate. A wonderful spot for sweet-tooths and enthusiasts for early 20C glamour.

🐾 **4 Mariage Frères** – *D4* - *Caroussel du Louvre, 99 r. de Rivoli- Mᵒ Palais-Royal-Musée-du-Louvre - ☎01 40 20 18 54 - www.mariagefreres.com - daily 12pm-9pm; brunch daily except Tue - €35-50.* Reputed the world over, this traditional establishment offers more than 500 teas collected from 30 countries, as well as jams, biscuits, chocolates, teacups and teapots. Rich antique décor.

Bars

6 Le Fumoir – *E5* - *6 r. de l'Amiral-de-Coligny - Mᵒ Louvre-Rivoli - ☎01 42 92 00 24 - www.lefumoir.com - daily 11am-2am; brunch Sun (€26).* A bar with a cosy atmosphere - think club armchairs and banquettes - between the Louvre and St-Germain-l'Auxerrois. Le Fumoir also a café, *salon de thé*, library and restaurant.

LE MARAIS AND LES HALLES

***Area map** p. 28-29*

Brunch

1 L'Ébouillanté – *F5* - *6 r. des Barres - Mᵒ Pont-Marie - ☎01 42 74 70 52 - summer: daily 12pm-10pm; rest of the year: 12pm-7pm - brunch Sun from 12pm (€21-25).* It may be tiny, but this *salon de thé* has one of the prettiest terraces in Paris. set in the little cobbled street at the back of Église Saint-Gervais-Saint-Protais. The varied menu includes salads, bricks (stuffed crêpes from North Africa), pastries, 30 varieties of tea and fruity cocktails. Everything is made on-site using fresh ingredients.

Salons de thé

71 Lily of the Valley – *G4* - *12 r. Dupandit-Thouars- Mᵒ Temple - ☎01 57 40 82 80 - daily 11am-7pm.* Chez Lily is a paradise for tea-lovers with its ceiling adorned with flowers and its organic made-in-France tea, sold loose. Tearoom classics, such as cheesecake, are given a lighter spin: the cookies are made with granola and the scones are made with cranberry. The owner Pauline is passionate about tea and is happy to advise on the smallest query. Note the charming old-fashioned crockery.

12 Carette – *G5* - *25 pl. des Vosges-Mᵒ St-Paul/Chemin-Vert/Bastille - ☎01 48 87 94 07 - www.carandte-paris.fr - daily 7.30am-12am - brunch €30.* The famous Place du Trocadéro pâtisserie-cum-*salon de thé* opened on Place des Vosges in 2010, with a charming terrace under the arcades, by the Pavillon de la Reine. The hot chocolate here is always delicious and the macarons delectable.

14 Comme à Lisbonne – *F5 - 37 r. du Roi-de-Sicile- Mᵒ St-Paul - ☎01 61 23 42 30 - www.commealisbonne.com - daily except Mon.* Visit in the afternoon and indulge in a light *pastéis de nata*, warm and powdered with cinnamon, just like in Belém!

Bars

22 Bubar – *G6 - 3 r. des Tournelles- Mᵒ Bastille - ☎01 40 29 97 72 - daily 7pm-2am.* There are no French vintages in this wine bar, only foreign wines selected by Jean-Loup, the "bubar" (a play on words of "barbu", meaning "bearded man"), which he knows like the back of his hand. Prop yourself up at the bar to chat with the owner and fill up on tapas graciously offered by the house.

9 Candelaria – *G4 - 52 r. de Saintonge- Mᵒ Filles-du-Calvaire - ☎01 42 74 41 28 - www.quixotic-projects.com/fr/les-lieux/candelaria - daily 6pm-2am; brunch weekends 12.30pm-4pm.* This cocktail bar is one of the best of the capital. You won't find the door on the street: you enter vie an unassuming *taqueria* (which serves delicious tacos) and go through the door at the back : expect a laid-back atmosphere where faithful customers sip on the wildly creative concoctions.

10 Le Mary Celeste – *G4 - 1 r. Commines - Mᵒ Filles-du-Calvaire - www.lemaryceleste.com - daily.* One of the trendiest bars of the Upper Marais, Le Mary Celeste is always busy: it's well worth a visit for the atmosphere

and the drinks. Oysters and tacos are also on offer, as well as wine, beer on tap and mezcal cocktails. Expect an international vibe and "world food". There's also a dinner menu.

72 Le Perchoir Marais – *F5 - 37 r. de la Verrerie - Mᵒ Hôtel-de-Ville - www.leperchoir.tv - 8.15pm-2am (Wed 9.15pm) - closed Sun and Mon - no reservations.* Rooftops are all the rage now on the Paris nightlife scene and the roof of department store BHV is a notable addition. The décor changes with the seasons (in winter you'll find wool blankets and fake fur) and there is always a party atmosphere.

Wine bars

7 Barav – *G4 - 6 r. Charles-François-Dupuis - Mᵒ Temple - ☎01 48 04 57 59 - www.lebarav.fr - Mon-Fri 12pm-3pm, 6pm-12am, closed Sat lunch and Sun.* A real wine bar, where vintages are tasted accompanied by meticulously selected market-fresh products, served in a typical Parisian bistro setting. Reservations advised after 6pm.

73 La Belle Hortense – *F5 - 31 r. Vieille-du-Temple - Mᵒ St-Paul - ☎01 48 04 71 60 - www.cafeine.com/belle-hortense - daily 5pm-2am.* Fancy a well selected glass of wine? In need of a book recommendation? La Belle Hortense will cater to all your needs! This unusual venue, a wine bar-cum-bookshop, is a quiet spot, perfect for wine-lovers and keen readers.

123

QUARTIER LATIN

Area map p. 40-41

Salon de thé

24 **Tea Lichou** – *F8* - 7 r. Broca- M° Les Gobelins - ℰ09 81 02 10 83 - www. tealichou.fr - Tue-Sat 11.45am-6.30pm. This child-centric spot is favoured by the parents of the area. You'll find swings and games as well as a tasty selection of cookies, muffins and chocolate fondants, made by the team.

18 **The Tea Caddy** – *E6* - 14 r. St-Julien-le-Pauvre - M° Cluny-la-Sorbonne - ℰ01 43 54 15 56 - www.the-tea-caddy.com - daily 11am-7pm (11pm Thur-Fri). This cosy tea room opposite St Julien-le-Pauvre , little changed since its opening in 1928, will make you feel like you're in England. The charming owner will happily provide paper and colouring pencils to little visitors, who contribute to the homely atmosphere. Homemade pies, scones and tarts are on offer.

87 **Odette** - *E6* – 77 r. Galande - M° Cluny-la-Sorbonne - ℰ01 43 26 13 06 - www.odette-paris.com - daily 10.30am-7.30pm. An excellent spot to try *choux à la crème*, either in the retro little room upstairs or to take away.

Bars

75 **La Tireuse** – *EF7* - 18 r. Laplace - M° Cardinal-Lemoine - latireuse.fr - Tue-Sat 6pm-2am. You won't be dealing with any grumpy waiters here because the beer is self-service! Some tables even have their own beer taps linked to kegs concealed under the table. Beer is ordered on a personal touch-screen, which activates the beer pump: your beer will serve itself, nice and frothy. The atmosphere is informal and sharing taps is common, so this isn't your place if you're after an intimate tête-à-tête.

20 **The Bombardier** – *F7* - 2 pl. du Panthéon - M° Cardinal-Lemoine - ℰ01 43 54 79 22 - www.bombardier pub.fr - daily 12pm-2am. A touch of *rosbif* in the Latin Quarter! Quiet and intimate during the week, this English pub is a great spot for weekend socialising with a pint of beer and maybe a sports fixture. Come early in summer when the terrace gets very busy

☺ 21 **Café de la nouvelle mairie** – *E7* - 19 r. des Fossés-St-Jacques- M° Luxembourg- ℰ01 44 07 04 41 - 8am-12am, daily except weekends. This bar is cherished by Parisians – and with good reason! Natural wines (sulphates are not welcome here) accompany generous helpings of Chavassieux sausage on a bed of mashed potato, or poultry liver terrine, to be devoured greedily at the zinc bar. The terrace is subject to invasion as soon as there's a little sun.

Wine bar

74 **Les Pipos** – *F7* -2 r. de l'École polytechnique - M° Cardinal-Lemoine - ℰ01 43 54 11 40 - 9.30am-2am (Sat 12am-2am). Closed Sun. Everything about this place evokes old Paris. In the heart of university district, Les Pipos continues to attract students on its terrace on the pretty Place Larue. The kitchen serves traditional cuisine.

ST-GERMAIN-DES-PRÉS-MONTPARNASSE

***Area map** p. 50*

Salons de thé

29 **Café Pouchkine** - **D6** - 155 bd
St-Germain - Mᵒ St-Germain-des-Prés
- ℘01 42 22 58 44 - www.cafe-
pouchkine.fr - daily 9am-11pm.

"After the fall of Lenin, we would go
to Café Pouchkine and drink a hot
chocolate", so sang French singer
Gilbert Bécaud and, thanks to his
song, you can indeed do just this in
St-Germain-des-Prés. Expect elegant
French ceilings and cosy wood
panelling, with Russian red tea and
sumptuous pastries on the menu.

The legendary cafés

St-Germain-des-Prés – Follow in the footsteps of the Existentialists of the 1950s (Sartre,
Simone de Beauvoir) at Le café de Flore, Les Deux Magots, la brasserie Lipp (see p.48).

Montparnasse – The Montparnasse haunts of the interwar artists and intellectuals have
become upscale brasseries, and sometimes tourist traps, but it is always an experience to
visit, even just for a coffee: you'll find Belle Époque chandeliers, chintzy mirrors and red
leather banquettes. La Coupole, Le Dôme, La Rotonde, Le Sélect, see p. 54-56.

And also: La Closerie des Lilas, 171 bd du Montparnasse, 6ᵗʰ - ℘01 40 51 34 50.

La Rotonde

© Gianluca Santoni/sime/PhotononStop

"Tea time" at the grand hotels

5 *Le Bristol* – **C3** - *112 rue du Faubourg-St-Honoré, 8th* - *Mo Miromesnil* - ✆ *01 53 43 43 42* - *tea time daily 3pm-6pm - 60 € per pers., 85 € for 2. The cherubs of the Fontaine aux Amours will watch over your summery tea in the "Jardin Français" while you tuck in to savoury nibbles, scones, muffins and delectable petits fours by head pâtissier Laurent Jeannin.*

92 *Le Shangri-La* – **A4** - *10 av. d'Iéna, 16th* - *Mo Iéna* - ✆ *01 53 67 19 98 - tea time daily 3pm-6pm - 39 €. This 100% vegan afternoon tea features an enticing selection of sweet treats: think almond and orange calisson, chestnut and blackcurrant mont blanc, chocolate tart, cookies, financiers and shortbread.*

11 *Le Ritz* – **D3** - *15 pl. Vendôme, 1st* - *Mo Opéra* - ✆ *01 43 16 33 74 - tea time daily 2.30pm-6pm - 65 € or 85 €. The Proust salon at the Ritz , with its fireplace and antique book cabinets, is a fittingly opulent spot for an indulgent afternoon tea. Head pâtissier François Perret excels in the art of the biscuit and his boudoirs, florentins and cigarettes russes, presented on beautiful white Limoges porcelain, will delight your taste buds.*

126

30 Bread & Roses – **D7** - *62 r. Madame* - *Mo Rennes* - ✆*01 42 22 06 06 - www. breadandroses.fr - daily 8am-19h30. Closed Sun.* This is a tearoom but also a *boulangerie* (delicious bread), *patisserie*, seller of fine foods and restaurant. You'll find a wide range of cakes, scones, muffins, cheesecake and carrot cake, as well as rum baba, crumble, *millefeuilles* and fruit tarts.

Bars

77 Le Bar du Marché – **E6** - *75 r. de Seine*- *Mo Odéon ou St-Germain -des-Prés* - ✆*01 43 26 55 15 – daily 8am-10pm.* The "BDM" is the best place to get a feel for the hustle and bustle of St-Germain. Take a seat on the heated terrace and sip on your tipple of choice, accompanied by a hot dog spilling over with melted cheese, an omelette or a hearty tartine smothered in rillettes.

25 La Palette – **E5** - *43 r. de Seine*- *Mo Mabillon* - ✆*01 43 26 68 15 - www.cafelapalandteparis.com - daily 8am-2am.* This quintessential St-Germain café has always been a favourite haunt of the students of the neighbouring Beaux-Arts; some famous former students have even left their paintings on the walls. The lovely shady terrace is usually packed in summer.

27 Le Hibou – **E6** - *16 carr. de l'Odéon* - *Mo Odéon* - ✆*01 43 54 96 91 - www. lehibouparis.fr - daily 8am-11.30pm.* A café-brasserie where people go to pose as much as to eat, but the Spritz (€12) is tasty, and the terrace is usually full: you'll hear regulars chattering long into the night.

28 Chez Georges – **D6** - *11 r. des Canandtes - Mo Mabillon - ✆01 43 26 79 15 - daily 3pm-2am (Sat 12pm-2am, Sun 7pm-2am).* One of the legendary bars of St-Germain, with its unchanged counter and old photos on the wall. Great for a glass of wine with friends.

31 Le Smoke – *D8* - *29 r. Delambre-Mº Edgar-Quinand - ☎01 43 20 61 73 - 12pm-2am (Sat 3pm) closed Sun.* In Montparnasse, if you don't fancy the famous cafés, head to Le Smoke : happy hour from 2.30pm to 7.30pm, where pints are 4 € and cocktails €5 (Mojito, Caipirinha, Margarita). You can also get lunch or dinner here. It's always busy and the vibe is friendly and a little bit jazzy.

Wine bar

76 Freddy's – *E6* - *54 r. de Seine Mº St-Germain-des-Prés - daily 12pm-12am.* This bar has no tables and no phone number, instead the emphasis is on its *raison d'être*: wine and a delicious tapas menu. You'll drink good wine and nibble on tasty small plates (€5-15): think crispy beef and tuna mi-cuit.

INVALIDES-TOUR EIFFEL

Bars

78 Café Central – *B5* - *40 r. Cler - Mº École-Militaire - ☎01 47 05 00 53 - www.cafecentralparis.com - daily 7am-1am.* In the heart of the quiet pedestrianised rue Cler, Café Central is a hotspot for the well-heeled youth of the 7th arrondissement. With New York stylings and a vast terrace, the atmosphere is nonetheless laid-back.

Salons de thé

33 Miss Marple – *C5* - *16 av. de la Motte-Picquand - Mº La-Tour-Maubourg - ☎01 45 50 14 27 - daily*

9am-7pm, Sun 10am-4pm, Closed Mon. With a décor featuring chandeliers, velvet and old-fashioned paintings of animals, patrons of this tearoom are immersed in the universe of the great Agatha Christie. Savoury tarts, scrambled eggs and exquisite scones served with cream and homemade raspberry jam are on offer. For brunch, there's a choice of organic boiled eggs with soldiers or pancakes submerged in maple syrup, paired with a steady flow of smoked tea, fruit juice or smoothies, prepared on the spot.

CHAMPS-ÉLYSÉES AND THE WEST

Salon de thé

35 Plaza Athénée – *B4* - *25 av. Montaigne - Mº Alma-Marceau - ☎01 53 67 66 65 - www.plaza-athenee-paris.fr - Mon-Fri 7.30am-10.15pm and Thur-Fri 12.45pm-2.15pm, closed weekends.* In the superlatively elegant Galerie des Gobelins, the pastry chef Angelo Musa creates sweet delights including the choux infiniment vanille.

Bar

34 Buddha-Bar – *D3* - *8-12 r. Boissy-d'Anglas - Mº Concorde - ☎01 53 05 90 00 - www.buddhabar.com - daily 12pm-2am (weekends from 6pm); brunch Sun 12pm-4pm - €39/46.* A giant Buddha dominates the vast restaurant and its attractive mezzanine, while the lighting creates a soft, slinky atmosphere. It's a beautiful spot and is usually busy: a favourite of glamorous Parisians and tourists alike.

OPÉRA-PALAIS ROYAL-VENDÔME

Area map *p. 83*

Bar

79 Le Café de la Comédie – *E4 - 157 r. St-Honoré - Mᵒ Palais-Royal-Musée-du-Louvre - ℰ01 42 61 40 01 - daily 7.30am-1am*. Between the Louvre and the Comédie-Française, opposite the beautiful Place Colette and its striking artwork (the Kiosque des Noctambules), this is the ideal place to take a breather in the heart of Paris, whatever the hour.

Salon de thé

45 Casse-Noisette – *D3 - 35 av. de l'Opéra - Mᵒ Opéra - ℰ09 80 62 57 72 - daily 8am-8pm*. Jeffrey Cagnes cut his teeth under Jean-François Piège before opening his own patisserie-cum-tea room. A few savoury dishes are available but the sweet treats here are the big draw: the famous cannelé; the false copper cake mould (you'll see); the blackcurrant-chocolate tart; the rum baba with raisin cream; and divine salted caramel choux buns.

36 Aki Artisan Boulanger – *E4 - 16 r. Ste-Anne - Mᵒ Pyramides - ℰ01 42 97 54 27 - www.akiboulanger.com - daily 7.30am-8.30pm. Closed Sun*. This boulangerie fuses the best of French and Japanese tradition, such is its recipe for success. Think Opéra pastries flavoured with green tea matcha, bento and baguettes Flavours always come first and the baker is never short of ideas.

MONTMARTRE-PIGALLE

Area map *p. 88-89*

Bars

91 Comestibles and Marchands de vins – *65 r. du Mont-Cenis - Mᵒ Jules-Joffrin - Mon-Sat 10.30am-9.30pm, Sun 10.30am-5.30pm*. At once a wine cellar, tapas bar, restaurant and fine grocer's, this multi-tasking space was conceived by Sébastien Arnaud, an enthusiast of fine French products. The menu includes Ospital charcuterie, conserves by La Belle-Iloise, duck breast, *bœuf bourguignon* and tartines (bread with a variety of delicious toppings).

90 Marlusse and Lapin – *E1 - 14 r. Germain-Pilon - Mᵒ Pigalle - ℰ09 51 56 23 62 - www.marlusse andlapin.fr - daily 4pm-2am*. The two barmen, nicknamed Marlusse and Lapin, certainly know how to party. Here happy hour starts at 4pm and "real" beer enthusiasts will enjoy the selection of Chouffe, Karmeliand etc. There's also a good range of cocktails. Don't miss the back room, which will transport you to another time.

53 La Guêpe – *E1 - 14 r. des Trois-Frères - Mᵒ Anvers - ℰ01 42 64 98 32 - 6pm-2am. Closed Mon*. The house tapas dishes are laid out in higgledy-piggledy fashion along the handsome earthenware bar: think fried snails with parsley butter, marinated beef brochettes, mackerel with lime and generous sharing plates of charcuterie. Ideal for an "aperitif".

38 Le Bâton Rouge – *E1* - *62 r. N.-D.-de-Lorandte - Mᵒ St-Georges - ☏06 52 90 36 42 - www.batonrouge. paris - 6pm-2am. Closed Sun.* This bar references Louisiana in more than just name. Packed with kooky voodoo-themed relics, this spot has a unique atmosphere. Expect Southern-style nibbles and exotic cocktails. .

39 Le Sans-Souci – *E1* - *65 r. Jean-Baptiste Pigalle - Mᵒ Pigalle-☏01 53 16 17 04 - daily 9am-2am.* The under-stated environs of this South Pigalle institution are HQ for the neighbour-hood's merrymakers. The Sans Souci is relatively calm during the day, but welcomes densely packed crowds at night who dance to DJ-spun rock and electro beats. The atmosphere is buzzy, with a trendy, laid-back crowd. At the end of rue Victor-Masse, to the right as you leave, you'll find Le Mansart, which is just a touch more "chic", and an excellent complement to the Sans Souci.

40 Le Dirty Dick – *E1* - *10 r. Frochot - Mᵒ Pigalle - ☏01 48 78 74 58 - daily 6pm-2am.* This former "hostess bar", from Pigalle's seedier bygone days, is testament to the change "SoPi" (South Pigalle), now one of Paris's trendiest districts, has seen in recent years. The atmosphere is fabulously kitsch, with a menu of Polynesian, Hawaiian and Mexican cocktails, made with house-made syrups and juice and served in tiki cups and conch shells.

42 Carmen – *E1* - *22 r. de Douai/34 r. Duperré - Mᵒ Pigalle - ☏01 45 26 50 00 - www.le-carmen.fr - 6pm-6am, Closed Sun and Mon.* Housed in the former mansion house of Georges Bizand, it may have the look of a grand hotel bar, but this club and cocktail bar attracts a more alternative crowd. The space is delightfully atypical, featuring grand columns, ornate mouldings and soft lighting. You can get drinks or listen to live music around the grand piano.

44 La Fourmi – *E1* - *74 r. des Martyrs - Mᵒ Pigalle - ☏01 42 64 70 35 - Sun-Thur 8am-2am, Fri-Sat 8am-4am.* La Fourmi is an attractive space decorated with mismatched second-hand pieces. It attracts a lively young crowd, a little less trendy than some of its neighbours – but it's always busy in the evening. Continue the festivities at the Divan du Monde club opposite or La Cigale

47 L'Étoile de Montmartre – *26 r. Duhesme - Mᵒ Lamarck-Coulaincourt ☏01 46 06 11 65 - daily 7.30am-2am.* This café-bistrot, with its distinct red-brick exterior, is a favourite with locals. Though the food isn't exceptional, it is a great spot for a drink, either inside or on the terrace. The vibe is young and laid-back.

48 La Divette de Montmartre – *136 r. Marcadand - Mᵒ Lamarck-Caulaincourt - ☏01 46 06 19 64 - 5pm-1am. Closed Sun.* It doesn't get much more Parisian or seventies retro than this rock-themed bar, covered in stickers and presided over by Serge, who takes great pride in his extensive vinyl collection. There's live music on Friday nights and in summer beer-drinkers fill the terrace from early in the evening. Good vibes guaranteed.

129

Wine bars

(37) **Albion** – *F2 - 80 r. du Faubourg-Poissonnière - M° Poissonnière - ℘01 42 46 02 44 - closed weekends.* Flavoursome dishes emerge from the semi-open kitchen, accompanied by fine vintages; prices are reasonable and the staff speak French and English.

(46) **Vingt Heures Vin** – *17 r. Joseph-de-Maistre - M° Blanche - ℘09 54 66 50 67 - www.vingtheuresvin.com - see also p. 120.* Let yourself be guided by the master of the house, whose wine cellar is full of unexpected delights, selected with care and passion. Expect delicious wines accompanied by simple but tasty dishes. Convivial atmosphere.

(80) **Le Persifleur** – *E1 - 3 r. Durantin - M° Abbesses - ℘09 83 64 57 94 - 6pm-2am. Closed Sun-Mon. www.persifleur.fr.* Here the cocktail is the star and the bar staff provide the show. The house twist on a mojito is a delight, as is the daiquiri: let the waiter advise you. Throw in gorgeous décor and a retro soundtrack and you've got the makings of a perfect night.

(82) **La Recyclerie** – *83 bd Ornano - M° Porte de Clignancourt - ℘01 42 57 58 49 - www.larecyclerie.com - Mon-Thur 12pm-12am, Fri-Sat 12pm-2am, Sun 11am-10pm.* La Recyclerie is full of character and there is no place in Paris quite like it. The team behind the space have converted the former Gare Ornano, a station of La Petite Ceinture railroad, into an eco-friendly bar, restaurant and cultural space. The old vestibule has become the bar-canteen; the baggage storage is transformed into a cosy corner and the side of the old train tracks forms an open-air terrace. The philosophy is 100% green and there is a vegetable garden, a chicken coop and even bee hives. There is also a DIY workshop area, complete with tools. It's well worth seeing—and you'll be supporting an eco-responsible initiative in the process!

CANAL ST-MARTIN-LA VILLETTE

***Area map** p. 96*

Bars

(51) **Le Floréal** – *G3 - 150 av. Parmentier/73 r. du Faubourg-du-Temple - M° Goncourt - ℘01 40 18 46 79 - Mon-Fri 8am-2am, w/end. 9am-2am.* This former Tabac has become one of the hippest spots in the 11th arrondissement. Décor is 1950s and 1960s-themed with booths and red and green moleskin armchairs and a bright pop-art style mosaic on the façade.

(52) **Le Comptoir général** – *G3 - 80 quai de Jemmapes - M° République - ℘01 44 88 24 48 - www.lecomptoirgeneral.com - daily 11am-2am.* There's always something happening in this atypical – and rather huge – venue. The ethos of Le Comptoir General is all about fair trade, solidarity and supporting minorities. Visitors can buy second-hand African clothes, peruse unusual artefacts (bones, rare bird feathers), dance to Franco-African music and taste cuisine from around the world. Extremely busy on weekends.

54 Le Syndicat Bar – *F3 - 51 r. du Faubourg-St-Denis - M° Château-d'Eau - ℘06 66 63 57 60 - www.syndicatcocktailclub.com - daily 6pm-2am.* Don't be deceived by the dodgy looking exterior: the shabby speakeasy façade hides a deliciously stylish bar furnished with marble and russet curtains. You will enter the "Organisation for the defence of French spirits", where only 100% French alcohols are on the menu. Old-school hip hop soundtrack.

56 Lavomatic – *G3 - 30 r. René-Boulanger - M° République - www.lavomatic.paris - Tue-Wed. 6pm-1am, Thur-Sat 6pm-2am.* This is one of the best-hidden bars in Paris thanks to its secret placement at the back of a launderette. Once inside, look for the camouflaged button and you will discover the idiosyncratic watering hole: think pop stylings, deliberately distressed walls, plump cushions and swings disguised as armchairs. The daring cocktail menu offers a range of concoctions mixed with spices, fruit and vegetables, including the DétoxOmatic made from beetroot, blackcurrant, gin, citrus and artichoke liqueur.

64 Le 25° Est – *G1 - 10 pl. de la Bataille-de-Stalingrad - M° Jaurès ou Stalingrad - ℘01 42 09 66 74 - daily 11am-2am.* This is one of the prettiest terraces in Paris. Located on the edge of the canal. Patrons are invited to have a drink on the water's edge in a lively atmosphere. Here the Happy Hours start at 3pm; bartenders keep the drinks flowing – think Cuba Libre, Pina Colada, Long Island Ice Tea and White Russians. There is also a food menu featuring salmon tartare, crispy goat cheese and burgers.

55 Point Éphémère – *G1 - 200 quai de Valmy - M° Jaurès - ℘01 40 34 02 48 - www.pointephemere.org - daily 12.30pm-2am (Closes 10pm Sunday).* This cultural space organises exhibitions, concerts and performances and also houses artists, but it's also known for its bar and restaurant, set in a glass-walled space and on a terrace on the edge of the canal. The rooftop opens in the warmer months, between June and September.

88 Le Glazart – *7/15 av. Porte de la Villette - M° Porte-de-la-Villette - ℘01 40 36 55 65 - www.glazart.com.* A mainstay of nightlife in the east of Paris, the Glazart continues to redefine the party scene with its summer beach (June-Oct) and popular concerts.

Péniche Antipode – *Off map H1 - Opposite 55 quai de Seine- M° Jaurès - ℘01 42 03 39 07. Between mid-July and August the barge moves to Bobigny (shuttle possible).*

83 Chez Jeannette – *F3 - 47 r. du Faubourg-St-Denis - M° Château-d'Ecau - ℘01 47 70 30 89 - daily 8am-2am.* Jeannette is a hot meeting spot for Paris's trendiest (the "bobos" and hipsters) and it's certainly not short on kitsch style with its neon signs and retro formica bar. Coffee, beers, cocktails and food.

Beer bar

84 Paname Brewing Company - *41 bis quai de Loire - M° Laumière - ℘01 40 36 43 55 - daily 11am-2am.* If the water starts to make your head spin, you may just have indulged in too many hop-based beverages at the Paname! The beers here are wittily named and thoroughly excellent; you also get to drink them more or less atop on the canal, which is a definite bonus. This new-generation brewery offers an expertly-selected range of artisanal beers in a delightful setting.

BASTILLE AND L'EST

Salon de thé

97 **Kopi Cream** – *G5* - *16 r. Daval-Mº Bastille* - *☎06 59 54 09 53* - *http://kopicream.com* - *Tue-Fri 8.30am-6.30pm, weekends 9.30am-6.30pm.* Founders Georges and Benoît set out to open an Australian and Indonesian inspired coffee shop. On weekdays, Kopi Cream serves a small good-value savoury menu including salads, quiches and sandwiches. Stop in the afternoon to try some of the best coffees from around the world or a chai latte served with a hunk of banana bread; brunch is on offer on weekends. Tasty, healthy food at modest prices.

Beer bar

😋😋 **49** **La Fine Mousse** – *H4* - *6 av. Jean-Aicard* - *Mº Rue-St-Maur* - *☎09 80 45 94 64* - *www.lafinemousse.fr* - *Mon-Sun 5pm-2am.* This is not your average beer bar: here you'll find only artisanal brews, both French and international. This a paradise for beer-lovers thanks to a selection of 20 beers on tap and an excellent range of bottled varieties. Located in trendy Oberkampf.

Bar à vin

57 **Les Caves de Prague** – *H6* - *8 r. de Prague* - *Mº Ledru-Rollin* - *☎01 72 68 07 36* - *10am-11pm. Closed Sun and Mon.* The magic of this place is hard to pin down. Set in the quiet rue de Prague, this wine cellar (*cave*) exudes a warm and woody atmosphere. Curious wine-seller Thomas will find the vintage to suit your taste buds, mercifully without selling you the most expensive bottles. Excellent charcuterie platters. In summer the few tables on the terrace are packed – you'll need sharp elbows!

Bars

67 **L'Incognito** – *H6* - *71 r. de Charonne* - *Mº Ledru-Rollin* - *☎01 43 72 06 34* - *daily 3pm-12am (Fri-Sat 2am).* Walid has transformed this former family green grocer's into a bar serving beers, natural wines and rare whiskies. The selection is hand-picked from around the globe and Walid will sometimes bring down his secret bottles from upstairs. An enthusiast and a connoisseur, he is extremely well placed to advise you

50 **Le Perchoir** – *H4* - *14 r. Crespin-du-Gast* - *Mº Ménilmontant* - *☎01 48 06 18 48* - *www.leperchoir.fr* - *daily 4pm-2am (Sat-Sun 2pm-2am).* This rooftop bar was a runaway success as soon as it opened. French actor Romain Duris and other names about town are often seen here. The view over Paris is hard to beat, but the food is worth your attention too: try the mind-blowing lobster sandwich.

😋😋 **58** **À la française** – *H5* - *50 r. Léon-Frot* - *Mº Charonne* - *☎09 82 49 02 69* - *www.coquandels.fr* - *daily except Sun 10am-2am.* Expert barman Stephen

Martin is behind this *très français* bar, which only uses French products. Here, long-neglected wines, liqueurs and aperitifs (la Suze, le Byrrh) are back in style, brought bang in to the 21st century in terrific cocktails.

Le Quartier rouge - Off map H5 - *52 r. Bagnolet^e - M° Alexandre-Dumas - ☏01 81 29 42 99 - daily 9am-2am. Closed Mon.* This bistro only recently moved in on rue de Bagnolet. Owners, Lorraine (in the morning) and Chérif (evening) welcome newcomers like old regulars. The chef Dimitri concocts flavoursome entrées (excellent foie gras) and more elaborate main dishes, like john dory on a bed of asparagus. There's dancing later on (sometimes on the bar!). Concerts on select evenings.

Les Chaises - Off map H3 - *33 r. de la Chine - M° Pelleport - ☏09 51 65 08 24 - 6pm-2am. Closed Sun* You won't find any tourists here: it's a typically Parisian bar, frequented by regulars, where you can drink Gallia, a beer brewed in Paris. The local clientele come to nibble on cheese and charcuterie plates and sip on wine, beer and cocktails. There are also occasional concerts, card games and writing workshops.

65 La Féline - H4 - *6 r. Victor-Landalle - M° Ménilmontant - www.lafelinebar.com - 6pm-2am. Closes Sun and Mon.* If you're in the area, you simply must visit La Féline, a bar inspired by the 1942 film of the same name, directed by Jacques Tourneur. Expect a rock atmosphere, lots of leather and ripped jeans!

66 L'Alimentation générale - H4 - *64 r. Jean-Pierre-Timbaud - M° Parmentier - ☏01 43 55 42 50 - www.alimentation-generale.net - Wed-Sun 7pm-2am (5am*

Fri and Sat). It may look like an old-school grocer's, but don't be deceived: this buzzy, down-to-earth bar hosts concerts and serves inexpensive but excellent food and drink. Check the website for concert listings.

Music bars

69 Le Vieux Belleville – H3 - *12 r. des Envierges - M° Pyrénées - ☏01 44 62 92 66 - www.le-vieux-belleville.com - daily except Sun.* A Local bistro with a warm, lively atmosphere. The room joins in with old Paris "chansons" and spontaneous sing-songs.

La Maroquinerie – Off map H3 - *23 r. Boyer- M° Ménilmontant - ☏01 40 33 35 05 - www.lamaroquinerie.fr - Mon-Fri 2pm-7pm, concerts 6.30pm-1.30am, closed in August.* This hip concert venue is also a bar, restaurant and exhibition space. Eclectic programme with mostly current and new artists. Great terrace.

© Philippe Michel/age fotostock

Le Vieux Belleville

Shopping

You will find the key shopping districts on the map p. 136-137.
Opening Hours: Most shops open between 10am and 7pm, and close Sunday with the exception of the shops at the Carrousel du Louvre, the Marais and the Champs-Élysées. Since 2015, Sunday opening has also been permitted for Paris's department stores and shops located in international tourist zones *p. 154.*
Sales: They start at the end of June and beginning of January; each official sale period last six weeks during which discounts can reach up to 70%.

CLASSIC SHOPPING

Les Halles and rue de Rivoli: This is the area for high street fashion: all the big international names (Zara, H&M, etc.) have a store on rue de Rivoli. The **Forum des Halles** and its canopy are a veritable open-air shopping centre. You'll also find lots of inexpensive souvenir shops here.

Open on Sundays, **le BHV Marais** has recently been renovated. You'll find everything here (the basement level dedicated to DIY is legendary). BHV Hommes (rue de la Verrière) is a five-floor space dedicated entirely to menswear.

On the Left Bank, **rue de Rennes** and the Montparnasse shopping centre offer clothes stores and French high-street staples, such as entertainment/electronics paradise, Fnac.

On nearby, **rues St-Placide and d'Alésia**, you will find big brand outlets and boutiques selling cut-label clothing with discounts of up to, 50%.

LUXURY SHOPPING

On **rue du Faubourg-St-Honoré** you'll find luxury boutiques (haute couture, and watches and jewellery around Place Vendôme) and *concept-stores* (the legendary Colette at 213 r. du Faubourg-St-Honoré closed its doors in December 2017, but there are many others). The new wave of haute couture (Marc Jacobs, Stella McCartney) has moved into Palais Royal. The most famous couturiers all have boutiques on **Avenue Montaigne** (Chanel, Dior, YSL) and **Avenue George-V** (Hermès, Givenchy) and they are gradually opening in the Marais too. On the Left Bank, luxury stores can also be found around St-Germain-des-Prés.

TRENDY SHOPPING

Le Marais: The designer boutiques and art galleries that fill this area attract tourists and hip Parisians alike. The retail experience is made more pleasant by the abundant café-terraces, ready to welcome stressed shoppers.

If you're into vintage fashion, second-hand shopping and design, head for the **Abbesses** area in Montmartre, and around **rue de Charonne**: in both you'll find small-batch designers and quirky boutiques.

135

Printemps

For a timeless shopping experience, explore the **covered passages** (Galerie Vivienne, Passage Verdeau), around Grands Boulevards.

LEFT BANK SHOPPING

St-Germain-des-Prés: Luxury ready-to-wear boutiques have replaced the bookshops that once dotted Boulevard St-Germain. You'll find antique dealers around Quai Voltaire and rue du Bac and art galleries on rue de Seine, rue Guénégaud and rue des Beaux-Arts. **Le Bon Marché**, the oldest of Paris's department stores, and the most luxurious can be found at Sèvres-Babylone. Don't miss the famous Grande Épicerie, a food lover's paradise.

TOURIST SHOPPING

Department stores: **Printemps** and **Galeries Lafayette**, on **Boulevard Haussmann**, attract thousands of tourists every day. You will find everything here, including the big names of haute couture. The sumptuous décor alone makes them worth a visit.

OUR PICKS

Unusual

❶ **Deyrolle** – *D5* - *46 r. du Bac - Mᵒ Rue du Bac - ℰ01 42 22 30 07 - Mon-Sat 10am-7pm (closed Mon 1pm-2pm) - www.deyrolle.com.* Deyrolle is a place like no other. This cabinet of curiosities,

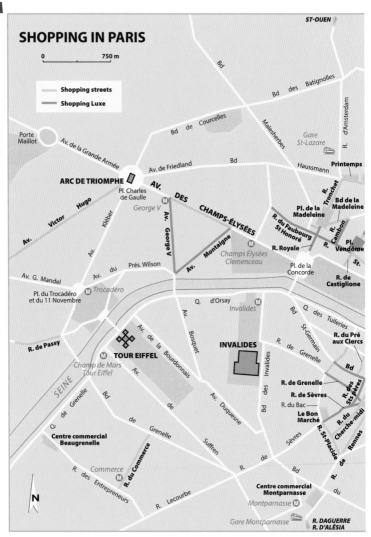

SHOPPING IN PARIS

0   750 m

- Shopping streets
- Shopping Luxe

ST-OUEN

Porte Maillot

Av. de la Grande Armée

Bd des Batignolles

Bd de Courcelles

Malesherbes

Gare St-Lazare

d'Amsterdam

Av. de Friedland

Bd

Haussmann

Printemps

ARC DE TRIOMPHE

Pl. Charles de Gaulle

AV. DES

CHAMPS-ÉLYSÉES

George V

R. Tronchet

Bd de la Madeleine

Pl. de la Madeleine

R. du Faubourg St Honoré

R. Cambon

Victor Hugo

Kléber

Av.

AV. George V

Av. Montaigne

Champs Élysées Clemenceau

R. Royale

Pl. Vendôme

St.

Prés. Wilson

Pl. de la Concorde

R. de Castiglione

Av. G. Mandel

Av. du

Q. d'Orsay

Invalides

Q. des Tuileries

Pl. du Trocadéro et du 11 Novembre

Trocadéro

Av.

Bosquet

Bd

Q. des

St-Germain

R. du Pré aux Clercs

Av. de la Bourdonnais

INVALIDES

R. de Grenelle

Bd

R. de Passy

TOUR EIFFEL

Champ de Mars Tour Eiffel

Av.

des Invalides

R. de Grenelle

R. des Sts Pères

SEINE

Av. Duquesne

R. de Sèvres

R. du Bac

Q. de Grenelle

Bd

Le Bon Marché

R. du Cherche-midi

Centre commercial Beaugrenelle

de Grenelle

Suffren

Sèvres

R. St-Placide

de Rennes

Commerce

R. du Commerce

R. des Entrepreneurs

R. Lecourbe

Bd

du

Centre commercial Montparnasse

Montparnasse

N

Gare Montparnasse

R. DAGUERRE
R. D'ALÉSIA

136

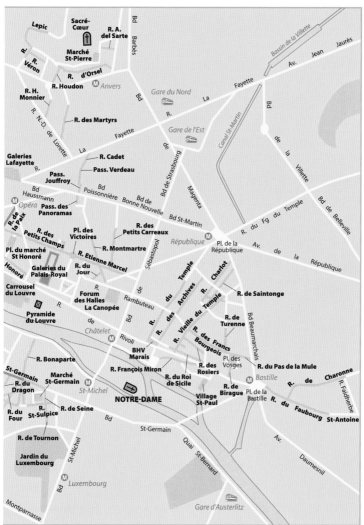

137

Lepic

Sacré-Cœur

R. A. del Sarte

Bd Barbès

Marché St-Pierre

R. Véron

R. d'Orsel

R. Houdon

Anvers

Bd

Gare du Nord

Fayette

Av. Jean Jaurès

Bassin de la Villette

R. H. Monnier

R. N.-D. de Lorette

R. des Martyrs

La Fayette

de

Bd

Gare de l'Est

Canal St-Martin

de

la

Villette

Bd de Belleville

Galeries Lafayette

Pass. Jouffroy

R. Cadet

Pass. Verdeau

Bd Haussmann

Bd Poissonnière

Bd de Bonne Nouvelle

Bd de Strasbourg

Magenta

Bd St-Martin

R. du Fg du Temple

Opéra

R. de la Paix

Pass. des Panoramas

R. des Petits Champs

Pl. des Victoires

R. des Petits Carreaux

R. Montmartre

Sébastopol

République

Pl. de la République

Av.

de

la

République

Pl. du marché St Honoré

Honoré

Galeries du Palais-Royal

R. Etienne Marcel

R. du Jour

de

Temple

Charlot

R. de Saintonge

Carrousel du Louvre

Pyramide du Louvre

R.

Forum des Halles

La Canopée

Rambuteau

du

R.

des

Archives

Vieille

du

Temple

R. des Francs Bourgeois

R. de Turenne

Bd Beaumarchais

de

Châtelet

Rivoli

BHV Marais

R. François Miron

R. du Roi de Sicile

Pl. des Vosges

R. du Pas de la Mule

R. Bonaparte

St-Germain

R. du Dragon

Marché St-Germain

St-Michel

NOTRE-DAME

R. des Rosiers

R. de Birague

Pl. de la Bastille

Bastille

R.

de

Charonne

R. Faidherbe

R. du Four

R. St-Sulpice

R. de Seine

Bd

Village St-Paul

R. du Faubourg

St-Antoine

R. de Tournon

Jardin du Luxembourg

St-Michel

St-Germain

Quai St-Bernard

Av.

Daumesnil

Bd

Luxembourg

Montparnasse

Gare d'Austerlitz

The St-Ouen flea market ("les puces")

It is impossible to exhaust this vast antiques market and open-air flea market. You'll find vintage clothes (jeans, leathers and much more) and never-ending bric-a-brac stalls (sometimes unlicensed) with ultra-low prices in a down-to-earth atmosphere. M° Porte-de-Clignancourt (line 4). Saturday, Sunday and Monday. www.marcheauxpuces-saintouen.com

founded in 1831 is an enchantment for the eyes. Here you'll find taxidermy versions of all the animals of the Savanna and meticulously catalogued collections of butterflies and other insects.

Decoration and beauty

2 Fleux – *F5* - *39 and 52 r. Sainte-Croix-de-la-Brandonnerie- M° Hôtel-de-Ville - ☏01 53 00 93 30 - Mon-Fri 10.45am-7.30pm, Sat 10.45am-8pm, Sun 1.30pm-7.30pm - www.fleux.com.* A temple of hip designer décor stocking everything from kitchen gadgets to designer furniture. The off-the-wall collection spans Jielde lamps and scented candles, with all manner of other quirky delights.

3 Buly 1803 – *E5* - *6 r. Bonaparte - M° St-Germain-des-Prés - ☏01 43 29 02 50 - Mon 11am-7pm, Tue-Sat 10am-7pm - www.buly1803.com.* This boutique, set up like a 17C dispensary—with a quaint walnut, marble and terra cotta décor—feels like a remnant of the past. Look a little closer, however, and you will find gorgeous natural

products like soaps, creams, rosewater and precious oils such as baobab and sandalwood. Warning: you may want to buy everything.

Food

4 Épicerie Izraël – *F5* - *30 r. François-Miron - M° St-Paul - ☏01 42 72 66 23 - Tue-Fri 9.30am-1pm and 2pm-7pm, Sat 11am-7pm.* You'll feel like you're in the cave of Ali Baba when you enter Épicerie Izraël. For more than half a century, this boutique has been supplying Parisians adept in exotic cuisine with spices and products from all around the world.

5 Maison Plisson – *G5* - *93 bd Beaumarchais- M° Saint-Sébastien-Froissart - ☏01 71 18 19 09 - Mon 9.30am-9pm, Tue-Sat 8.30am-9pm, Sun 9.30am-7pm - www.lamaison plisson.com.* Organic, locally-sourced products and healthy eating are at the heart of this new- generation fine food store. From boulangerie to charcuterie and even market garden stalls, everything here is appetising. You can eat here too.

9 Stohrer – *E4* - *51 r. Montorgueil – M° Les Halles - ☏01 42 33 38 20 - www.stohrer.fr - daily 7.30am-8.30pm.* This patisserie, the oldest in Paris (1730) is a must-visit. It is here that Nicolas Stohrer invented desserts for the royal court. You can get tasty sandwiches for lunch, but the sweet specialities are definitely the biggest draw: try the *religieuse*, *puits d'amour*, babas or the delicious éclairs.

Concept-Store

6 Merci – *G5* - *111 bd Beaumarchais - M° Saint-Sébastien-Froissart - ☏01 42 77 00 33 - 10am-7pm - www.merci-*

merci.com. This centre for all things fashion and design never ceases to surprise. Always on the lookout for new trends, Merci displays across 1500m^2 /4921.26ft^2 a curated selection of objects and clothing. The collections of household linens and tableware are well worth a peruse. There are three café/ restaurant spaces for those wishing to take a break.

8 Sergeant Paper – *F4-5* - *38 r. Quincampoix - M° Rambuteau - ✆01 44 93 50 79 - www.sergeant paper.com - Tue-Sat 12pm-8pm.* This concept store, specialising in graphic art, subtly mixes street art and photography by promoting a rotating roster of young artists, which changes every month. The establishment promotes accessible art and every print is printed with great care and comes with a certificate of authenticity. Pretty little stationary items are also on sale.

Fashion

10 Brand Bazar – *D6* - *33 r. de Sèvres - M° Sèvres-Babylone - ✆01 45 44 40 02 - daily 10.30am-7.30pm - www.brandbazar.com. Closed Sun.* A paradise for fashionistas, Brand Bazar sells a range of brands with a collection that is at once curated and accessible. Spanning big designers and young French and international creators, the stock is undeniably of-the-moment. Jewellery is fine and colourful, bags are bohemian and the shoes are of the best quality, but nobody takes themselves too seriously here and the welcome is friendly.

Bazaar

11 c – *G3* - *15 r. Beaurepaire - M° Jacques Bonsergent - ✆01 42 40 10 11 - Tue-Sat 11am-7.30pm, Sun 2pm-7pm - www.bazartherapy.com.* In this "gift drugstore", you are guaranteed to find the ideal gift (or souvenir for yourself!). Have a go on the delightful "tirette" machine, inspired by a vintage fairground attraction, which dispenses mystery gifts, or check out the wall of tableware gadgets. The owners of the shop now also collaborate with artists to make eccentric decorated tables and accessories.

13 Boutique de Paris – *F5* - *29 r. de Rivoli - M° Hôtel-de-Ville - ✆01 42 76 43 43 - daily 10am-7pm. Closed Sun. http://boutique.paris.fr.* You'll find the CIty of Light represented in just about every form in this shop, from mugs, tea towels, and carafes to chocolate and colouring sets. The items, many stamped with an Eiffel Tower, are pretty and there is an extensive range: it's the perfect spot for buying souvenirs.

Bijoux

12 Babylone – *G5* - *11 r. des Francs-Bourgeois - M° Saint-Paul - ✆01 44 54 03 84 - www.babyloneparis.com - daily 12pm-7pm.* Christine Laaban creates all her jewellery herself by hand. Over the last twenty years she has developed a distinctly Parisian style: at once laid-back and chic. The designer mixes pâte de verre (glass casting), natural stones and crystal to create unique pieces. Earrings from €30, necklaces from €45.

Nightlife

The City of Light is famous for its theatre, live music, cabaret and dance and there is a stunning diversity of entertainment on offer. In the audience at a show is one of the best ways to experience Paris.

♿ Find the addresses on our maps using the numbers in the listings (ex. ❶). The coordinates in red (ex. C2) refer to the detachable map (inside the cover).

PROGRAMMES

L'Officiel des spectacles (€0.70 in press kiosks www.offi.fr) is an indispensable resource for organising nights out: every Wednesday it publishes the complete programme of shows on in Paris. Inside you'll find all the useful information on cinemas, theatres, concerts, cabarets and dinner-shows, plus suggestions for walks around Paris.
See http://evene.lefigaro.fr/and app and more general websites:
www.parisbouge.com;
www.sortiraparis.com;
www.timeout.com/paris.

Kiosque Théâtre
Half-price tickets for shows on the same day (for the most expensive). More than 100 shows and 120 and plays are on offer. No card payments. Come half an hour before opening to increase your chance of getting tickets.

Kiosque Théâtre de la Madeleine – *D3* - Pl. de la Madeleine (8th) - M° Madeleine - Tue-Sat 12.30pm-8pm, Sun 12.30pm-4pm.
Kiosque Montparnasse – *D7* - Parvis de la gare Montparnasse (15th) - M° Montparnasse-Bienvenüe - Tue-Sat 12.30pm-8pm, Sun 12.30pm-4pm.
Kiosque Théâtre Ternes – *B2* - Centre of Place des Ternes (17th) - M° Place-des-Ternes - Tue-Sat 12.30pm-8pm, Sun 12.30pm-4pm.

Kiosques Jeunes
Here, those ages 13-30 can get pairs of free or reduced tickets.
Kiosque Jeunes la Canopée - 10 Passage de la Canopée – (1st) - M° Châteland - Tue-Sat 11am-7pm.
Kiosque Jeunes Champ de Mars - 101 quai Branly – (15th) - M° Bir-Hakeim - Tue-Sat 1pm-6pm.

CONCERTS

For the big concert halls (La Philharmonie de Paris, l'Auditorium de Radio France and La Salle Pleyel and Salle Gaveau) it is essential to reserve in advance. There are concerts every night in more intimate venues, such as churches, bars, clubs. See www.lylo.fr and www.offi.fr for full programme.

OPERA AND DANCE

The two homes of the **Opéra national de Paris**, l'Opéra-Bastille (*G6* - M° Bastille) and l'Opéra-Garnier (*D3* - M° Opéra) programme operas,

© Arnaud Chicurel/hemis.fr

141

Opéra-Garnier

concerts and recitals and classical and contemporary ballets. Tickets must be reserved several months in advance for some shows. Consult the website: www.operadeparis.fr/billandterie.

The **Opéra-Comique Salle Favart** (***E3*** - Mᵒ Richelieu-Drouot) also hosts operas and recitals. www.opera-comique.com.

For contemporary dance, consult the programme of the **Théâtre de la Ville** (***F5*** - Mᵒ Châteland) as well as **Théâtre national de Chaillot** (***A4*** - Mᵒ Trocadéro). See www.theatredelaville-paris.com; http://theatre-chaillot.fr.

REVUES PARISIENNES

Paris owes its glamorous international reputation in no small part to its fabulous revues, some of which date from the second half of the 19C: the **Folies-Bergère** (***E2*** - Mᵒ Grands-Boulevards or Cadet); the **Moulin-Rouge** (***D1*** - Mᵒ Blanche); the **Lido** (***B3*** - Mᵒ George-V); the **Crazy-Horse** (***B4*** - Mᵒ Alma-Marceau) and the **Paradis Latin** (***F6-7*** - Mᵒ Jussieu).

CULTURAL CENTRES

Maison des Métallos (***H3*** - In 1937 this former factory became the Maison des Métallurgistes (House of Steelworkers), an assembly point for trade unionism. Today it's a cultural

© Bertrand Gardel/hemis.fr

La Bellevilloise

centre with a packed programme of theatre, dance, digital art, exhibitions, meetings and debates. www.maisondesmandallos.org.

La Bellevilloise (*Off map H3* - M° Gambetta or Ménilmontant - 20th arr.) Founded in 1877 in the wake of the Paris Commune, this cooperative, the first of its kind, is now an independent, multi-discipline cultural space which hosts, among other events, film projections, jazz brunches, festivals and private parties. The charming premises is a big draw with its indoor olive trees plated under a vast glass atrium. Jazz and electro concerts. www.labellevilloise.com.

Le 104 (*Off map G1* - M° Riquet). ♿See p. 94.

DANCING

Paris is not short on clubs. See www.soonnight.com/paris (flyers for free and reduced entry); www.timeout.com; and www.villaschweppes.com. Entry is often free for women before midnight; men will usually have to fork out €10-15, depending on the venue. To get back home use Noctiliens (♿ *p. 158*) or a taxi. Metros start again at 5.30am.

Tips: You will sometimes need to book in advance. ID often required on entry: most clubs are 18+.

Our selection of clubs

❷ **Le Duplex** - *A2* - R&B and electro - *2 bis av. Foch - M° Charles-de-Gaulle-Étoile – www.leduplex.com - daily* Free before 12.30am with flyer. Two floors with different ambiances. Different themes every night. Contact to arrange private parties.

3 La Concrete – *G7* - *69 port de la Râpée, 12th - M° Bercy - www. concreteparis.fr - Thur 6pm-3am, Fri-Sat 6pm-7am, Sun 7am-2am.* This barge made its name with its after-parties, which quickly became a favourite with Paris's night hawks looking for a trendy spot to continue the party until midday. If you love techno and electro, this venue is made for you. The barge also has a terrace with a superb view over the Cité de la Mode et du Design.

8 Le New Players – *E3* - general - *161 r. Montmartre - M° Grands-Boulevards - daily except Mon - free entry with guestlist.* Lively themed nights.

9 Social Club – *E3* - international - *142 r. Montmartre - M° Bourse - www.parissocialclub.com - Thur-Sat.* Concerts and club nights, eclectic range of music.

10 Rex Club – *EF3* - electro- *5 bd Poissonnière - M° Bonne-Nouvelle - www.rexclub.com - Thur-Sat.* Iconic Paris club where well-known DJs preside over the decks.

12 Badaboum – *H6* - electro - *2 bis r. des Taillandiers - M° Ledru-Rollin - www.badaboum.paris - Fri-Sat.* Concerts followed by club nights mixing sound and visuals.

13 Le Mix Club – *D7* - general - *24 r. de l'Arrivée - M° Montparnasse-Bienvenüe – www.mixclub.fr - Thur-Sat.* Different themed nights every evening. Erasmus nights on Thursday, free for all before midnight.

143

Les quais de Seine (Left Bank)

The banks of the Seine have been given a new lease of life in recent years. The closing of roads on the rivers banks by the Invalides and the development of the area around the Bibliothèque François-Mitterrand (BNF) have opened up new spaces, which are particularly popular in summer months.

The banks of the 7th arrondissement

You'll find restaurants, barge-bars (péniches) and clubs concentrated on the stretch between Pont Royal and Pont Alexandre-III.

6 Concorde Atlantique – *D4* - *barge club - opposite 23 quai Anatole-France - M° Assemblée-Nationale - www.bateau concordeatlantique.com - Fri-Sun Three floors with a view over the Seine make this a very pleasant spot for summer nights.*

14 Rosa-Bonheur sur Seine - *C4* - *37 quai d'Orsay - M° Invalides - ✆ 01 47 53 66 92 - www.rosabonheur.fr - daily except Mon 12pm-2am (Sun 10pm and Tue 12am). New bar-barge Rosa has got a relaxed and friendly vibe with a terrace for summer and a dance floor that fills up as the night. goes on. Tasty tapas is also on offer. Just sit back and admire the view.*

Showcase - **C4** - electro/concerts-
Port des Champs-Élysées, under Pont
Alexandre-III - M° Invalides - www.
showcase.fr -Thur-Sat This historic venue
has a packed concert programme (see
www.showcase.fr).

The Rive Gauche of the 13th arrondissement

The banks of the Seine between Pont
de Bercy and Pont de Tolbiac offer a whole
host of party venues, some pop-up and
some permanent.

⑯ **Batofar** - **Off map H8** - barge
bar, restaurant, café-concert - 11 quai
François-Mauriac - M° Bibliothèque-
François-Mitterrand - www.batofar.org.
Véritable institution de la nuit parisienne,
A veritable institution of the Parisian
nightlife scene. The Batofar continues
to reinvent itself. Beyond the concerts
(7pm-11pm) and club (11.30pm-6am), you
can also come here for brunch or a casual
drink. Beach from May to September.

⑮ **Le Nüba** - **G8** - Bar, restaurant,
club - 34 quai d'Austerlitz - M° Gare
d'Austerlitz - www.lenuba.com - Tue-Sat,
6pm-5am, Sun 12pm-12am Pecherd on the
roof of the Cité de la Mode et du Design,
Le Nüba attracts a hip party crowd in a
bohemian setting. Ambiance guaranteed.

144

Le Batofar

© Bertrand Gardel/hemis.fr

Where to stay

Each area of Paris has its own distinct atmosphere. Some arrondissements are residential (7th, 15th, 16th), some known for their nightlife (3rd, 10th, 11th), others chic (6th, 7th, 8th), while some are more family-orientated (12th, 13th, 14th, 15th).

♿ *Find the addresses on the detachable map (inside the cover) using the numbers included in the listings (ex. ❶). The coordinates in red (ex. D2) refer to the same map.* *Our price ranges are established on the basis of one night in a standard double in low/high season. You may also find special promotional prices.*

LA CITÉ AND LES QUAIS

From €85 to 130

❶ **Hôtel de Nesle** – *E5* - *7 r. de Nesle, 6ᵗʰ - Mᵒ Odéon or St-Michel - ℘01 43 54 62 41 - www.hoteldenesleparis.com - 🅿 - 19 rooms.* A characterful hidden gem in the heart of the Latin Quarter. The rooms – some without en-suites – are each inventively decorated around a theme (colonial, oriental, countryside, Molière). The garden features Tunisian palm trees.

LE MARAIS AND LES HALLES

From €130 to 150

❷ **Hôtel Andréa Rivoli** - *F5* - *3 r. St-Bon, 4ᵗʰ - Mᵒ Châtelet - ℘01 42 78 43 93 - www.andreahotel.fr - 32 rooms.* You will not be disappointed with this very centrally located hotel. The whole property is entirely renovated (reception, rooms and breakfast rooms); the décor is contemporary and there is air-conditioning throughout.

From €160 to 230

❸ **Hôtel Crayon** – *E4* - *25 r. du Bouloi, 1ˢᵗ - Mᵒ Palais-Royal-Musée-du-Louvre - ℘01 42 36 54 19 - www.hotelcrayon.com - 26 rooms - Breakfast €12.* A welcoming and colourful hotel with décor courtesy of artist Julie Gauthron, who has given character to each room. The atmosphere is cosy with a homely bar space and a delightful hotchpotch of second-hand furniture.

From €195 to 250

❹ **Hôtel du Petit Moulin** – *G4* - *29 r. de Poitou, 3ʳᵈ - Mᵒ St-Sébastien-Froissart – ℘01 42 74 10 10 - www.hoteldupanditmoulin.com - ♿ - 17 rooms - Breakfast €17.* Christian Lacroix is behind the décor of this hotel. The look is unusual, sophisticated and flashy, blending tradition and modernity: think free-standing baths and kitsch patterns.

QUARTIER LATIN

From €99 to 169

😊 ⑯ **Hôtel Henriette** - *F8* - *9 r. des Gobelins, 13ᵗʰ - Mᵒ Les Gobelins - ℘01 47 07 26 90 - www.hotelhenriette.com - 32 rooms - Breakfast €12.* Located a few short steps from the Latin Quarter, Hôtel Henriette has got bags of charm with its pastel-toned colour scheme, designer light fixtures and

© Hervé Goluza/Hotel Henriette

Hotel Henriette

vintage 1960s furniture. This stylishly renovated hotel has a distinctly homely feel. The picture-perfect fairy-lit winter garden is made for Instagram.

From € 135 to 165

⑤ **Hôtel des Grandes Écoles** – *F7 - 75 r. du Cardinal-Lemoine, 5th - Mo Cardinal-Lemoine - ✆01 43 26 79 23 - www.hotel-grandes-ecoles.com - ♿ - 51 rooms- Breakfast €9.* The three houses that comprise this hotel have a distinctive country cottage feel, with a pretty secluded garden. The main building has conserved its old-fashioned charm, while the other two have been tastefully renovated.

ST-GERMAIN-DES-PRÉS

Set price €89
Solar Hotel – *Off map D8 - 22 r. Boulard, 14th - Mo Denfert -Rochereau - ✆01 43 21 08 20 - www.solarhotel.fr - ♿ - 34 rooms.* The owner of this hotel is a passionate environmentalist and the name Solar is, in part, an allusion to the solar panels on the façade. You will also find organic food and an adorable flower-filled terrace, while waste is recycled and water reused. It is the first completely environmentally friendly hotel in Paris. Bicycles available for hire.

From € 110 to 240

Fabe Hotel – *Off map C8* - 113 b r. de l'Ouest, 14ᵗʰ - Mᵒ Pernety - ☎01 40 44 09 63 - www.lefabehotel.fr - ♿ - *17 rooms - Breakfast €10*. Expect green and chocolate-toned décor and evocatively named rooms (Mona Lisa, Rugiada, French Romance). Headboards and furniture feature large flower prints. Cosy and practically-designed.

⑦ Hôtel de Sèvres – *D7* - 22 r. de l'Abbé-Grégoire, 6ᵗʰ - Mᵒ St-Placide - ☎01 45 48 84 07 - www.hotelde sevres.com - *32 rooms - Breakfast €13*. Shopping enthusiasts will appreciate the placement of this hotel, just next door to Le Bon Marché. The feel is cosy, dominated by brown and beige hues. The breakfast room opens onto a small flower-adorned courtyard. There is also a well-being space.

INVALIDES-TOUR EIFFEL

From €125 to 290

⑧ Le Bailli de Suffren Hotel – *C7* - 149 av. de Suffren, 15ᵗʰ - Mᵒ Ségur - ☎01 56 58 64 64 - www.lebailliparis.com - ♿ - *25 rooms - Breakfast €13*. Ideally situated between the Eiffel Tower and Invalides and Montparnasse, the hotel has been renovated in pared-down style, while retaining its Parisian charm. Rooms are bright, comfortable and effectively sound-proofed.

From €285

Paris Perfect – *Off map C7* - ☎001-888-520-2087 - www.parisperfect.com - ♿ - *60 apartments*. Larger groups or those who want amenities like a washing machine would do well to rent one of Paris Perfect's gracious apartments (studios to 3-bedrooms). The palatial Macon (3-bed, 2.5-bath, from €928) is ideal for families. It sleeps 6, has a spacious, well-equipped kitchen, and boasts an Eiffel Tower view through its tall windows.

TROCADÉRO-CHAILLOT

From €80 to 180

Hôtel Hameau de Passy – *Off map A5* - 48 r. de Passy, 16ᵗʰ - Mᵒ La Muette - ☎01 42 88 47 55 - www.hameaud epassy.com - ♿ - *32 rooms* A cul-de-sac leads to this discret *Hameau* and its charming interior courtyard, covered in greenery. Quiet nights guaranteed in the small but modern and well-kept rooms.

OPÉRA-PALAIS-ROYAL

From €59 to 148

⑪ Hôtel des Arts – *E3* - 7 cité Bergère, 9ᵗʰ - Mᵒ Grands-Boulevards - ☎01 42 46 73 30 - www.hotel desarts.fr - *25 rooms - Breakfast €7*. Nestled in the heart of the Cité Bergère, this hotel has the charm and quiet of the provinces. Rooms are light. You will be welcomed by a (56 year-old) talking parrot who may just want to have a chat!

From €97 to 147

⑩ Hôtel Chopin – *E3* - 46 passage Jouffroy (entrance 10 bd Montmartre), 9ᵗʰ - Mᵒ Grands-Boulevards - ☎01 47 70 58 10 - www.hotelchopin.fr - *36 rooms - Breakfast €8*. In a covered passage from 1846, which houses Musée Grévin, this little hotel enjoys a surprising level of quiet even though it's in the middle a lively neighbourhood. Reserve its brightly-decorated rooms well in advance.

MONTMARTRE-PIGALLE

From €90 to 140

17 **Hotel Basss** – *E1* - 57 r. des Abesses, 18*th* - M*o* Abbesses - ☎01 42 51 50 00 - www.hotel-basss.com - ♿ - 36 rooms - Breakfast €12. You'll be charmed by the soft colours of this hotel in the heart of Montmartre. The entrance hall is so pleasant that you will be tempted to linger (sweet treats are always put out). The clean and simple rooms are tastefully decorated.

From €190 to 285

18 **Le Pigalle** – *E1* - 9 r. Frochot, 9*th* - M*o* Pigalle - ☎01 48 78 37 14 - http://lepigalle.paris/ - 40 rooms. This hotel has bags of personality and has been meticulously decorated in line with the hip and bawdy spirit of Pigalle. On top of the trendy (and just slightly naughty) décor, the hotel is also a hub for the area and organises collaborations with local artists, artisans and businesses. Some rooms have their own record player and vinyl selection and all have a minibar, iPad and beautiful retro bathrooms. For a quieter night, opt for a room at the back of the hotel.

From €225 to 480

12 **Hôtel Les 3 Poussins** – *E2* - 15 r. Clauzel, 9*th* - M*o* St-Georges - ☎01 53 32 81 81 - www.les3poussins.com - ♿ - 40 rooms - Breakfast €14. Located on a quiet street, this hotel has bright rooms decorated with photographs of Paris. Some are equipped with a kitchenette. There is also a little patio, perfect for lazing around or taking breakfast.

CANAL ST-MARTIN

From €98 to 278

13 **Best Western Hôtel Faubourg Saint-Martin** – *F3* - 6 r. Gustave-Goublier, 10*th* - M*o* Strasbourg-St-Denis - ☎01 40 40 02 02 - www.hotel-faubourg-saint-martin.com - ♿ - 42 rooms - Breakfast €12. This comfortable hotel is well-placed close to Gare du Nord and Gare de l'Est, and near the Canal St-Martin. The well laid-out rooms have different themes: nature, feathers, polka dots.

From €170 to 240

19 **Hôtel Providence** – *F3* - 90 r. René-Boulanger, 10*th* - M*o* Strasbourg-St-Denis - ☎01 46 34 34 04 - www.hotelprovidenceparis.com - 18 rooms - Breakfast €18 The essence of Parisian chic: think elegant mouldings, Hungarian parquet, velvet and a fine wood bar. This gem of a hotel is ideally placed for making the most of the east of Paris. It also has a terrace, perfect for enjoying a morning coffee.

© Benoit_Linero/Le Pigalle

Le Pigalle

BASTILLE AND THE EAST

From €99 to 209

Mama Shelter – *Off map H3* -
*109 r. de Bagnoland, 20ᵗʰ -
Mᵒ Gambandta - ☎01 43 48 48 48 -
www.mamashelter.com - ♿ - 🅿 -
171 rooms. -Breakfast €16.* The stylings
come courtesy of Parisian design
legend Philippe Starck and the look is
at once imaginative and cutting-edge.
The hotel has a large bar and lounge
area, a restaurant with huge windows,
and a long terrace over the abandoned
Petite Ceinture railway. Ultra-popular
brunch on the weekend.

From 99 to 179 €

⑮ Hôtel du 20 Prieuré – *G4* -
*20 r. du Grand-Prieuré, 11ᵗʰ -
Mᵒ Oberkampf - ☎01 47 00 74 14 -
www.hotel20prieure.com - ♿ - 32
rooms - Breakfast 13 €.* Renovated in
2007, this hotel has a contemporary,
city feel and offers small, pleasant
rooms, decorated in shades of white,
with design furniture and huge prints
of Paris on the walls.

Planning Your Trip

151

Cycling on a Vélib' bike in front of Le Bon Marché
© François Renault/Photononstop

Know before you go

BY TRAIN

All stations are very well served by public transport and taxis and have Vélib' (bike share) stations. Information and reservations for **SNCF trains:** ☎ 3635 - www.voyages-sncf.com

Gare de Lyon (12th arr.): trains from southwest France, Italy and Switzerland. Lines 1 and 14, RER A, B and D.

Gare de Bercy (12th arr.): trains from Clermont-Ferrand, Burgundy and some from Lyon. Auto Train service. Lines 6 and 14.

Gare d'Austerlitz (13th arr.): trains from southwest France and Spain. Lines 5 and 10, RER C.

Gare Montparnasse (15th arr.): trains from the Grand-Ouest. Lines 4, 6, 12 and 13.

Gare du Nord (10th arr.): trains from the north of France,the United Kingdom, Belgium and the Netherlands. Lines 2, 4 and 5, RER B, D and E.

Gare de l'Est (10th arr.) : trains from the east of France and Germany. Lines 4, 5 and 7. RER D, B and E est accessible at Gare du Nord, one station away from Gare de l'Est.

Gare St-Lazare (9th arr.): trains from Normandy. Lines 3, 9, 12, 13 and 14, RER E.

For buses and Transilien network, consult www.ratp.fr and ♿ *p. 160.*

BY PLANE

Paris is served by two international airports: **Roissy Charles-de-Gaulle** 23 km/14.3mi to the north of Paris on the A1. It is served by the RER B, the Roissybus, the shuttle bus, nightbuses (N143 et N140) and taxis. The 350 bus also provides a link between Gare de l'Est and Roissy (70 min, €6); the 351, between Place de la Nation and Roissy (70 min, €6).

Orly airport is 11 km/6.8mi to the south of Paris on the A 6. It is served by the Orlybus, OrlyVal, the T7 tram, the shuttle bus and taxis. Orly is also linked to "Pont de Rungis" station on the RER C by the "GO C Paris" bus service (35 min, €6.25).

Beauvais airport, 80 km/49mi to the north of Paris is a base for some low-cost carriers.

For timetables, real-time flight information and access information: **www.parisaeroport.fr.** ♿ *p. 3 for details of public transport access.*

WHEN TO GO

Paris attracts visitors all year round. New Year celebrations, Easter and summer are the busiest periods, as well as during the major professional salons. During these periods it is therefore advisable to book your stay well in advance. Some hotels offer price promotions in low season (from November to Mars, outside of New Year and major events).

SOME PRICE IDEAS FOR BUDGETING	
SERVICES OR ITEMS	**PRICE IN EUROS**
A bed in a hostel	from 26 per person
A double room in a comfortable hotel	100-150
A double room in a superior category hotel	150-250
A meal in a simple restaurant	20-25 per person
A meal in a mid-range restaurant	35-50 per person
A meal in a gourmet restaurant	75-150 per person
A glass of wine	3-5
A cocktail in a bar	6-11
Entry to a national museum	8.50-12
A single metro ticket/book of 10 tickets	1.90-14.50

TOURIST INFORMATION

Office du tourisme and Congrès de Paris – www.parisinfo.com. For all the latest information on events, museums, walks, hotels and restaurants. Hotel reservations and booking for tourist sites, museums, cruises, RATP pass, Paris City Pass.

Paris Île-de-France regional tourism committee – www.visitparisregion.com

Mairie de Paris (city hall) – www.paris.fr

Que faire à Paris - http://quefaire. paris.fr. This website from the city of Paris has all the latest on going out, exhibitions and weekly-updated activities.

BUDGET

Use the table above to help you set your budget.

Emergency numbers

Samu (Paramedics) – ☏15
Police – ☏17
Pompiers (fire) – ☏18
Brûlures (burns) – ☏01 42 34 17 58
Poison Centre (24hr advice and help line on toxic risks of medical, industrial and natural products) – ☏01 40 05 48 48
SOS Médecin (medical emergencies: sends doctor to a residence) – ☏01 47 07 77 77
Stolen bank card – ☏0 892 705 705 (€0,34/mn)

Basic information

CHILDREN

Paris is a great town for children. They love the Eiffel Tower, the Bateaux-Mouches and of course the big parks (Tuileries, Luxembourg, Buttes-Chaumont, etc.). But don't forget these fun-filled spots:

- Le jardin des Plantes, with its Muséum, Grande Galerie of evolution and zoo *(p. 46)*
- Parc de La Villette, with La Cité des Enfants and la Géode *(p. 94)*
- Le musée de la Chasse et de la Nature *(p. 32)*
- Le 104 *(p. 94)*
- Le jardin d'Acclimatation *(p. 78)*
- Le musée Grévin *(p. 84)*
- Le Palais de la Découverte *(p. 76)*

CYCLING

Thanks to the bike-friendly policies of the current city hall, cycling has become a good way to get around Paris : 220 km/136.7mi of cycle paths cover Paris and new routes are constantly being created to ensure the safety of cyclists.

For more detailed information, consult the *Paris à vélo* map, available in town halls (mairies de Paris) and the Office du tourisme de Paris.

Obligations – Bell, lights for night-time; using the designated bike stations to lock up bikes (it is illegal to attach bicycles to street furniture). No riding on the pavement.

Vélib'

The system of the Vélib'or "vélo en toute liberté" is simple : take out a bike anywhere and return it to any of the 1800 stations of the capital and 30 neighbouring areas. 📞01 30 79 79 30 - www.velib.paris - subscription : 1 day/ €1.70; 7 days/ €8; First ½hr free, then 1 € for the next ½hr; 2nd additional ½hr €2; €4 per additional ½hr starting from the 3rd additional ½hr - €150 deposit (to be removed from card if bicycle not returned).
Michelin Vélib map n° 61.

Bike rental

You will need ID documents for any rental. Rental will include helmet, basket, lock and sometimes child seat.
Paris à vélo, c'est sympa ! – 22 r. Alphonse-Baudin - M° St-Sébastien-Froissart - 📞01 48 87 60 01 - www.parisvelosympa.com - Mon.-Fri 9.30am-1pm, 2pm-6pm, Sat-Sun 9am-7pm - €12/½ day, €15/1 day, €25/2 day - allow €250 for deposit-themed guided tours (3hrs): €35 (under 12 years: €20).
Valmy Cycles - 179 quai de Valmy - M° Louis-Blanc - 📞01 42 09 68 16 - http://valmy-cycle.blogspot.fr-9am-8pm. Along Canal St-Martin.
AICV (Animation insertion culture et vélo)– 38 quai de la Marne - M° Ourcq - 📞01 43 43 40 74 - www.aicv.net - Tue-Sun 10am-6pm - €10/3hrs (adults), €8/3hrs (children). Ideally situated by the Bassin de La

Villette, this non-profit association also provide cycle itineraries.

Bike-taxi

Bike-taxis are a recent addition to the Paris tourist offer

Trip Up - www.tripup.fr - ☎09 70 40 66 69 - Mon-Sat 10am-6pm - €15 pick-up charge and then €5/km.
Cyclopolitain - www.cyclopolitain. com - ☎01 46 33 25 19 - tours of Paris from €55 (1hr).

DISABLED ACCESS

In this guide, the ♿ symbol indicates sites that are accessible to people with reduced mobility. ♿On the tourist office website (*parisinfo.com*), consult the "visiting Paris with a disability" section where you will find the (downloadable) Accessible Paris guide and a good deal of useful information (transport, restaurants, adapted tourist sites, etc.).
Museums – Most museums and tourist sites are wheelchair accessible. Musées de la Ville de Paris (www. paris.fr) organises a range of activities for disabled visitors: workshops, tactile visits, conferences in sign language or for lip readers and specific visits for people with learning difficulties.
Toilets – All toilet facilities provided by the city of Paris are accessible to people with disabilities (♿*see p. 159*).
Transport – All bus routes are wheelchair accessible, with a retractable ramp at the back of the bus. However, only the line 14 of the metro and some RER stations are fully accessible.

The website www.infomobi.fr will help you to find adapted routes. Finally, **Taxis G7 Access** (*☎01 47 39 00 91, www.g7.fr and smartphone application*) operates a fleet of 120 vehicles adapted to accommodate people with reduced mobility (with ramps to access the vehicle) and 900 low-floored cars.
Guided tours – The association Parisien d'un jour (*www.greeters. paris*) organises personalised adapted visits for people with disabilities (♿*see p. 158*).
The association AICV rents out **bicycles** (handbikes, tricycles) for people with disabilities (♿*see p. 154*).

ECO TRAVEL & MEETING LOCALS

Information

www.parisinfo.com – The Paris tourist office proposes a list of green/ eco recommendations: sustainable classed accommodation options, shopping destinations and ideas for alternative and unusual tours, lead by Parisians.
www.voyageons-autrement.com – The leading portal for responsible tourism in France. Articles, official designations and plenty of ideas for travelling responsibly.

Alternative accommodation

Une chambre en ville – www.chambre-ville.com.
For guestrooms (chambre d'hôtes) in Paris. A federation of professionals who developed their own B&B accreditation, Clef verte (green key), in 2011.

www.goodmorningparis.fr – Leading guestrooms (chambre d'hôtes) agency for experiencing a local's Paris.

France-Lodge Locations – www. authenticbandbparis.com. Federation of professionals of guest rooms (chambre d'hôtes) in Paris (FPPCH).

Eating with locals

Voulez-Vous Dîner ? – www.voulezvousdiner.com. This private club connects visitors to Paris with Parisian hosts, wishing to share their cuisine.

EMERGENCIES

♿Box : *Emergency numbers, p. 153.*

FREE ENTRY

Most museums and national monuments are free for under 26s from European Union countries. For over 26s, national museums are only free on the first Sunday of the month. Entry to the permanent collections of the **Musées de la Ville de Paris** is free for everyone, with the exception of the Catacombs, the archaeological crypt of Notre-Dame and the Palais Galliera. ♿ *www.parismusees.paris.fr*

GARDENS AND PARKS

The French capital has 490 parks and gardens. They open between 8am and 9.30am in the week and at 9am on the weekend; closing times vary depending on the season: 9pm to 10pm from mid-April to August; 8pm September-October, 7pm from March to mid-April; 6pm in February and end of October until mid-November; 5.30pm rest of the year. ♿Detailed opening times at: www.paris.fr. Most of Paris's parks and gardens have lawns and some have designated picnic areas. It is possible to take guided discovery visits of the great gardens of Paris (♿*see p. 157*).

GUIDED TOURS

Guided visits of monuments, areas and exhibitions run every day in Paris. They are listed in some major daily newspapers, the theatre/nightlife publications (like *L'Officiel des spectacles*) and on posters at the entrance of monuments. Programmes are also available at the Office du tourisme de Paris and, of course, online. In general, you will not need to book, and will just need to go to the meeting point; payment at the location.

Walking tours

Centre des monuments nationaux – ☎01 44 54 19 33 - www.monuments-nationaux.fr - €9 excluding tickets for access to monuments (18-25 years €7). Offers visits of monuments, as well as some areas of the city, themed around architecture, run by state-qualified professional guides (*conférenciers*).

Association pour la sauvegarde et la mise en valeur du Paris historique – 44-46 r. François-Miron - 4th arr. - ☎01 48 87 74 31 (11am-6pm, Sun 2pm -7pm) - www.paris-historique.org - visites guidées (2hr) - €12 (under 25s €6).

Guided tours of parks and gardens – The Mairie de Paris (city of Paris) proposes guided tours of the parks and gardens of the capital. Programmes available in the town halls of each arrondissement, at the Hôtel de Ville or on request at: environnement@paris.fr.

Bus tours

Through a bus window or from the top deck is another good way of discovering the town, with or without a commentary. You have a few options. One is the **tourist buses and coaches**, of course, but you may also wish to explore the city surrounded by real Parisians, on the **RATP buses**, some of which pass through the capital's historic districts. (see p. 160).

Montmartrobus – Circuit of the hill of Montmartre between the Mairie du 18e arr (town hall) and Place Pigalle (1 ticket t+).

Balabus – Crosses Paris from east to west, taking in the key tourist sights, between Gare de Lyon and La Défense (bus stops marked Balabus Bb) - April-Sep: Sun and public holidays 12.30pm-8pm (departs La Défense), 1.30pm-8.30pm (departs Gare de Lyon) - duration: 1hr30min (1 ticket t+).

Big Bus Paris (red coaches) – http://fra.bigbustours.com - &. - tours with commentary in nine languages in double-decker coach - stops : Eiffel Tower, Champ-de-Mars, Musée du Louvre, Notre-Dame, Musée d'Orsay, Opéra, Champs-Élysées-Étoile, Grand Palais, Trocadéro - route with commentary - total duration:

2hr15min, but you may hop on and off during the course of the route - 1st departure at 9.38am on the Champs-Élysées (Étoile), then every 10min, in summer - €33 (4-12 years €16), 10% reduction if ticket bought online - tickets can be bought on the bus or online (less expensive).

Tour Cityrama – www.pariscityvision.com - route with commentary in coach taking in the capital's most famous monuments - departs 214 r. de Rivoli (Mo Tuileries). Various route options.

Open Tour – www.paris.opentour.com - four routes with commentary in double-decker open-top bus; option to hop on/off at 50 different stopping points. €37 for 2 consecutive days or €33/1 day. (under 15s/€17). The Pass Open Tour can be bought directly on the bus, at the Open Tour office (13 r. Auber - 9th arr. - Mo Havre-Caumartin and Opéra), at the Paris tourist office or at RATP ticket offices.

Boat tours

Bateaux-mouches – Pont de l'Alma (Right Bank) - ☎01 42 25 96 10 - www.bateauxmouches.fr - 10.15am -11pm depending on the time of year - €13.50 (under 12 years/€6) - duration: 1hr10min approx. - various lunch/dinner cruise packages available.

Bateaux parisiens – Port de la Bourdonnais (at the foot of the Eiffel Tower) - RER C Champ-de-Mars, Mo Bir-Hakeim ou Trocadéro - ☎0 825 01 01 01 (€0.15/min) - www.bateauxparisiens.com - cruise with commentary April-Sep: 10am-10.30pm (departs every 30 min); rest of the year: 10am-10pm (departs every hour) - €15 (under 12 years/ €7); specific cruises (dinner, children's) are scheduled; details online.

Vedettes de Paris – Port Suffren (at the foot of the Eiffel Tower) - RER C Champ-de-Mars, M° Bir-Hakeim or Trocadéro - ℰ01 44 18 19 50 - www.vedettesdeparis.com - cruise with commentary (1hr) April-mid-Sep : 10.30am-11pm (departure every 30 min; every 20min in July/Aug); mid-Sept-March: 11am-9pm (departure every 45mins) - €15 (under 12 years/ €7).

Paris Canal – ℰ01 42 40 96 97 - www.pariscanal.com - reservation obligatory - cruise on the Seine and Canal St-Martin between the Musée d'Orsay and Parc de La Villette - mid-March-mid-November: departs 9.30am at Musée d'Orsay (M° Solférino) OR 2.30PM at Parc de La Villette (M° Porte-de-Pantin) - duration 2hr30min - €20 (child/€13).

Canauxrama – ℰ01 42 39 15 00 - www.canauxrama.com - reservation obligatory - departs from Port de plaisance Paris-Arsenal, opposite 50 bd de la Bastille (M° Bastille) : 9.45am and 2.30pm; departs Bassin de La Villette, 13 quai de la Loire (M° Jaurès) : 9.45am and 2.45pm - route (2hr30mins approx.) from Bastille to La Villette or vice versa - €18 (under 12 years/ €9).

Unusual tours

Ça se visite – 63 av. Parmentier - 11e arr. - ℰ01 43 57 59 50 - www.ca-se-visite.fr - €12 (€10 10-26 years). Urban walks with locals and artists from the traditionally working-class communities of the northeast of Paris. There are also tours incorporating the centre of Paris and the suburbs, as well as night-time tours and scooter (!) tours.

Paris par rues méconnues – ℰ01 77 17 11 06 - www.paris-prm.com - annual membership €20 and tour €20 (including one welcome drink) - duration: 2hr. For something a little bit different. Themed tours lead by enthusiasts and specialists: a great way to see another side of Paris and meet real Parisians.

Parisien d'un jour – www.parisgreeters.fr. These Parisian volunteers work with the **Paris Greeters** organisation. They lead tours on request with small groups of 1-6 people: a different way to discover the city.

Douce Banlieue – www.tourisme93.com. More than 150 different walks exploring the north-east of Paris and suburb la Seine-St-Denis through "quartiers populaires" (traditionally working-class communities).

HEALTH

Pharmacies open 24hr/24 and 7/7
Pharmacie Les Champs-Élysées - 84 av. des Champs-Élysées - M° George-V - ℰ01 45 62 02 41.
Pharmacie Européenne - 6 pl. de Clichy - M° Place-de-Clichy - ℰ01 48 74 65 18.
Grande Pharmacie Daumesnil - 6 pl. Félix-Éboué - M° Daumesnil - ℰ01 43 43 19 03.
&See www.pharmaciesdegarde.com.

LOST PROPERTY

Before you do anything else, try to retrieve your lost object in the place where you think you lost it. Otherwise: **Services des objets trouvés** (found objects service)– 36 r. des Morillons - 15th arr. - M° Convention - ℰ0 821 00 25 25 (€0.12/mn) - Mon-Thur 8.30am-5pm, Fri 8.30am-4.30pm. Declare a lost object at: www.service-public.fr or servicedesobjetstrouves-paris@interieur.gouv.fr.

NIGHTLIFE

Paris still merits its historical reputation as a "ville festive". You will find abundant theatres and legendary cabarets. The site **www.parislanuit.fr** lists all the shows and night-time events by day(& *Nightlife, p. 140*).

OPENING HOURS AND PUBLIC HOLIDAYS

Shops : around 10am-7pm, daily except Sun.
"Commerces de bouche" (boulangerie, patisserie, butcher's, charcuterie) : often open Sun morning and closed Mon.
Local grocer's: many open late in the evening.
Supermarkets: 9am-8pm, daily except Sun. (some big chains like Monoprix are open until 10pm).
Department stores : 10am-7pm; late-night shopping one night a week, until 9.30pm or 10pm.
Museums and monuments: ticket offices generally close half an hour before the closing of the building.

Churches: No tourist visits during services; generally closed between 12pm and 2pm.
Certain tourist sites and shops may be closed on the following public holidays: 1 January, Easter Monday, 1 and 8 May, Ascension Day (Holy Thursday), Whit Monday, 14 July (National Day), 15 August, 1 and 11 November, 25 December. Museum openings on public holidays vary. Check in advance

POST OFFICE

Bureau de poste (post office) (Due to building works, the Louvre bureau is closed) – 16 r. Étienne Marcel - M° Étienne-Marcel - ℰ36 31 - open 7/7 and almost continuously from Monday to Saturday, except between 6am and 7.30am; on Sunday it is open from 10am to 12pm - only for sending post and parcels.

PUBLIC TOILETS

The town's 400 "sanisettes" (self-cleaning public toilet cubicles) are open from 6am to 10pm. They are free and wash themselves automatically after every visit (allow 3 min between each person). You will also find free toilets in department stores, commercial galleries and major parks and gardens, You pay a small fee to use toilets in stations but they are free in airports. There are various free smartphone applications to help you locate toilets in Paris.

PUBLIC TRANSPORT

Metro

The most simple, rapid and economical mode of transport. Fourteen lines cross the capital with a train coming on average every 2 to 4 minutes (6 to 8 minutes after 8.30pm and on weekends). It runs from 5.30am to 1.15am in the morning (2.15am on Friday, Saturday and public festivals). The main drawback is the rush-hour crowds (8am-9.30am; 5pm-6.30pm). To work out how long your journey will take, allow 2 minutes for every stop and 3 minutes for changing lines (for example, for a journey with 15 stops and 2 changes, allow 35 minutes). Consult the website *www.ratp.fr*, Visiting Paris section or ☎3246 (€0.34/mn). The free RATP smartphone app (App Store and Google Play) "Next Stop Paris" is available in nine languages and can be very useful (geolocation, journey planner).

♿ A map can be found at this back of this guide, on the reverse side of the cover and the back of the detachable map.

Bus

This is without a doubt the most pleasant mode of transport. The metropolitan network is comprised of 60 bus routes. Some pass Paris's most famous monuments and districts (the 24 and 72 in particular). Disadvantages: you need to know the routes well (route maps in bus shelters) and the frequency can be irregular, especially on Sundays.

Night bus (Noctilien) – 47 routes run all night (from 12.30am to 5.30am), between Paris and the suburbs of greater Paris: these are the Noctilien, routes, of which the number is preceded by the letter N. In Paris they leave from five different stations: Gare de Lyon, Gare de l'Est, Gare St Lazare, Gare Montparnasse and Châtelet; circular lines N01 (interior circular) and N02 (exterior circular) stop at popular Paris night spots. Frequency of routes N01-N02: every 17mins (10mins Fri-Sat).
Routes N140 and N143 link Gare de l'Est to Roissy Charles-de-Gaulle airport (12.30am-5.30am, €7.60), see www.vianavigo.com.

RER

Ideal for getting to the outskirts and suburbs of Paris (La Défense, Versailles, Disneyland, Roissy and Orly airports), but less practical for Paris proper (*intra-muros*): even though it's faster than the Metro, it's usually more complicated to get to the RER platforms than the Metro platforms. Be careful not to throw away your RER ticket before reaching your destination: you will need it to get out.
The network has five lines, with three running through the central Châtelet-Les-Halles station (lines A, B and D).
Line A, which runs through the East-West axis of Paris, serves Disneyland.
Line B, which runs North-South, goes to Roissy Charles-de-Gaulle airport.
Line C, which runs West-East, serves Versailles-Rive-Gauche (Château).
Line D runs from the North to South-East of the city.
Line E circulates from West to East.

Tram

This is environmentally-friendly mode of transport does not cover many typically "touristy" routes. Lines T3a and T3b run across the Boulevards des Maréchaux, connecting to bus, metro and RER routes. There are plans for the tram line to loop the whole of Paris by the end of 2019. The practical T3a line links the Porte de Versailles (Parc des expositions) to Porte de Vincennes (Bois de Vincennes) via Parc Montsouris and Bibliothèque François-Mitterrand.

Batobus

A novel but expensive way to cross Paris via the Seine, taking in some of the most popular areas and monuments. Passes are valid for 1 or 2 days or the whole year. Stops: Eiffel Tower, Musée d'Orsay, St-Germain-des-Prés, Notre-Dame, Jardin des Plantes, Hôtel de Ville, Louvre, Champs-Élysées and Beaugrenelle - ℘0825 05 01 01 - www.batobus.com - 6 April-2 Sept: 10am-9.30pm, every 20min; 3 Sep.-5 April: 10am-7pm, every 25 min - €16/1 day. (under 16s/€7), €19/2 days. (under 16s/€10), €60/annual pass.
Combined ticket with Open Tour bus (*see p. 157*) €45/2 days, €49/3 days.

Transport tickets

The ticket t+ – On the Metro and RER (Paris *intra-muros* only) the ticket t+ ticket will give you access to the whole network and allow you to change between lines. However, prices for RER tickets outside of central Paris vary depending on the distance, so you will not be able to use a Metro ticket. On the bus, a ticket t+ will allow you to travel across the whole network (except lines 299, 350 and 351) and to make bus/bus, bus/tram and tram/tram changes for journeys not exceeding 1hr30min between the first and last ticket validation.
Ticket t+ can be bought as single tickets or in sets of 10 (*carnets*) in Metro and RER stations, on the bus and in the Bureaux de Tabac.
Prices – ticket t+: €1.90 ; a "carnet" (10 tickets) full fare: €14.50 ; reduced fare (4-9 years): €7.25.

Tourist offers

"Paris-Visite" – Allows unlimited travel on the Metro, bus, tram, RER and Transilien. The coupon is valid for 1,2,3 or 5 days and also gives access to airport connections (only with a zones 1-5 coupon). It also carries reductions for certain sights and activities (around €100 of reduction with 13 partners).
Adult price (zones 1-3): €11.65/1 day ; €18.95/2 days ; €25.85/3 days and €37.25/5 days.
Adult price (zones 1-5): €24.50/1 day ; €37.25/2 days ; €52.20/3 days and €63.90/5 days. ℘ *See www.ratp.fr.*

SUNDAY

In Paris, shops in tourist districts are open on Sundays. All shops are open in the **Marais**, including the section around rue du Temple/rue des Francs-Bourgeois, as well as the boutiques of **Village St-Paul**, the **Les Halles** area, the **Champs-Élysées**

Bateau-mouche on the Seine.

and the **Carrousel du Louvre**. Some **department stores** - Galeries Lafayette by Opéra, le Bon Marché, BHV Marais- the shopping centres at Beaugrenelle, Bercy Village, and 4 Temps at La Défense and the major **stations** are now open Sunday.
♿ *p. 134.*

TAXIS

Where to find a taxi

You will easily find a taxi near the stations and along the main traffic thoroughfares. It is customary to hail a taxi by putting your arm out. A green light will be on if a taxi is free, a red light if it is occupied. You may also book a taxi on the phone or online.
Taxis bleus – ☎36 09 (€0.15/mn, 7/7, 24hr/24)/01 41 52 54 25 - www.taxis-bleus.com.
Taxis G7 – ☎36 07 (€0.15/mn)/ 01 47 39 47 39 - www.g7.fr. Cards accepted. Taxis **G7 Access** accessible for people with reduced mobility - ☎01 47 39 00 91.
Taxis G7 MaxiCab people carriers for 5-7 passengers and luggage - ☎36 07 (€0.15/min).
If you wish to pay by card or cheque, specify at the time of booking. The price of the journey to reach you is added to your journey.
There are also almost 200 callboxes located on big public squares and near Metro stations, as well as 470 taxi stops, indicated by a blue Taxi panel, though you will often find nobody at them.

General phone number – ☎01 45 30 30 30. This number connects you to the nearest taxi station and, if this one doesn't respond, the call is automatically transferred to another nearby taxi point.

Prices

Minimum cost of a journey: €7.
Minimum pick-up charge: €3.83.

TOURIST OFFICES

Office du tourisme and Congrès de Paris

Permanent welcome points
Main tourist office (Bureau central d'accueil) – 25 r. des Pyramides - M° Pyramides - ♿ - May-Oct: 9am-7pm; Nov-April: 10am-7pm - closed 1 May - www.parisinfo.com (♿*see p. 153*).
Gare de Lyon – M° Gare-de-Lyon - 8am-6pm - closed Sun and public holidays.
Gare du Nord – M° Gare-du-Nord - 8am-6pm - closed 1 Jan, 1 May and 25 Dec.
Gare de l'Est – By international TGV arrivals - M° Gare-de-l'Est - 8am-7pm - closed Sun and public holidays.
Anvers – 72 bd de Rochechouart - M° Anvers - 10am-6pm - closed 1 Jan, 1 May and 25 Dec.

Other tourist organisations

Mairie de Paris – 29 r. de Rivoli - M° Hôtel-de-Ville - ☎01 42 76 40 40 - www.paris.fr - Mon-Fri 10am-6pm.
Paris Info – ☎39 75 - Mon-Fri 8.30am-6pm, Sat 9am-2pm. The call centre for the city of Paris (Ville de Paris) will answer all your questions about local life.
Syndicat d'initiative de Montmartre – 21 pl. du Tertre - M° Abbesses - ☎01 42 62 21 21 - 10am-4pm (*w/end closed from 1pm to 2pm; Fri 10am-6pm*) - www.montmartre-guide.com.
Comité régional du tourisme Paris Île-de-France – Information points in Charles-de-Gaulle and Orly airports. Welcome, information and sale of tourist products - www.visitparisregion.com

TOURIST RATES

Paris Museum Pass – Valid for 2, 4 or 6 consecutive days, it offers direct and unlimited access to 60 museums (permanent collections) and monuments in Paris and the Paris region – on sale at www.parismuseumpass.com, in museums, (bureau de) Tabac and the Office du tourisme de Paris – 2-day pass/€48, 4 days/€62, 6 days/€74.
The financial advantage is significant for those who wish to visit several museums in a day, even more so because it allows holders to skip the queue.
Paris City Pass – Available in 2-, 3-, 4- or 5- day, this package from the Paris tourist office can be used for a transport pass, a museum pass, a river cruise etc. On sale at tourist office information points and at www.parisinfo.com.
♿ See also "Paris-Visite" transport pass, offering special deals on tourist sites p. 161.

Festivals and events

Below you will find a selection of events. For a full list, visit **en.parisinfo.com** and **www.timeout.com/paris/en**

Autumn 2018
▶**Franz West** – 12 Sept-10 Dec 2018 – Centre Pompidou – www.centrepompidou.fr
▶**Cubism** – 17 Oct 2018-25 Feb 2019 – Centre Pompidou
▶**Venice in the Time of Vivaldi and**
▶**Tiepolo** – 24 Sept 2018-21 Jan 2019 - Grand Palais - www.grandpalais.fr/en
▶**Joan Miró: This Is the Color of My Dreams** – 3 Oct 2018-4 Feb 2019 – Grand Palais

164

Winter 2018
▶**Michael Jackson, icône de l'art** – 23 Nov 2018-17 Feb 2019 – Grand Palais
▶**Zao Wou-Ki: Space is Silent** – Through an 2019 – Musée d'Art Moderne – www.mam.paris.fr/en
▶**Chinese New Year** – 5 Feb 2019 - Grande parade in Chinatown (13th arr) and Belleville - www.chine-informations.com

Spring 2019
▶**Salon du Livre** – 15-18 March 2018 – Paris Expo Porte de Versailles – www.livreparis.com
▶**Mois de la photo** (Photo Month) – Apr 2019 – around Paris - moisdelaphotodugrandparis.com
▶**Marathon de Paris** – 7 April 2018 – www.schneiderelectricparis marathon.com

▶**Foire de Paris (Paris Fair)** – late Apr-early May - Porte de Versailles – www.foiredeparis.fr
▶**Foire du Trône** (traditional funfair) – Until end of May 2019 – Bois de Vincennes, Pelouse de Reuilly – www.foiredutrone.com

May
▶**Kiosques en fête** – Free concerts in the kiosques (bandstands) of Paris until end of October - www.parisinfo.com
▶ **Saint-Germain-des-Prés jazz festival** –Mid-May for 15 days. - www.festivaljazzsaintgermainparis.com
▶**Nuit des musées** – End of May – Late opening and events in the museums of Paris (Louvre, Orsay, Pompidou) – www.nuitdesmusees.culturecommunication.gouv.fr
▶**Roland-Garros** (French Open) – End of May, 15 days – Porte d'Auteuil – www.rolandgarros.com

Summer 2019
▶**Fête de la musique** – 21 June - www.fetedelamusique.
Paris Jazz Festival –Mid-June through late July at Parc Floral – www.parisjazzfestival.fr
▶**Festival Jazz Musette des Puces** – A music festival at the St-Ouen flea markets - www.festivaldespuces.com
▶**Tour de France** (ends in Paris) – July 21 - www.letour.fr/en
▶**Japon Expo (Japan Expo)**–early July - Parc des Expositions de Paris-Nord Villepinte – www.japan-expo-paris.com/fr/

© Paris Tourist Office - Photographer : Sarah Sergent

Fête de la musique at the Archives Nationales

▶**Les Pestacles** – Until September at Parc floral – festival for children – www.lespestacles.fr

▶culturecommunication.gouv.fr

▶**Marche des fiertés lesbiennes, gays, bi et trans** – Gay Pride Parade through all of Paris – www.gaypride.fr

▶**Festival Paris-Cinéma** – Until mid-July – www.pariscinema.org

▶**Solidays** – 3-day festival: last weekend of June – Longchamp Racecourse – music festival; proceeds go to organisations fighting against AIDS – www.solidays.org

▶**Fête foraine des Tuileries (Tuileries Fun Fair)** – Jardin des Tuileries until end of August.

▶**Fête nationale du 14 Juillet (Bastille Day)** – Dance parties and fireworks; military parade on the 14th on the Champs-Élysées.

▶**Festival Fnac Live** – Free concerts in front of the Hôtel de Ville - early July.

▶**Paris Plage (Paris Beach)** – Until mid-August – www.quefaire.paris.fr/parisplages

▶**Paris Quartier d'été** – Music, theatre and dance events. Until mid-August - www.quartierdete.com

▶**Cinéma en plein air** – Until mid-August, Parc de La Villette – www.lavillette.com

▶**Festival Classique au Vert** – Weekends until end of Sept at Parc Floral (Bois de Vincennes) – free classical concerts - www.classiqueauvert.paris.fr

▶**Festival Cinéma au Clair de Lune** – Start of Aug – free open air film projections all around Paris – www.forumdesimages.fr

Autumn 2019

▶**Jazz à La Villette** – Until mid-Sep - Jazz festival at Parc de la Villette - www.jazzalavillette.com

▶**Fête de Ganesh** – 23-26 Aug – www.templeganesh.fr

Picasso. Blue and Rose – 18 Sept-6 Jan 2019 - Musée d'Orsay - www.musee-orsay.fr

▶**Festival d'Île-de-France** – World music concerts in Paris and the Île-de-France region, until end of Oct - www.festival-idf.fr

▶**Biennale internationale des antiquaires** – Antique dealers' festival, at the Grand Palais - www.sna-france.com

▶**La Nuit des Publivores** – A grand show, with music dance and entertainment, themed around advertising films from around the world - Grand Rex - www.nuitdespublivores.com

▶**Journées du patrimoine (National Heritage Days)** – www.journeesdupatrimoine.culturecommunication.gouv.fr

▶**Portes ouvertes des ateliers d'artistes de Ménilmontant** – Ménilmontant artists' studios open day – ateliersdemenilmontant.org

▶**Techno Parade** – Mid-Sep – www.technoparade.fr

L'Alimentation – Oct 2018 to June 2019 – Musée de l'Homme

▶**Nuit blanche** – Early October – All-night festival: installations and artistic performances across Paris – http://quefaire.paris.fr/nuitblanche

▶**Fête de la Science** – Workshops and conferences at La Villette and the Palais de la Découverte – www.fetedelascience.fr

▶**Fête des Vendanges** – Harvest festival of the Butte de Montmartre – www.fetedesvendanges demontmartre.com

▶**Renoir Father and Son. Painting and Cinema** – 6 Nov-27 Jan 2019 – Musée d'Orsay - www.musee-orsay.fr Harvest festival of the Butte de Montmartre – www.fetedes vendangesdemontmartre.com

▶**Jean-Michel Basquiat (1960-1988)** – 3 Oct-14 Jan 2019 – Fondation Louis Vuitton – www.musee-orangerie.fr

▶**The cruel stories of Paula Rego** – 17 Oct-14 Jan 2019 – Musée de l'Orangerie – www.fondationlouis vuitton.fr

Winter 2019

▶**Sérusier's 'The Talisman'. The right to dare all** – 29 Jan-28 Apr 2019 – Musée d'Orsay - www.musee-orsay.fr

▶**Black models: from Géricault to Matisse** – 25 Mar-14 Jul 2019 – Musée d'Orsay – www.musee-orsay.fr

Summer 2019

▶**Berthe Morisot: female Impressionist** – 18 June-22 Sept 2019 – Musée d'Orsay – www.musee-orsay.fr

Find Out More

169

Port de l'Arsenal, Colonne de Juillet in the background
© Bertrand Gardel/hemis.fr

Distinctive features

THE SNAIL'S SHELL

From an administrative standpoint, Paris resembles a snail's shell: in the centre is the Seine and 1st arrondissement with the 2nd, 3rd, 4th and 5th arrondissements, which constitute the historic heart of the city (ancient and medieval), uncoiling around them. Next, and continuing the spiral, the 6th, 7th, 8th, 9th, 10th and 11th arrondissements encompass the old "faubourgs" (dating from the Ancien Régime); finally the 12th,13th, 14th, 15th, 16th, 17th, 18th, 19th and 20th arrondissements finish the loop, having officially been re-classed as arrondissements (instead of villages) of Paris in 1860.
See the map inside the cover at the start of the guide.

A SPECIAL ADMINISTRATION

At the head of the Marie de Paris (city of Paris) is the mayor, appointed by the Conseil de Paris, composed of 163 advisers, chosen every six years by 518 arrondissement-level advisers, directly elected by Parisian voters in every arrondissement.

The mayor possesses the same powers as the mayor of any other municipality, with the exception of powers of the police (traffic circulation, public peace and public hygiene) which are the responsibility of the Préfet de Police (prefect of the police), an employee of the state named by decree of the President of the Republic in the Council of Ministers
Twenty arrondissement councils, based in each one of the mairies (town halls) of the arrondissements serve as bridge between the administration and the population. They have no decision-making power but assist the mayor and the Conseil de Paris (Paris council). These councils are composed equally of councillors directly elected by Parisian electors, municipal officers named by the mayor of Paris and members elected by the Paris council. The first mayor of Paris elected by universal suffrage was Jacques Chirac (1977). In 2001, Parisians elected a Socialist mayor for the first time, Bertrand Delanoë, who was re-elected in 2008. Since 2014, Paris has been run by its first female mayor, Anne Hidalgo.

Staying for longer?
⊚ *Discover the comprehensive Guide Vert Paris with walks and listings for each arrondissement.*

Metamorphosis of a city

A "SMALL" CAPITAL

Paris is encircled by the 1973 ring road (the boulevard périphérique), a loud and noisy boundary, and flanked by two green lungs (the Bois de Boulogne and the Bois de Vincennes). The city within is roughly circular, yet slightly squashed, as it extends for 12km/7.5mi from east to west but only 9km/5.6mi from north to south; it is bisected by the River·Seine. It's a relatively small capital at 87 km² (Madrid is 607 km² and Moscow 879 km²) but is very densely packed with 25,000 inhabitants per square kilometre (versus 3300 per kilometre squared in Marseilles). This little self-enclosed territory is home to 2, 211 297 Parisians and is the beating heart of France.

URBAN GROWTH

The first city "defence" of the little island occupied by the Parisii of Lutecia from the 3C BC, was natural. The incessant demographic growth, the necessity of a military defence and to set and collect taxes to finance the development of the town and the growing political role of Paris, lead to the construction of six different city walls over the centuries. Little by little, Paris annexed its "faubourgs".

The Gallo-Roman Wall

♿*See the wall on the map on the facing page.*

The Parissi, taking advantage of the Pax romana, emerged from Lutetia, built by the Gauls and defended by the river and surrounding swamps, to settle along the Left Bank and the river Seine in the 1C and 2C: the area stretched from the present-day St-Michel to Place Maubert and, higher up, from rue Descartes to Luxembourg. But the Barbarians (around 276-285) later forced them to retreat to the Cité, where they would build fortifications and a rampart using the stones of Roman monuments. Eight or nine hectares spread out inside these walls. In 4C and 5C Paris (Lutetia took its inhabitants' name in 360) Paris stated enclosed by this little wall.

From Clovis to Suger

Clovis, king of the Francs, chose Paris as his capital in 508 for its strategic placement. He installed himself on the island, which from this point became known as Île de la Cité. From the 6C to the 10C, swamps were drained and cultivated, while river harbours were established near Place de Grève and it became a commercial area.

Different sanctuaries were constructed during the Merovingian period, of which nothing now survives, apart from a few remains in the chapel of

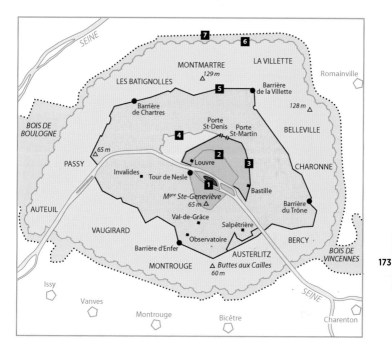

St-Symphorien in the Église Saint Germain des Prés.

Under the reign of Hugh Capet, the town spread out onto the two banks of the river, with the Right Bank superseding the Left Bank. The king made the Palais de la Cité (on the site of the current Palais de Justice) a royal residence. Grand sanctuaries were built, some on Île de la Cité, by Suger, a minister under Louis VI and Louis VII and abbey of St-Denis.

The Philippe Auguste Wall

♿ *See the wall marked **2** on the map below.*

Between 1180 and 1210, a massive wall was erected on the order of Philippe Auguste, who wanted to protect Paris and its inhabitants while he left to go on Crusade.

Running over more than 5 km/3mi, reinforced upstream by a chain barrage across the river and downstream by the Louvre Fortress and Nesle Tower (where Institut de France is today).

The activity of the town was concentrated on the Right Bank around Châtelet and the Grand Pont (linking Île de la Cité and the Right Bank), to the west of Place de Grève (where the Hôtel de Ville is today). The roads were paved, contributing to improved circulation and hygiene. The number of fountains increased as the management and distribution of the water grid became more sophisticated, regularly drawing from local springs, including one in Belleville.

It is also during this period that Paris would begin to look like a great world capital: the construction of Notre-Dame began in 1163 (the construction would last more than a century) and the Université de Paris (later the Sorbonne) would be established in 1225.

The Charles V Wall

🔄 *See the* **3** *wall on the map p. 173.*
It was Étienne Marcel, the provost of the merchants of Paris, who, after seizing power in 1356, undertook to restore the old Philippe Auguste Wall and to begin the construction of a new fortification, which would be completed under Charles V (and which would take his name).

This new fortification was supported in the east by the fortress of Bastille and surrounded by ditches. The Paris ramparts enclosed just under 440ha/1087ac and protected some 150,000 inhabitants.

Roads lead to the village of Montmartre, the St-Denis basilica, the commandery of the Temple and the Château de Vincennes; as such the town developed on the Right Bank, as opposed to the Cité and the Left Bank, where the university developed.

The Louis XIII Wall

🔄 *See wall* **4** *on the map p. 173.*
In the 16C, neither the Wars of Religion, nor the siege of the city by Henri de Navarre succeeded in slowing down the multiplication of civil and religious buildings and the extension of the city of Paris. The Place Royale (today called Place des Vosges) was constructed, as well as the hospitals St-Louis and Charles IX between 1560 and 1574; later, Louis XIII would enlarge the Philippe Auguste Wall to the west, partially in order to accommodate the Louvre Palace (which had itself been enlarged) and the St-Germain district. Constructed between 1633 and 1636, the Louis XII Wall would stand until 1754. Under the reign of Louis XIII, Paris would become a great world capital: Richelieu constructed the Palais-Royal (1629) and founded the Académie Française (1635), while the Marais was sumptuously developed.

Louis XIV and Paris

Louis XIV moved the royal court to Versailles in 1682 and would spend little time in Paris itself. However, he did not forget Paris and would carry out numerous grand building projects including the construction of the Place Vendôme and the Place des Victoires. In 1660, when returning by carriage from Vincennes, Louis XIV was struck by the unappealing spectacle of the old Charles V fortifications: they were dilapidated and had lost all use since his last victories. He ordered to have them demolished and replaced with a courtyard planted with four rows of trees. The ditches were filled and a raised terrace built with a view of the surrounding countryside.

The redevelopment of these "grands boulevards" began the process of extending the town towards the "faubourgs" (suburbs): Faubourg St-Germain and St-Marcel were joined to the city and Faubourg St-Antoine was constructed. It was also at this time that Le Nôtre designed an east-west axis in line with the Allée des Tuileries, predecessor of the Champs-Élysées.

The Farmers-General Wall

ⓒ*See wall* **5** *on the map on p. 173.* From 1784, the limits of Paris were set by the Farmers-General Wall. It was no longer a protective wall but a fiscal wall erected to enforce the payment of a toll on goods coming in to Paris. Constructed between 1784 and 1797, today its line is traced by the exterior boulevards of Paris. The elevated sections of the Metro (lines 2 and 6) run along the site of the former Farmers-General Wall. It was 23km/14ft long and 3m/9.8ft high and was punctuated with 57 toll-houses, designed by architect Ledoux, of which four still remain: the rotundas at Monceau and La Villlette (now a bar) and the square pavilions of Denfert-Rochereau and Nation.

All the villages neighbouring the wall did not have to pay the same taxes that Parisians were subject to in order to bring in goods such as wine, coal and wood. As a result, these villages saw a huge influx of a population forced out of Paris due to expensive living conditions and increasing difficulties with housing.

The Thiers Fortifications

ⓒ*See wall* **6** *on the map p. 173.* This wall was built for military purposes. The Russian Army's invasion of France and then Paris in 1814 and 1815 proved the need to protect Paris. President Thiers came up with the idea to construct a fortified wall 1-3km/0.6mi-1.8mi from the Farmers-General Wall, which would withstand enemy fire. The idea was adopted in August 1841. A 39km/24mi wall was erected, protected on the interior by a 15m/49ft ditch (now the site of the Boulevards des Maréchaux) and the exterior by a 200m/656ft-wide military zone, punctuated by 94 bastions.

Though the Thiers fortifications were never used to defend Paris, they would nonetheless play an important role 18 years after their construction when a bill would decree that the Paris city limits be moved to interior ditch that lined the wall.

The annexation of 1860 – From 1860, all the land situated between the Farmers-General Wall and the Thiers Fortifications was annexed to Paris. Four municipalities were fully absorbed into Paris (Vaugirard, Grenelle, La Villette and Belleville), seven others were partially absorbed (like Passy, Auteuil), while 13 others would give up a small part of their land (Vanves, Issy, Neuilly, St-Ouen).

From the Commune to 1900

The fires of the 1871 Commune would lead to the reconstruction of most of the grand public edifices of Paris including the Hôtel de Ville, the Richelieu wing of the Louvre (seat of the Ministère des Finances) and the

Légion d'honneur. The Palais-Royal and le Palais de Justice were also restored ; the Opéra Garnier was finished in 1875 and the construction of the Sacré-Cœur was started.

For the Exposition Universelle (World's Fair) of 1889, the Eiffel Tower, icon of modern Paris, appeared on the Paris skyline. 1900 (the year of the next World's Fair) would also be a prolific year for the urban architecture of Paris: the Pont Alexendre-III was built, linking the Champs-Élysées to the Invalides; the Gare d'Orsay went up across the river from the Louvre. It was also the year that Paris's metro opened with its first line running between the Porte de Vincennes and Porte Maillot; the Hector Guimard Metro entrances created at the same time would also become iconic.

176

The present limits

👣*See wall* 🔳 *on the map p. 173.*

The Thiers wall was razed by the Third Republic in 1919 and the definitive city limits of Paris were fixed between 1925 and 1930: the Bois de Boulogne, Bois de Vincennes and a narrow ring of land encircled the city. During the Second World War, Paris lost is status as capital as the government installed itself in Vichy. The town was bombed and declared an "open city", before being occupied.

On 26 August 1945, cheering crowds gathered to watch Général de Gaulle march triumphantly down the liberated Champs-Élysées. The population of Paris reached 2 700,000 inhabitants. ,

After the War

As part of reconstruction efforts after the War, Paris embarked upon great building works initiated by various presidents of the Republic (in the model of the great projects of French kings). At the beginning of the 1950s, the government decided to build a business district, La Défense, impressive enough to compete with the best in the world. This grand project was installed at the end of a historically grand perspective, stretching from the Louvre to the west of Paris, taking in the Champs-Elysées. After the construction of the Maison de Radio-France (1963) and the redevelopment of Beaugrenelle (the first tower was finished din 1970) under de Gaulle, Paris inaugurated one of its most controversial buildings, the Pompidou Centre, inaugurated in 1977 on the initiative of president Georges Pompidou.

Under the presidency of Valéry Giscard d'Estaing, it was decided that the Gare d'Orsay would become a gallery and the abattoirs of La Villette would become a science museum (both inaugurated under Mitterrand in 1986).

The Mitterrand years

The grand architectural projects of president Mitterrand are famous the world over. Of all the projects, only one the Grand Louvre and its pyramid, inaugurated in April 1989, was directly commissioned by Mitterand. All the other monument designs were the winning entries of national competitions: the Finance Ministry; the Institut du Monde Arabe; the Cité de la Musique. The Opéra de la Bastille, Bibliothèque Nationale de France and Arche de La Défense were the product of international competitions.

Un patrimoine religieux à préserver

The 85 churches of Paris are the city's best free museums, packed with artistic treasures, but they are often in poor condition. It is not uncommon to find crumbling stonework and dingy interiors. Decades of insufficient maintenance has put these important cultural heritage sites in danger and does little for the image of Paris, perhaps giving the impression that the city cares more about leisure activities than preserving its history. A key issue for the coming years.

New directions

Though Jacques Chirac's presidency saw the construction of the Musée du Quai-Branly, built in 2006, more generally, grand monument building had given way to improving the "ordinary city". The emphasis was on the everyday environment of the city and looking after its architectural heritage.

From 1990 to 2010 – The city of Paris introduced a number of measures designed to improve circulation around the city and create a less car-heavy environment. "Axes rouges", specially designated major roads with fewer traffic lights and a higher speed limit, were introduced; other areas were pedestrianised or reserved for bicycles. Improvements were also made to public transport and a tram line developed around the edge of Paris. The self-service bike rental scheme Vélib was launched in 2007, followed in 2011 by Autolib, a self-service electric car sharing facility. With space to build increasingly rare, defunct railways and industrial spaces have been cleverly utilised to build new districts, like **ZAC Paris Rive Gauche** - which has changed the face of Austerlitz, Tolbiac and Masséna - as well as **ZAC Pajol** in the 18th arrondissement. Since 2015, the three branches of the army and the entire Ministry of Defence (a kind of French pentagon) have been regrouped in a new site in Balard, in the 15th.

What next ? – More former railway land is being developed, including a new "écoquartier" at Clichy-Batignolles, which is already part-completed: it will feature housing, public facilities and offices. Housing and offices will also be created across 200ha/494ac between Porte de la Chapelle and Porte de la Villette, as part of the ongoing 'Paris Nord-Est Project'.

Finally, there is inevitably talk of integrating the city more closely with its "petite couronne" (little crown), its three neighbouring suburban municipalities. Sections of the périphérique ring road (Porte des Lilas, Porte de Vanves and Porte des Ternes) have already been or will be covered to make way for the creation of gardens or open public spaces, taking in the current suburbs. The debate on whether to integrate the "petite couronne" into the city proper is already underway and is a controversial issue. The question "How to enlarge Paris?" is becoming the more politicised "Why would we want to enlarge Paris?".

"GRAND PARIS"

In 2009 then-president Nicolas Sarkozy enlisted ten international teams of experts from a range of

© Franck Guiziou/hemis.fr

178

Halle Pajol, Jardins Rosa Luxemburg in the 18th

spheres (architects, urban planners, sociologists) to come up with big ideas on how to develop the conurbation of Paris and present their vision for what Paris might look like in the coming decades. The objective was to create urban and social continuity between the capital and its "banlieue" in order to develop a better-performing economic region, a more welcoming space for an increasingly cosmopolitan population, while continuing to welcome a steady flow of French and international tourists. All of these plans would have been impossible without extensive transport development and the form this would take was debated at length: in May 2011, a compromise was reached between the government and the region and the "Grand Paris Express" project was launched. By 2025, a new network of 200km/124mi of "autmomatic supermétro" will be constructed, transporting 2 million passengers a day and facilitating links between suburbs, reducing their isolation. Work began in 2014 on the "supermétro", with the first operations to take place in 2018. The plan also includes improving the RER network and extending the line 14 metro, linking airports Orly in the south and Roissy-Charles-de-Gaulle in the north.

Paris and its revolutions

The history of Paris has been marked by a series of revolutions and great movements of social and political protest that have often had repercussions for the country as a whole. The function of the mayor of Paris (considered too dangerous) was removed in 1794 and was only really restored in 1977!

ST BARTHOLOMEW'S DAY MASSACRE

The bells of St-Germain-l'Auxerrois, tolled on the night of 23-24 August 1572, marking the beginning of the Wars of Religion with the **St-Bartholomew's Day Massacre**. Thousands of protestants were savagely executed by the people. The staunchly Catholic city was hostile to the marriage of protestant Henri de Navarre (future Henri IV) with Catholic Marguerite de Valois and the royal policy of civil concord. Henri IV only entered Paris on 22 March 1594 after converting to Catholicism.

THE FRENCH REVOLUTION

In the febrile atmosphere following the meeting of the Estates General in May 1789, the fuse for revolution was lit when popular finance minister Necker was dismissed by the king on 12 July 1789 The angry population of Paris rose up. On the morning of 14 July, they looted the Hôtel des Invalides, before moving on to the Bastille fortress (then a prison) for arms and munitions. At the end of the afternoon, when the government saw that the French guards had deserted their barracks and arrived on the scene it agreed to back down
The Bastille was taken and, very quickly, its demolition began. The prison that had become a symbol of despotism was no more and by the following year people were dancing on its former site.

THE REVOLUTION OF 1830

The July Revolution or "Trois Glorieuses" (Three Glorious Days) took place in Paris on 27, 28 and 29 July 1830. When the elections held in July went against him, King Charles X refused to submit to the chamber of deputies and decided to

bolster his power. He drew up four ordinances that were a direct attack on the deputies, proclaiming the dissolution of the chamber elected less than one month earlier and setting a date for new elections. He abolished the freedom of the press and tried to exclude the bourgeoisie from elections. The population reacted violently. The next day, under the influence of Aldophe Thiers, journalists published calls for insurrection. On 27 July, people took to the streets and blocked the roads with barricades. Less than ten days after the publication of his ordinances, Charles X was forced to abdicate. The July Revolution put an end to the Bourbon Restoration and proclaimed the July Monarchy on 29 July 1830.

THE REVOLUTION OF 1848

Just like the Revolution of 1789, the 1848 Revolution was the result of an economic crisis affecting France's peasants and workers. The events unfolded in Paris on 23, 24 and 25 February 1848. On 22 February 1848, one of the political meetings known as "banquets des républicains" was banned, leading to riots. On the evening of the 23 February, troops stationed outside the Ministry of Foreign Affairs opened fire on the demonstrators and the riot turned into a revolt. The victorious insurgents invaded the Chateau des Tuileries, the residence of the King Louis-Philippe and forced his abdication. The Republicans imposed a provisional government, putting an end to the July

Monarchy, and created the Second Republic on 25 February 1848.

⊛ The Colonne de Juillet in the Place de la Bastille commemorates both the 1830 and 1848 revolutions.

THE COMMUNE (1871)

Following French defeat at the Battle of Sedan, Paris called for the deposition of Napoleon III and on 4 September 1870, the Empire came to an end and the Third Republic was proclaimed. The Prussians had taken 83,000 prisoners, including the emperor on 2 September. Faced with the threat of enemy troops encircling the city, a Government of National Defence was formed, but the capital was nonetheless placed under siege by the Prussian army during the winter of 1870-1871. Parisians withstood the siege heroically and were enraged when the government forced the capital to capitulate on 28 January 1871. The people of Paris seized power and on 26 March 1871, the "Commune de Paris", a proletarian government run by workers, was proclaimed at the Hôtel de Ville, setting itself against the government seated in Versailles. In May (21-28), there would be a week of brutal repression conducted by the Versailles troops on behalf of the government. During this "bloody week", the Hôtel de Ville, the Tuileries Palace (a wing of the Louvre) and many other Paris monuments would be burnt down and the column at Place Vendôme toppled. The construction

of the Sacré-Cœur, after the defeat of 1870 was a response to a public desire for penitence for the errors committed during the violence and the basilica became a work of reparation for France.

MAY 1968

On 22 March 1968 a student and workers' revolution against what they perceived as a Bourgeois and static society begun at the University of Nanterre, just outside Paris. On 13 May, young factory workers joined the students. The Latin Quarter was blockaded as students and protesters pulled up paving stones, and a general strike was called. This social crisis, first sparked by a crisis in universities, quickly became a political crisis as De Gaulle's hold on power was called into question. The left-wing opposition in parliament called for the president to step down while publicly supporting the young protesters. On 30 May, De Gaulle announced his refusal to withdraw from political life and dissolved the National Assembly and called elections; 100 000 demonstrated in support of the general. In early June, work resumed in state-run companies. On 30 June, the Gaullists won the elections.

Capital of the image

There is no denying that Paris is photogenic, from the secular spire of the Eiffel Tower to the glitter of the Champs-Élysées at night and the unmistakable banks of the Seine. The city has long been a source of inspiration to artists who have repeatedly reproduced the town's famous monuments and its lively neighbourhoods, striving to capture its eternal mystery.

PHOTOGRAPHY

Eugène Atget (1857-1927) was one of the first people to immortalise the street scenes and small trades of Paris, systematically documenting the city for a collection designed to be used by painters at the end of the 19C. **Robert Doisneau**'s (1912-1994) witty and tender images are among the most famous of Paris, including the iconic Baiser de l'Hôtel de Ville (Kiss by the Hôtel de Ville). His photos capture charming scenes from daily life: children playing, cafés and markets. **Henri Cartier-Bresson** (1908-2004), co-founder of Magnum Photos agency, himself captured the capital through striking watercolour-like photographs. Paris deserves as much as ever its title of world capital of photography. The Maison Européenne de la

Cinéma en Plein Air, Parc de la Villette

Grand Rex

Photographie, the Bibliothèque nationale de France and the Galerie du Jeu de Paume all regularly welcome major photographic exhibitions. Events (like Paris Photo at the Grand Palais) and smaller galleries are also a delight for photography enthusiasts.

CINEMA

Paris is the most filmed city in the world: an average of 10 shoots take place in the capital every day spanning cinema, TV films, advertising and more. Over the years, French directors have repeatedly made Paris itself the star of their films: think *Hôtel du Nord* (1938), *Amélie* (2001) or *Zazie dans le métro* (1960) and *Les Amants du Pont-Neuf* (1991).

The city has captivated international directors too, with films such as An American in Paris (1951) Last Tango in Paris (1972) and more recently Midnight in Paris (2011) prompting viewers across the world to fall in love with the City of Light. The first ticketed public projection of cinematography was organised on 28 December 1895 by Auguste and Louis Lumière at the Grand Café on Boulevard des Capucines. In 1886, Charles Pathé (1863-1957) turned cinema into an industry by installing studios at au 6 rue Francœur in the 18th arrondissement. Today, this building is occupied by film and television school Fémis. Though many of the first cinemas have gone, Studio 28 and the Luxor preserve the memory of their glorious past. The Grand Rex (see p.84) is still the biggest cinema in the capital.

Today, Paris is still one of the world capitals of the 7th art with 376 cinema screens (of which 93 are dedicated to art films and experimental cinema) and 27 million movie-goers a year.

Two key cultural institutions help cement its status: the Cinémathèque Française in the 12th arrondissement and the Forum des images, located within the Forum des Halles. There are also a number of film festivals that take place every year such as Festival Paris-Cinéma, Cinéma en Plein Air at La Villette, L'Étrange Festival and Mon premier festival (aimed at children).

182

© Nathan Alliard/Photononstop

Architecture

Every century has left its mark on the architecture of the city, with two particular periods – the 16 and 17C and the Haussmann project of the Second Empire – giving the town the characteristics that make it unmistakably recognisable.

IN SERVICE OF THE GRANDEUR OF THE KINGS

Henri IV, the first town planner of Paris

Taking control of a town devastated by the Wars of Religion, Henry IV undertook a series of major building projects to embellish and improve his capital. The Pont-Neuf, built in 1606, was the first direct link between the two banks of the river. The king also wanted to add grandeur to the emblematic centre of his kingdom by establishing or adding to symbolic sites (the Louvre, the Tuileries) and using noble materials (cut stone instead of cob and wood). He created impressive public spaces such as the elegant Place Dauphine and most famously, Place Royale, the present-day Place des Vosges; flanked by 36 brick and stone pavilions, the construction of the latter marked the height of the aristocratic golden age of the Marias. To accommodate for the growing number of horse-drawn carriages, wider roads were created, generally lined with exquisite new mansion houses, such as the Hôtel de Soubise and the Hôtel Carnavalet.

Louis XIII et Louis XIV

Louis XIII continued the building projects started by his father. The population of Paris went from 275,000 inhabitants in 1571 to 500,000 around 1680; the changing demographics prompted the multiplication of residential lots in the "faubourgs". New neighbourhoods grew on Île Saint-Louis and in Faubourg St-Germain. Richelieu would encircle Faubourg Montmarte and Faubourg St-Honoré inside a new wall.

This preoccupation with city building would quickly fade under Louis XIV, who was more interested in demonstrating his power than rationalising his cities. The Louis XIV style would be defined by rigour, grandeur, harmony and symmetry, recurring themes that most importantly underlined the absolute power of the monarchy. The monumental colonnade on the east façade of the Louvre (1667), 176 m/577ft long, is emblematic of the Sun King's imposing brand of Classicism. Similarly, the Hôpital des Invalides displayed a long 196m/643ft façade with a monumental central portal, dedicated to the glory of the king. The Places des Victoires and Place Vendôme, laid out by Jules Hardouin-Mansart (1646-1708), demonstrate this same motif of symmetrical lines converging at a statue of the king in the centre. Nature was not forgotten either, bur rather domesticated: the Sun King employed landscape gardener André Le Nôtre (1613-1700)

The Haussmann building

Today nobody would dream of calling Haussmann buildings inelegant, but they were criticised by many at the time of their construction. Though their façades were in cut stone (pierre de taille) and court-facing walls in brick, fitting with aristocratic style (Versailles combined brick côté ville and stone côté jardins), their uniform structure was considered unworthy of the moneyed classes who were intended to occupy them. To allow light in, the height of the buildings had to be equal to the width of the road (18m/59ft). Each building was fitted with balconies running along the 2nd and 5th levels, while the top floor (5th) would be topped with mansard roofs with dormer windows, for the servants. As for the interior layout, the "noble" rooms (salon, boudoir, dining room) would be lined on the street side of the buildings with the "common" rooms (kitchens and toilets) on the courtyard side. Modernity, in particular the addition of lifts, would desacralize the noble level "par excellence" of the Haussmann building, the 2nd floor. With its balcony and high ceilings, this level of the building also presented a good compromise of some view, relatively easy access (by stairs) and good access to water supply. Various decrees would loosen Haussmannian building regulations: for example, one decree in 1882 would permit "façades en saillie" (bow-windows).

184

to create a large tree-lined alley stretching from the Tuileries Palace to the Chaillot "mount". The "French garden" style was born and the first version of the Champs-Élysées was traced.

THE GREAT HAUSSMANN RENOVATION

Baron Haussmann (1809-1891), prefect of the Seine, was entrusted with the task of transforming the city into a capital fitting with its Second Empire material prosperity. Under the aegis of Napoleon III, he developed major new traffic thoroughfares. The North-South axis was easy to achieve – boulevards St-Michel and Sébastopol were quickly opened and joined with the new railway stations in the east and north (Gare de l'Est, Gare du Nord). The East-West axis was more difficult to extend, partially because

the population of the constituent Louvre, Tuileries and Marais housed a high concentration of aristocratic residences and these populations were harder to expropriate. Sanitary preoccupations also concerned Haussmann: Paris at this time had over one million inhabitants and cholera had hit in 1832. Haussmann would completely gut the centre of the city: the narrow, insalubrious roads that had comprised the Île de la Cité were almost completely razed. 600km/373mi of sewers were constructed between 1852 and 1870 and no less than 100,000 new buildings shot up. Straight lines of trees would appear across the city (80,000 trees were planted in total). The Bois de Boulogne and Bois de Vincennes, as well as artificial parks (Buttes-Chaumont in today's 19th arr., Monceau in the 8th and Montsouris in the 14th).

N

O

P

Q

R

S

Photo credits

Page 4
Notre-Dame: © Brian Jannsen/age fotostock
Eiffel Tower: © M. Gaspar/Michelin
Louvre: © Bruno Perousse/hemis.fr
Musée d'Orsay: © Bertrand Gardel/hemis.fr
Champs-Elysées: © Pascal Ducept/hemis.fr

Page 5
Seine, quais & bridges: © Bertrand Gardel/hemis.fr
St-Germain-des-Prés: © travelstock44/Look/age fotostock
The Marais: © Paris Tourist Office
Latin Quarter: © Guido Cozzi/Sime/Photononstop
Montmartre: © Bertrand Gardel/hemis.fr

Maps

Inside
La Cité *p16-17*
Le Marais *p28-29*
Quatier Latin *p40-41*
St-Germain de Prés *p50-51*
Opéra Palais Royal *p80*
Montmartre Pigalle *p88-89*
La Villette *p96*
Shopping in Paris *p136-137*

Cover
Neighborhoods of Paris
  Inside front cover
Paris metro map
  Inside back cover

THEGREENGUIDE short-stays **Paris**

Editorial Director	Cynthia Ochterbeck
Editor	Sophie Friedman
Translator	Hannah Meltzer
Production Manager	Natasha George
Cartography	Peter Wrenn, Nicolas Breton
Picture Editor	Yoshimi Kanazawa
Interior Design	Laurent Muller
Layout	Natasha George

Contact Us	Michelin Travel and Lifestyle North America
	One Parkway South
	Greenville, SC 29615
	USA
	travel.lifestyle@us.michelin.com

	Michelin Travel Partner
	Hannay House
	39 Clarendon Road
	Watford, Herts WD17 1JA
	UK
	✆01923 205240
	travelpubsales@uk.michelin.com
	www.viamichelin.co.uk

Special Sales	For information regarding bulk sales, customized editions and premium sales, please contact us at:
	travel.lifestyle@us.michelin.com

short-stay

- ◆ Charleston
- ◆ London
- ◆ New Orleans
- ◆ New York
- ◆ Paris

Visit your preferred bookseller for the short-stay series, plus Michelin's comprehensive range of Green Guides, maps, and famous red-cover Hotel and Restaurant guides.

Michelin Travel Partner

Société par actions simplifiées au capital de 11 288 880 EUR
27 cours de l'Ile Seguin - 92100 Boulogne Billancourt (France)
R.C.S. Nanterre 433 677 721

No part of this publication may be reproduced in any form
without the prior permission of the publisher.

© Michelin Travel Partner
ISBN 978-2-067230-22-4
Printed: April 2018
Printer: IME